Gadfly

Reading Church Through Reading Jesus

Gadfly

Reading Church Through Reading Jesus

John George Arthur

Circle Books

Winchester, UK
Washington, USA

First published by Circle Books, 2014
Circle Books is an imprint of John Hunt Publishing Ltd., Laurel House, Station Approach,
Alresford, Hants, SO24 9JH, UK
office1@jhpbooks.net
www.johnhuntpublishing.com
www.circle-books.com

For distributor details and how to order please visit the 'Ordering' section on our website.

Text copyright: John George Arthur 2013

ISBN: 978 1 78279 325 0

A CIP catalogue record for this book is available from the British Library.

Design: Lee Nash

Printed and bound by CPI Group (UK) Ltd, Croydon, CR0 4YY

We operate a distinctive and ethical publishing philosophy in all
areas of our business, from our global network of authors to
production and worldwide distribution.

CONTENTS

To Mark Greene, for his conspiracy of grace.

To Dave Gooderidge, for being the genuine article.

To Helen Arthur because, when I burn, she is the most often scorched.

The Gadfly & the Eagle

Gadfly. John Stott. Not a juxtaposition of words you might expect. But it was indeed he who inspired the title of this book.

But we'll come to that.

This book is like a roisterous border collie bounding out of the sea and shaking itself dry right by you but just a lot more serious than that. It's like one of those days when you're lazing languidly in the sun in your back garden with a few friends with the Kings of Leon wafting through the open windows, and then someone puts ice down your back – you're irritated, amused, outraged, oddly grateful all at once, and if you are in a good mood you enter into the puckish mischief of it all and leap out of your chair in search of ice, buckets, hoses, water, lakes – intent on some exultant, good-natured but wet and definitely cold, revenge, your breathless laughter drowns out the asthmatic tones of the Kings of Leon wafting through the open windows... And when it's done, suddenly you don't want to lie back in the sun any more, you're re-energized, ready to do something, ready to play. This book is like that – except it's calling us out to much, much, much more than a playful romp in the sun.

The best books change us. And change us for the better. They aren't necessarily right in every detail but they open up a vista, like the view you see for the first time when you reach the top of a hill. And the best books don't just open up a vista, they invite you to walk into it. This, I think, is one of those best books and it opens up a fresh vista of what following Jesus looks like, a fresh grasp of what it might feel like to be shaped, commanded, led into a riskier, deeper, less predictable, less legalistic, more frankly forceful, certainly intimate and costly following of the One.

It's a journey John has been on, and is on. So every word

comes not only from the mind and the heart but from the gut. It's emerged out of his life with Christ, out of a profound love for the church and a deep determination to seek to read the Bible through the lens of the one who is the word of God.

Along the way I was gripped by his insights into Gideon and Samson, Moses and Elijah, into the curiously open-ended parables of Jesus, into seeing deeper, more challenging significance in his miracles, in finding uncomfortable truths in his way of relating to followers and opponents, and radical challenges to my view of the normative Christian life in Jesus' terrible sacrifice. John's wrestling with the Bible leads inexorably to a profound challenge to the church that John loves to become something much more like the authentic community of accountable, risky friendships and of accountable, risky, engaged love for the world that her founder and commander has in mind.

It shakes some things up.

Gadflies do that. But they aren't always welcome – precisely because they shake things up.

Which brings me to John Stott.

It was 2010. November. John was 89 years old at the time and living in a care home for retired clergy. He was quite frail physically and though clearly able to process everything people said to him, found it easier to talk in sentences than paragraphs. He was, as you no doubt know, one of the most globally influential Christians of the twentieth century, the author of some fifty books, a Biblical scholar of the first rank, a preacher of acuity and concision, a disciple-maker of depth and loyalty, a voice for the poor, an encourager of the young, and a champion for deep engagement with the world. He was also one of the founders of the Lausanne Movement that had in 1974 released the Evangelical Protestant Church into an understanding of the inseparability of the Gospel proclamation and Gospel action. Personally, he was one of the most courteous, orderly, self-disciplined people I have ever met.

Now in November 2010, I had just come back from the third Lausanne Congress for World Evangelization in Cape Town and had gone down to see him with my son to share my reflections. He'd heard many others before mine. When I finished, the eagle whose inner vision was as sharp as ever said, "It lacked a gadfly." "Well", I said, somewhat defensively, I think, "it was pretty hard to get anywhere near the microphone." "In 1974", he said, "they didn't ask for permission, they just grabbed it."

I was blown away. Here was the master of decorum and order celebrating the gadflies, celebrating the passionate interrupters, the people who are so impelled by their convictions that they cannot but speak, the people who grab the microphones, not out of ego but because something too important is at stake not to. We need gadflies – even if by their very nature we may find their interruptions uncomfortable, even if maybe they haven't quite got everything neatly tied up and systematized, even if they may be wrong about a thing or two... The church needs gadflies.

John Arthur is a gadfly.

A passionate gadfly. Yes, he's done his best not to offend for offense's sake, not to take the cheap shot, but I can't guarantee you won't find some things that you don't like or totally disagree with. Still, I'm pretty confident you'll find plenty to be grateful for... like ice cubes on a hot day – and that as a result you'll have a yearning for a different life in Christ for yourself, for all of us.

I did.

I do.

Mark Greene

"...And no one pours new wine into old wineskins. Otherwise, the new wine will burst the skins; the wine will run out and the wineskins will be ruined. No, new wine must be poured into new wineskins. And no one after drinking old wine wants the new, for they say, 'The old is better.'"

Introduction

It's Kenya, January 2013. I've just traveled hundreds of kilometers by car from Kericho to Nairobi over the Great Rift Valley. Even on that single journey I've seen so many things that give rise to profound questions about my place on this earth. My heart aches to remember what my head cannot hope to contain.

I've seen a young Masai – walking behind a lone cow with ox-goad in hand – looking at me straight from the pages of the geography text books of my own childhood. He was followed by two more riding an ancient Masai-Fergusson silhouetted now against a lone tree in an endless horizon laughing. Later, there were four in a BMW seven series. I couldn't see if they were laughing. This *is* Africa and I cannot get enough of being beneath the biggest sky in the world. Today is my last day in the country before I return home to the UK. Before this day is out I'll turn down an ostrich ride.

Before I do that, I'll meet Ellen.

My company had arranged a driver and a schedule of sight-seeing before my flight home. First stop, the National Museum of Kenya. Ellen was an intern at the Museum working to complete her degree in tourism studies. It was a surprise to discover that the few shillings I paid to come in had also secured me her services as a guide. So it was that we came to be walking together among the ancient things. As we went, in the space between that which was carefully rehearsed, we spoke – one human to another – about all manner of things that were not. Here's a brief idea of some of what we covered in that two hours:

The forthcoming elections and the concern over tribal violence and civil unrest (the reason I am in Kenya at all); the theory of evolution; a comparison of the Scottish clan system with African tribalism; the liberation of Kenya under Kenyatta; the customs and practices of marriage and fidelity in the UK; the transformative value of education in Africa; the impact of David Livingstone on the region; the retro-impact of Pastor John (of Blantyre, Malawi) dumbfounding the good Methodist folk (of Blantyre, Scotland) in a BBC documentary by insisting that to be Christian they must preach the gospel; the evils of female circumcision; Ellen's rejection by her tribe for refusing the practice; the way her boyfriend contrived to split up with her because she no longer wore tribal dress when really it was because some African men do not like their wives to be clever; the way because of her choices she could not now hope to marry in her own home...

As we passed through the art gallery section Ellen asked me if I was artistic at all. I confessed to a low output there besides some poetry and, of course, preaching. "You are a preacher in the church", says Ellen, "then you must preach for me from the bible when we get to the end of our tour".

My text was Mary's song.

I related with passion the young Mary's strength of character to reject the accepted values of her culture. I extolled her refusal to live in the shadow of the fear of men. I rejoiced in her willful defense of the God who chooses to reveal His character through young women who have the strength to accept a curse. To wear with pride that which their culture considers shameful as a way to rejoice through their inmost being in the God who made all. I commended Mary's sacrifice as her way to testify before God that the proud should be rejected and the powerful sent away empty...

I commended Ellen to take Mary as her firebrand. To trust in the God who has already shown us in the bible how much He can, and will, rejoice in all the young women who are like her...

I'd like to say it was a brilliant sermon, but it was really only passable. Come on I had five minutes warning!

What was I doing? Well, to even begin to fully understand that you have to rewind the story three hours. I was sitting on the bed in my hotel that morning and I prayed the simplest of things to the God in whom I believe. Give me one chance this day to be the man in whom heaven touches earth. Give me one person this day that I can tell about you and your kingdom and, when the chance comes, don't let me mess it up.

But what was I doing in speaking to Ellen like this? Was I merely allegorizing? Or was I attempting to create a post-modern feminist polemic from a first-century manuscript? Although it might look like that, I wasn't. I was engaged in something much more profound. I was simply reading Ellen through reading Mary, all the while aware in the moment that this reading had become something sacred.

Now that you have read this story we are in a Gadfly moment, you and I. Since here then, in microcosm, are both the introduction and the conclusion to this book. It has become my profound belief that we all need to read like this in a much deeper way. It's just that the person we need to read is the church. We all need to face the challenge and the risk of reading our church through reading Jesus.

There is, of course, a more academic name for this process. It is called hermeneutics. A hermeneutic, for all that it sounds complex, is simply "a way" of reading a text. It's the filters that you operate when you read, even if you are not fully cognizant of them. It's the triggers, the buttons, the wiring of your reading brain, deep subtle things that cause some part of the meaning of what you read to resonate. That is how your hermeneutic becomes one aspect of how the bible can be a living text for you.

Hermeneutics *can have* enduring shapes. These, for the bible, tend to make sense when they are widely agreed. A good modern example of that would be trying to hear Paul's words in a first-century Jewish historical context. He was initially writing some of his letters to people in a first-century Jewish context, so this is one of the ways we need to understand what he was trying to say in them. This might strike you as so obvious that it's a surprise that I say it is "modern". I say that because it is. The bible, for centuries, *may not* have been being read this way.

R.W. Davies' book in 1948 changed the whole face of the debate, and that was only published relatively few decades ago.

Of course it's never simple and not all hermeneutics are agreed by everyone. They can be any random bit of post-modernism, for example take a look at 'the Jesus wars'. If you don't know what those are, don't worry it's not important. If it helps, think of a bizarre version of robot wars – everybody builds their own Jesus from the parts they have to hand and sets that Jesus off (controlled by them) to destroy all the other Jesuses. Hermeneutics can do that too.

That is not what I am up to though. But you will have to be judge of that for yourself. For Christians, what I want to argue is that the text we are reading is a conduit to the life of God and all His passion for your life. So the effect of reading a text like that cannot solely be about what you "notice" in it, or even about what you then go on to "believe". It has to be about which particles of it you have imbibed into your *being*. How you read God into the very substance of your life.

So, if you are interested in that, then we will be traveling together. My hope is for a journey on the open plain for the most part. After all, why would I just rehearse you what you already know? You *could* take the train that rumbles unendingly along the doctrinal, behavioral and often pseudo-intellectual tracks of the latest best-seller list sermonologue. That might be a more comfortable ride but, as my friend Heather Kelcey says, uncritically reading popular Christian books *over* a critical reading of the bible is a bit like Christian fast food – although you may feel fed, you are sometimes a long way from being nourished.

So, the subject of this book is reading the church through reading Jesus. Without defining the term whatsoever, what I want to say is that "the church":

- More than ever, needs a bigger Jesus
- Has to wrestle with a God who does not want our best

- Is losing the art of authentic, accountable friendship
- Sings a song of exclusion, sometimes the wrong one
- Was designed by Jesus as a place of sustenance not counsel
- Has a God who meets us at our edge not at our center
- Needs to rediscover, for its teaching, joy in its reading of Jesus

Buckle up...

Chapter 1

We're Gonna Need a Bigger Jesus

Do you think Sir Ian McKellen is sick of being prevented from entering night clubs by bouncers who say "You... shall not... passss!" For some actors a single line, in the thousands that make up their career, will be inextricably linked to them. Roy Scheider may have been ambivalent, more than thirty years later, for the line I've corrupted as my title here to be quoted back at him in an advert for Orange phones of all things. The reason it was repeated back is because it was (verbally) iconic. When it comes to Jesus one of my favorite verbally iconic lines is:

> you travel over land and sea to win a single convert and when you do you make him twice as much a son of hell as you are.

Another is:

> you diligently study the scriptures supposing that by them you possess eternal life, these scriptures testify to me and yet you won't come to me to have life

I'm guessing these are not in the readings list for your nativity play this Christmas.

Jesus, despite attempts to MAKE Him do so, does not have that killer line that defines Him. Rather, *every* line He has defines Him in some way. Every one is a killer somewhere for someone. All of them should be killers in the church. That's how it should work. Jesus comes to us through these lines. They confer a kind of 'textual life' onto the church, one we very much need.

That's why, in the church today, we are in danger, by omission or by design, of reducing the number of "admissible lines" for

Jesus to speak to us. We risk, in our rehearsal and celebration of Him, and in our over-familiarity with certain lines/under-familiarity with others, making Him smaller. What that means is, at some point, we either fade into the boredom of ritual obscurity (perhaps even to ourselves) or we are gonna need a bigger Jesus. Reading for a bigger Jesus we'll come to certain conclusions:

- Jesus read Himself in the scriptures and thus altered their reference point and their meaning
- Jesus announced His kingdom (the church) as continuous with God's storyline in the scriptures and fulfilling of it, thus altering their reference point and their meaning
- Jesus claimed to supersede all of the reference points yet given for the approach to God and viewed himself as consummating them
- Jesus thus calls the church to read itself as His life in this world

Here's how that works, here's a story of Jesus from the bible:

On one particular Sabbath, with His disciples in tow, Jesus is on the move. It's the Sabbath, the set apart day, the day for doing business with your God. The particular day for demonstrating your fidelity to God by your publicly observable behavior. Jesus, the rabbi, is out in the open. He has not set up a house church, calling people to sign up to Him and receive. He has not cornered a place in the temple, accepting reflected glory from austerity, longevity and depth of tradition. He has not rented a room in His home synagogue to carve out a geographical reputation. He is not waiting for people to come to His message (which in fact supersedes all of these institutions). He's taking it to them and seems to be in a hurry.

In this form of movement, like the prophets of old, Jesus is already a threat. It is not a surprise that He is shadowed now. Presumably He is reported back in His speech and deeds.

7

Pharisees, Teachers, Scribes, Sadducees, Zealots, Rulers and others, they all have a stake in him. Will He help their cause; will they lose territory (authority) to Him (he does miracles after all, that's pretty cool); will they lose disciples to Him? They dog His steps now, waiting.

An apparently minor controversy comes into view when Jesus' disciples pick a few ears of grain from the stalk and eat them as a snack on the way. Presumably they are not trampling brazenly right through the center of this farmer's field, presumably they are using the path along the edge. The edge of the field was a gleaning space, God told his people not to reap right to the edge (as this was greedy, and greed is idolatry). That way any poor or alien in the land could find a little food in God's economy – a kingdom promise if ever there was one. Presumably it's this kingdom grain that the disciples are picking because they are hungry. Did they forget to bring any food?

Jesus' detractors leap up and say "aha", look how your disciples break the Sabbath (picking a few ears being equated to full on reaping obviously). What does such Sabbath-breaking behavior say about you as their teacher, hmm?

Jesus, as He frequently does when challenged, responds with a question. It's not just any question, it's a killer question. To the people who by the age of thirteen may have memorized (get that, memorized) the old testament to qualify for their status. To the people who now teach and preach, and use these texts for their authority. To the few people in the radius of His hearing who are allowed to read publicly from these sacred manuscripts. Jesus says:

"haven't you read?"

For years now reading has defined these people's lives. Of course they have read, they of all people have read for goodness sake. Who does this guy think he is talking to?!

For Jesus, that's just the opener insult. He goes on:

"Haven't you read what David did?"

A classic rabbinical introduction to controversy and challenge. Then He proceeds to tell them a bible story which has, at its center, illegitimate eating. They'll know it well.

The protagonists of the story are none other than David (their hero) and his mighty men. The eating, which is noteworthy, is taking place when they are fleeing the wrath of Saul (in the days before David has taken the kingdom). The context in which they do this is a paradigm shift. God has given the kingdom to one whom He has secretly anointed king. This one is now moving subversively on a trajectory to capture this kingdom God has given him. David and his disciples will not just be successful in capturing any kingdom, it will be the greatest kingdom yet seen in Israel. It will, therefore, remain *the* kingdom which the Messiah must aspire to inherit.

So David – the soon to be true king after God's heart – is anointed by God and traveling in a hurry with his men at arms and, as they have need, they stop to eat. Going into God's temple tent they eat the bread that was laid before God, the bread that only priests are permitted to eat. They break God's law. Pointedly, in that story, they are not punished with fire. Their quest is thus shown to be surpassing of the authority of God's law concerning what may be eaten when.

In my visualizing this scene, I see Jesus stopping there. To let the insult really sink in, before He hits them with the killer line (literally, since this next line will be a nail in His own coffin, as so many of the things He says from here on are). With that next line they will be invited into Jesus' worldview. He will use the vehicle of an enacted parable within which they are, when they go home and think about it, being invited by Jesus, as we are, to see Him as a *bigger* threat than they already think He is. Here's how that works:

The power of precedent was a key teaching method for the

Jews and their rabbis. As with Abraham, Moses and their forefathers. As with the "traditions of the elders". Your 'observance' was heavily symbolic of who you wanted to be. That made them big on footstep following. It said something about you, who you followed (Apollos, Paul, Jesus, Antipas). Here, of course, they were, somewhat unwillingly, following Jesus around to watch Him.

Jesus then, as a rabbi might, invites them, by direct allusion, to see the behavior of His disciples (which they are criticizing) as a re-enactment of a Davidic storyline. In this re-enactment, Jesus is casting himself as a new David (we know anyway, and they may do too, that He is a direct descendant). To suggest that you are some kind of new David is, of course, a Messianic claim. Jesus is casting His disciples as the new 'David's mighty men' (mightiness clearly being at a bit of a premium for Jesus' budget so they weren't all that mighty). Importantly, therefore, Jesus is casting His critics as Saul's men.

His hearers won't be at all pleased that they have been put onto the side of Saul's mighty men, the men who were against God's true king. His detractors will not like being given the role of the illegitimate ones who pursue God's anointed judging him a dangerous pretender to the throne. As those who aid the rejected and worthless king to try and snuff out God's true choice. They won't like that at all.

All are invited in this to see Jesus' own trajectory in this story arc as nothing less than an overture of His intention (as God's new secretly anointed king), with His mighty men at hand, to fulfill again this Davidic story. He is going to take the kingdom. Just like it was in the time of David, ritual is of little account with such an agenda.

Jesus, the rabbi, uses this scripture story to point to four pregnant facts about His own mission in four killer lines:

He starts by saying look, God allows the temple priests to break the Sabbath by their work, yet they are innocent. Clearly in this, His second nod to priests, He is suggesting that His disciples somehow *are* like priests who can eat what they like on the Sabbath.

This is shock claim number one, since what does that make Him if not a high priest? Well the High Priest is not going to like that...

Jesus continues, almost casually, anyway:

"one greater than the temple is here".

Greater than God's house on earth, the place of God's glory, the place you go for forgiveness, the hope of Israel, is He MAD?!

This is shock claim number two; He thinks He is God's home, God's glory, God's hope and forgiveness incarnate. Well the temple rulers are not going to like that...

Jesus keeps going, undeterred by the granite faces that must surely now be forming, He says they don't understand the scriptures (Eek! Don't understand the scriptures!). This is because the scriptures, according to His reading, proclaim God's desire for mercy not sacrifice. This is a quotation that they will know (because some of them have memorized it) and it goes on to criticize the priests in the temple as a band of murderers.

This is shock claim three; He dares quote that at us! Dares to come round here with his law-breaking friends and cast us as the pious evil! Well we don't like that...

Then, all of a sudden, He snaps an apparent argument about the Sabbath shut in their faces. He says, my friends are innocent, not really because of the Sabbath or any of this but because "the son of man" (A.K.A. Jesus himself) is 'Lord of the Sabbath'.

This is shock claim four, and this one's a biggie. Jesus wants to exercise authority OVER and ABOVE God's law. He wants to do so with the title "son of man". *Now* we know who this guy thinks he is. He thinks he's in the place of God! He thinks He's God's chosen one, sharing God's authority and power. Well no one is going to like that! (Note to self, especially Caesar).

Jesus re-interprets a story found in the scriptures to reveal something deeper about Himself. It reveals that He is a much bigger threat than they already thought He was. This is a far bigger Jesus than a would-be Messiah – which is what they suspected they were dealing with (having already made their way through a few of those).

So you can see what I mean when I say we need to have a hermeneutic of Jesus. Jesus, right before our eyes, is re-reading these scriptures through His own mission and through His identity. Our task is to copy Him, to have a reading of church through a reading of Jesus. He is showing us the way.

So how do you read Him in this? Here is an apparently simple story in our bible about our Jesus that takes only ten lines to tell. On close inspection, if you read it as I suggest here, an apparently minor controversy is nothing of the sort. It is a major statement of Jesus' kingdom intentions (and his eschatological ones). It's fighting talk. If the church's reading is like this, then potentially here is a far bigger Jesus than the one we thank for saving us every Sunday.

Now, am I saying that if you read this story of Jesus and His disciples and *for your hermeneutic* it is just a minor controversy – between petty Pharisees who base their faith on excruciatingly small works and a free-thinking Jesus who thinks it's to do with a twenty-first century notion of 'faith' – that you are in the wrong?

Well, yes, that's exactly what I am saying. Wrong, because that's a small Jesus agenda. It has a complete poverty of ambition, and that will not do.

Am I saying that the church can't learn from this episode unless it has something like the dubious exegetical tools I am using at its disposal? Well, yes, that's exactly what I am saying. Thankfully for us, many gifted theologians are saying that more clearly. I just wish that many more people in pulpits and life-groups were doing likewise.

I'm not saying this because I'm some stuffed shirt of superiority (I hope). I'm saying it because when I read this cornfield battle story with my hermeneutic in place (that Jesus was enormously cool, incredibly shrewd, wickedly funny, unswervingly rehearsing the mandate His Father had given Him, and that He had the number of anyone who challenged this) fireworks are going off in my brain about Him. He becomes so much more present in the text.

(I say "my hermeneutic", clearly I got it from somewhere, blame Alistair Brown, John Bell and N.T. Wright for starters, but then blame that list of people who have set me on fire rather than sent me to sleep...)

A bigger Jesus is 'a greater than' Jesus
Reading Jesus in this way, I am absolutely loving Him – I thirst to know if He does more of these sorts of things, and Jesus does not disappoint me. In similar confrontations across the gospels He goes on to say and demonstrate that He is not just "greater than the Sabbath", as if that wasn't enough of a claim. He uses "greater than" credentials all over the place to show Himself to be a bigger Jesus, a bigger threat.

You want more? Jesus claims to be greater than all the greats of the Jewish-God-story so far:

- David – whom Jesus claimed referred to *Him* as 'Lord'.
- Jacob – whom Jesus was challenged to prove He was greater than – in the water/life giving credentials area – in the famous Samaritan woman at the well incident. This He promptly did.
- Jonah – which would take a book on its own to describe the reasoning for – but suffice to point out one obvious thing, a prophet who survives sacrifice and, from the depths of death, brings back an invitation to effective repentance and life.

- Solomon – in terms of wisdom and getting right what Solomon left half-baked, as well as being a son of Solomon/son of David himself.
- Moses – whom he not only corrected, but superseded (in line with Moses' own prophecy).
- Abraham – God covenanted with all nations in Abraham. Jesus claimed to be greater than Abraham as well – now things are getting shocking – whom He claimed to know.

More? Jesus claimed to be greater than the temple, which He personally cleansed of a corrupt priesthood. A priesthood who, behind closed doors, were disenfranchising those who could only draw near but not come in – by throwing up a pious Market in their way. A temple that Jesus claimed, with great intentional zeal and anger, to be what the prophet said, God's house of prayer for all nations (I say 'intentional anger' because anyone who takes time to fashion a whip is coolly planning what he is going to do with it). A temple, He, for a few glorious hours, restored and cleansed. A few hours in which – within temple precincts – He accepted Messianic praise from children before healing and restoring all who CAME TO HIM. Not to "it", you see.

Of course Jesus, ever the two-edged sword, is also explicitly cursing the temple in the long run. Its rulers' complicity with the way of war (revolutionary war) was going to herald its destruction. A fully ironic prophecy from the one who wept over warring Jerusalem because it would not recognize the day it was visited by the way of peace. And who usually visits the temple to bring Shalom? God does. Jesus later claimed that by so doing in person He had *replaced* the temple. He even cryptically refers us to His literal body (and, after the resurrection, therefore, church) as the new temple.

Still more? Jesus claimed to be greater than Satan who cannot tempt Him, cannot subvert Him, cannot display corruption's ultimate authority over Him – this is even as those present accuse

Jesus to His face that Satan is really who He is working for. Satan's house is looted by Jesus, because Satan has been bound up, and this loot taken (back) to another house.

He doesn't even stop within a first-century Jewish hermeneutic because Jesus claims to be greater than all of the house of Israel, and the fig tree which symbolizes it. Salvation comes from the Jews, but, in the end, God would need only one amazing Jew to bring it. Since the house of Israel was not found to be large enough for God to dwell in, God just gets a bigger house – and we have come to call that house "the church". Jesus is, of course, greater than the church, which is really His house and not ours. It's time we displayed that more.

So it comes to this, the church inherits *all these claims* from Jesus now. So we must see to it that in the church the hermeneutic of Jesus, therefore, is permitted to run wild! We have a bible which maintains that Jesus is "the image of the invisible God" and that "God was pleased to have all His fullness dwell in Him". That's a pretty huge claim. In reading Jesus like this I'd expect to find evidence of such a deep agenda. I mean if He'd had that agenda He'd court more than a bit of controversy wouldn't He?:

Your father Abraham rejoiced at the thought of seeing my day; he saw it and was glad. "You are not yet fifty years old", the Jews said to him, "and you have seen Abraham!" "I tell you the truth," Jesus answered, "before Abraham was born, I am." At this they picked up stones to stone him, but Jesus hid himself, slipping away from the temple grounds.

The Jews gathered round him, saying, "How long will you keep us in suspense? If you are the Christ, tell us plainly". Jesus answered, "I did tell you, but you do not believe. The miracles I do in my Father's name speak for me, but you do not believe because you are not my sheep. My sheep listen to my voice; I know them, and they follow me. I give them eternal life, and they shall never perish; no one can snatch them out of my hand. My Father, who has given them to me, is greater than all; no one can snatch them out of my Father's hand. I and the Father are one." Again the Jews picked up stones to stone him, but Jesus said to them, "I have shown you many great miracles from the Father. For which of these do you stone me?" "We are not stoning you for any of these," replied the Jews, "but for blasphemy, because you, a mere man, claim to be God."

Here are two accounts from Jesus' earthly life where He has increasingly confrontational interchanges with the ruling religious order of His day. Both result in the red mist coming down and those present feeling that, in the zeal they have for God, they have a mandate to instantly and brutally execute Jesus without further recourse to any judiciary. Why?

Jesus claims not only to be older than someone who died centuries before, but He claims to be *"I am"* which is one of the only given names for God. Jesus claims not only to be a good shepherd (coded language that, as He says elsewhere, the current shepherds are corrupt). Jesus, in fact claims to be *the* Good Shepherd (coded language for God's Messiah which the prophets told the people to wait for).

He claims that He has the power to grant eternal life (get that, grant it) and that He holds this life (this water, this bread, this wine) in His hands in an interchangeable way to the way that God does. He claims to be one with His father.

Even if Jesus' claims were abstruse in some way (which, to me, they are not) those gathered around Him at the time conclude that He is claiming to be God. Those who witnessed this recorded that reaction because it would have been more than a little sphincter-tightening for them too, scary Jesus, bad Messiah.

So we read Jesus *reading Himself* as equivalent to God and that is slippery to hold onto. It supersedes our experience completely – because it points to a supremacy which, even in this highly advanced age, we cannot ever hope to get our heads around and that makes Jesus bigger and more controversial still. He carries on making claims and showing this supremacy over, well, everything from life to death and back again, scooping up the cosmos along the way. That's a big agenda, that's a big Jesus.

As more clever people than me are constantly pointing out, that agenda made the greatest of sense, and the greatest of controversy, on the stage that it was first played out. This is certainly one part of the hermeneutic that we need, AND, somehow supernaturally, it also makes the greatest of sense on our stage, cue The Church – inheriting all this. How does that work?

Well it CAN work with a small Jesus, the timeless moral example Jesus, the infinitely allegorical Jesus, the pre-critical Jesus, the 'a funny thing happened to me this week when I fell asleep preparing this sermon' Jesus and that's my worry. Mainly because that Jesus makes no *real* claims today and cannot create, for today's people, the controversy that I love.

Maybe you don't agree. I'm in love with the bigger Jesus to whom these original writings point so powerfully. I love the Jesus who, upon their reading, leapt off the page and into the room. Here's a snippet of my story...

Alone in 1988 in an upper room in a flat in Orchard St., Aberdeen, a young man was reading the scriptures. Scriptures he had developed an appetite for mainly to settle a challenge from a friend, certainly not to find God. Scriptures which had, however, become compelling, interesting and, to be fair, a bit angering. His anger related to Jesus. He had, through the fault of no one really, his whole life been fed a line, given an impression, drawn a picture of Jesus which was dull, dull, dull. Then one day he actually read the core text and Jesus exploded on the page as cool, cool, cool. Hip, confrontational, heroic even, but not dull. Why had he been lied to all this time?

On this day in Orchard Street the young man had been attending church for something like six months, it was a shock for both parties, no doubt about that. He hadn't gone to become one of them; the closer he got to them the more they troubled him. He went, and only continued to go initially, because church was the place where these weird texts were explained and Jesus, presumably, was unpacked a little. Truth was, for all his University educated blah, blah, blah, there was just a load of stuff in the bible that was just too damn hard to comprehend. The place he knew that they explained Jesus and all that, was church.

He knew church was the place where they explained Jesus.

On this particular day in 1988 the young man was alone in the middle of the day and was finishing reading this weird thing called the gospel according to John. His intellect had been mighty stirred it had to be said, not something he had been expecting. The street was quiet, the world was quiet, a pale sunlight lit up the dowdy furniture. Pages turned, if he'd only read his textbooks as diligently... but anyway.

He gets to the end of this wholly remarkable book (a book that is largely testified by secular and religious commentators alike as a work of literary genius). In its closing stanza he notices something odd, something snags on his brain. Jesus has become interesting no doubt, challenging no doubt, someone to be like really, no doubt 'Jesus the concept' was a rich concept, but then there was this:

Jesus did many other things as well. If every one of them were written down, I suppose that even the whole world would not have room for the books that would be written.

Well, that was odd and, as the wheels started turning in his head, it went from odd to a huge problem. Jesus could not logically live up to this closing bravado – scientifically this was incorrect. There was only one way it could even hope to approach the truth at some future point and that would be if Jesus were still alive today.

That's when He showed up... Like you knew He would. That's when He became impossibly big. Nothing was to be the same ever again. Without a hermeneutic in sight – just one set of damaged goods and a bible.

Here's the Gadfly moment then. Am I saying that the church is gonna need a bigger Jesus because:

- It does not illuminate the scriptures with proper excitement
- It has a poverty of ambition about the mission and the identity of its central figure

Well, yes and no. In my experience of church this excitement and ambition have been intermittent at best, hard to find even. This level of debate about the bigger meanings and spiritual challenges of Jesus in any life-group, church meeting – or even most sermons – seems to exhaust people and I don't know why that is. What about you? Maybe the Jesus experienced at your place is big enough?

What I am saying is that I *believe* the Church needs a bigger Jesus because it can never hope to have one that is big enough. *I believe* the church should take that responsibility on the chin and stretch for it, for all she is worth, especially given her mandate and who she is supposed to reach. To do that better she needs to know her Lord in *at least* these sets of terms, grounded in His culture, exalted to His kingdom and, therefrom speaking directly into the 'viscerality', loving directly into the hearts, challenging directly into the minds – and washing the feet of all who come anywhere near her places and her people all at the same time. Anyway, this IS getting a bit preachy now...

...it's just that, the bible refers to the church as the keeper of this great mystery revealed. In an accompanying mystery that we cannot hope to fathom, isn't it true that we, above all people – who have been so fully affected by this – will want to combine our expressions of it, presided over by the Spirit whom Jesus sent, into one almighty common explosion of it? So mighty that all the forces of darkness and Hell don't stand a chance when faced with its onslaught on this world.

So mighty and beautiful that God himself wants His son to marry it and hold the mother of all parties. Shorthand: we take His name, 'the Church of Christ'.

The church that bears such a name does not need some rambling aspiration to be faithful, relevant and nice. It needs rather to wield *a reading of Jesus* that fires our imagination drawn from the well of His authentic model. So, here is one such model that I am going to look at in this book, one reading that Jesus hinted about and riddled about in His earthly life: At the end of space and time, or the end of all things, or the end of the age, or the coming of the kingdom of heaven, whatever language you want to use here, there is to be the mother of all parties. It's called the wedding feast of the lamb. We are all invited.

What I want to now say throughout this book is that, in a foretaste of this party, an immanent realized eschatological position if you will, the church is already the champagne at that party. You are not the wine of the kingdom (sorry Graham) you are its champagne. And it is time somebody opened the champagne.

Chapter 2

God Wants Our First, Not Our Best

Now, to think of a clever way to start a tricky second chapter: There's a boy-man called Jerub-Baal who invented the stealth-torch and, in a strange pre-cursor to Kate Bush, did find a sound that could kill someone.

Not bad.

Even after all the powerful and elaborate claims I have just made for it in chapter one, we have to face up to the fact that church is a real thing made up of real people. People have needs, worries, emotions, behaviors and can, if we are completely honest, be prone to certain pathologies. These all come together in the complex way church experiences and expresses its corporate self. This corporate self can deeply affect us as individuals because, to state a slightly obvious truth, we all have a stake in the storyline of church. This depends on our emotional investment in a particular local expression of church, its cultural givens and its people. It also depends on whether I agree with everyone else about the future storyline of both of these churches.

When I start comparing the storylines of churches I know and the storylines that I find in the bible, I see that there are times when the church's storyline might be significantly challenged as 'misaligned'. Repairing that misalignment is what this book, in one sense, is trying to be about. Part of the misalignment seems to me to come from the church's historical and current pathologies around the notion of "giving God our best".

Let me give you a silly example of this. In times gone by it was a given to dress nicely to be in God's presence, this was even called the Sunday Best. Although that outward appearance example has largely faded, I would argue that its psychological equivalent, especially in serious evangelical churches, remains. Thus, it remains a widely assumed fact frequently derived from the scriptures that Christians need to be a people who, individually and corporately, are striving at all times to give God our best. As my chapter title gives away, I think this is nonsense and creates a force in the church which is, if not destructive, then a source of inertia at least.

The problem with this inertia is that it is very distracting from Jesus' trust that we are to be (forcefully) advancing His kingdom. Let's begin to explore two illustrative arguments around this idea of giving God our best. To do this, I need to go a little bit dark for a second and take a pop at some problems I see in church. I know this doesn't seem to sit well with the whole "you are champagne" thing, but it will be necessary in almost every chapter. The problems I want to look at here are just two example pathologies. These I will call "ministry monasticism" and "personalized prioritization".

Once I've looked at these, I want to explore the concept of "textual life" in relation to them. I want to search for 'a reading' which could serve us as their viable counterpoint. We will then tentatively explore some alternative storylines that might come to be read through my hermeneutic.

If I get that right this gives us some possible principles for the life of a modern church as well as an example of how my hermeneutic might work. I can give you the conclusions already and that might be a useful steadying post for my erratic writing style, they are:

- Individualism in the church consents to a tradition that allows me to define what's best to give to God around my own agenda
- Even when we define the best to give God by consensus it can quickly become a cultural definition and will be free from any real risk

- For God, our failure and particularly our risk might actually be a vital source of deepening relationship with us
- We need to realign our thinking to be supporting God in His best by bringing Him our first.

Obviously for the last two I'll have to lay out what that means in some sort of depth. But first, let's take a pop at the church:

Ministry Monasticism

I knew a church secretary once who would always send me a very formal letter to help me understand the "usual guidance" for visiting preachers even though I'd been many times. This would contain an order of service, a list of preferred songs and so on. Much to his annoyance, I always ignored it (I wasn't being rude, they used to ask me to do youth services and they were meant to be more funky). I would be met at the door by him and he would press upon me any important notices. He would take me into a room and then invite "the diaconate" to join us for prayer. This involved ten people filing into a small room and standing in a circle. Two pre-selected ladies would then pray short prayers, one for me, one for the church and, on his signal with no one saying anything else, they all filed out. He would then accompany me to two doors and ask me to enter by the one on the right whilst he entered on the left (both doors went to the same open area). He repeatedly invited me to sit in the larger "mercy seat" chair at the front during the service (I never did, preferring to sit in the pew with everybody else). He was always mildly irked that I wouldn't preach from the pulpit.

You're getting it, aren't you? This loving but rigid man had a view about how things should be done and sought to see to it that they were done that way. I have no doubt in my mind that he was doing his best for God. Here's the thing though, he'd defined what that best was himself – it was dominated by his experience of church culture and his expectation of the storyline of that culture to continue unchanged. This fuelled his view of God and his view of ministry. He held everybody else to ransom with the passive aggression of it. He is guilty of ministry monasticism.

Ecumenical terminologies aside, let's agree that any modern church is loosely made up of many "ministries", like the one our friend above was discharging. These ministries with a small 'm' are the range of services that can be given by the, largely volunteer, forces that make up the church. Ministry leaders are people, and people, particularly in something that is as objectively important to us as the church, can become prone to pathologies of giving their best.

Ministry monasticism kicks in when that minister is allowed (passively or actively) to define how we, the church, should give God our best through how they give God theirs. I know it sounds harsh to call this pathological but this is really monasticism masquerading as service. This is an individual using church as a vehicle to concentrate on giving God their own best possible personal offering.

In the past I think this had rather a lot to do with organ music, but it is very diversified now since modern churches have many more logistical and spiritual components than their forebears. Many of these components have come to be considered defining of the church for the members. If the church is tight on resources the link between the small 'm' ministry and its "minister" can be next to permanent and therefore very hard to evaluate or challenge, but here's a five point checklist to see if it qualifies as a monasticism:

1. Does your small 'm' minister come over, well, a little obsessive about how things should be done "properly"?
2. Do you get the feeling that your small 'm' minister has invested this service with their personal story of 'faith actualization'?

3. Is your small 'm' minister and his/her ministry essentially synonymous?
4. Would the idea that your small 'm' minister be asked to step aside for a time horrify them?
5. Would certain people in your congregation happily punch the small 'm' minister, or at least roll their eyes at the very mention of their name?

When a person responsible for a small 'm' ministry *accepts* the idea that they should give God their best, there is danger. Something which starts out with the desire to be serving everyone can become an amplified expression of a very individual worship of God.

A church's storyline should be plural and it will always falter when it is based instead around that of a range of individuals acting *individually*. Calcifying at the center of that will be that whole set of *private* assumptions on worship, preaching, pastoral visiting, evangelism, Christmas celebrations etc. about "the way things are done properly". This is actually unchallenged individualism which consents to a tradition that allows me to define what's best to give to God around my own personal agenda. That just leads to inertia.

Personalized Prioritization

Whilst ministry monasticism is an idea of someone giving their, rather intense, best to God gone awry it has an anti-thesis. This is where whole sections of the community can come up with a diverse set of reasons why God cannot be given their best. This I will call personalized prioritization but note that this is a behavior of groups. To any church leadership who want to organize God's church in line with a God-given mission, a serious long-term planning problem will always present itself. It is people who are the main resource. They are sometimes only randomly available and their volunteering *has to be* done on a budget of time. Evidentially this is a tight one. Managing that budget leads to an uneasy balance, because sometimes people want to validate how little time they can *afford* to prioritize for church and mission.

You know where I am going with this, so I might as well say it. Personalized prioritization kicks in when the leadership finds that it can only deploy kingdom resources once it has taken into account the immutability of certain things, here's an incomplete list: a five-day working week; a pleasure day on Saturday; a family lunch (at lunchtime!) on Sunday; no more than two nights a week out of the house; the regrettably finite amount of annual large scale time due to family holidays; and the unavailability of numerous, but random, weekends per year. The latter are needed by busy moderns to 'get away from it all' and one is left feeling that Church is very much included in that 'all', and might sometimes be the focus. Once all of that is taken into account, the leadership has its resource.

Let's not make it sound like this pathology is always the work of the assertive, self-assured middle classes. It comes in a passive version too. The person in the second year of a timid marriage who hopes that it should be obvious that quality time alone with one's spouse is an inalienable pre-cursor to marital health. Couples with young children at various stages who hope it will be obvious that there is a need to withdraw from responsibility (and evenings) because everyone agrees you raise your children well. People with middling kids who hope it will be obvious that, when they had to seek another fellowship with more kids that age, they "left for the sake of the children".

Nor is this pathology always deliberate, spare a thought for that more beleaguered group of parents in painful relationships with teenagers (or younger) who let every Sunday morning turn into a sour shouting match about how boring and irrelevant church is – something that might be an astute observation in any case. Quietly and inadvertently these parents can come to resent the church's (and sometimes, more deeply, their own) failure at engaging said children in the way of faith. That resentment can manifest itself in a passive aggression towards upbeat externally facing mission.

When the leaders do try to have a conversation with all of these groups about prioritizing how much time and commitment is (perhaps sacrificially?) available for church and mission, this can quickly descend into a post-modern argument about "importance" and "unimportance". The offering I can afford compared to my priorities. The church might be held in a bond of gratitude for anything that's given from such a valuable place as "my" at all. The conclusion? Busy or beleaguered modern people just simply can't prioritize consistently enough to be relied on after personalized prioritization is given adequate consideration.

The personalized prioritization pathology might be the other side of the historical coin from where the church used to be using guilt as its primary method of motivating giving and keeping people rather servile to its authority. Today it is just the story (perhaps even reaction) of a slight deregulation of the need to serve the church and the expression of personal faith and judgment. It's just the story of busy, faithful people who are compelled to prioritize. When that prioritization is (privately) done along the lines of a culturally endorsed, but somewhat invisible, set of givens they are happy to give to God's church. God's church therefore, from a lot of its people a lot of the time, gets the "best of the rest".

Corporately when we leave this individualism unchecked we consent to define by silent consensus that God only deserves the best of the rest of our lives. That quickly becomes a cultural definition free from accountability, risk of failure or any real risk at all in the church. It becomes a way that we are allowed to see our lives played out *in the church as one of our contexts*, rather than *as those who are* the church. Aided and abetted by this poor theology and a dubious history of practice we thus accept a post-modern individualistic storyline which is this: we get to define the best that should be given – we get to set the agenda.

Two of the best then:

Ministry Monasticism: one who defines, on God's behalf, the best offering to give.

Personalized Prioritization: those ones who are complicit in endorsing the idea that God should be pleased with being offered the best of the rest.

Now that's a mean and cheerless line to take, what happened to all that talk of champagne?

Well, church is tough. Loving church, in a way that doesn't damage something or someone, is tougher. Calling the modern church into the truly plural entity God has designed is toughest of all. What we have to do in the storylines of these (and other) pathologies is locate a cushion. It's a cushion that could be smothering your church. We need to find the cushion of 'culture and expectation', and when we do, we need to knock the stuffing out of it. How would we do that? Well, I'm glad you asked, we could begin by recognizing that the starting point is all wrong. God doesn't want our best. He wants our first.

Here's a story from the bible:

There's a young man in the bible who always draws my eye whenever I think about questions of dealing with an unsatisfactory status quo. I know you thought that this book would be all Jesus, Jesus, Jesus but let's take a new look at a blast from the Sunday school past. The features of his memorable story, like the storylines at the start of the chapter, seem a fixed part of the furniture.

I've always interpreted this young man as angry; the text about him gives me that feel. Even if he was, in fact, a sweet delight, little of the core of what I want to say changes for that. So let's leave him interesting. We encounter Gideon threshing wheat in a wine press. What an idiot. Only a fool threshes wheat in a wine press. A wine press is protected from the wind, a threshing barn is high on a hill to take advantage of the full force of said wind to blow away the lighter chaff when you throw the whole lot up in the air (just in case you don't know what threshing is). Gideon's chaff is raining on his head, maybe in more ways than one.

His story in the bible opens with the reason why he is apparently an idiot. An enemy force is so oppressive that it subjugates Israel completely and keeps it that way by deliberately wrecking crops and livestock. The story says that they did not spare a living thing for Israel. For seven years they annually invaded the land with a great force and with one purpose *"to ravage it"*. The once proud folk of Israel were living in caves and dugouts. After seven years of this they called out to God. Maybe God can save us.

God shows up and says, to paraphrase, now you remember all that I did in Egypt because Egypt is upon you again. You know how mighty I was and you want some more of that action, well, the answer is no, you reap what you sow, you brought this on yourselves. Unpacking that reaction is not my aim, but just one of the reasons the answer is 'no' is because half of them are still worshipping Satan and all his little wizards in the midst of all this and, whatever that is, it ain't no generation God's going to listen to.

But to the God of innovation, the God who works secretly, the answer wasn't all 'no'. The answer was a new thing, something unexpected. The angel of the Lord – a big news angel who frequently turns *into* God – came and sat down. Conveniently right next to where this young man was, however feebly and chaff covered, defying the oppressor. Angels speak counter-intuitively.

"The Lord is with you, mighty warrior".

The gravity of this statement completely fails to land because it hits a cushion of culture and expectation which maybe has a little bit of personal baggage sitting on top of it. Now, this is where you get to choose a milk-sop Gideon or a raging furnace of post-teenage angst, it's all in the voice, here's my interpretation, and mine's as good as any, if a bit Scottish:

"Aye right! God with us! What do you call this pile of crap then? Where is this God our fathers (but not my father since he's gone over to Satan) talk so much about? When the elders bang on about mighty out-stretched arms, nation-crushing, sea-crossing, fire-blazing, supernatural rescuers taking us gloriously out of Egypt. If we were brought gloriously out of Egypt, how come I can still see Egypt from here? If He did rescue us then it was to abandon us."

I think Gideon got this spectacularly wrong and he would keep getting it wrong until what I call an 'I am' moment came along for him. In that 'I am' moment he is going to get an insight about God so powerful that it will change his view of God and of the people of God forever. He is going to discover that God doesn't want their best. He's going to realize that God wants the first.

Of course I am going to say that churches sometimes badly need their own "I am" moments too in order for God to get His calling across to them. Let's look at how Gideon's 'I am' comes. As we do this let's keep some things in mind:

- Gideon is perilously close at times to ministry monasticism
- The people of Israel have adopted personalized prioritization
- Jointly, their best response to God's mission is evidently not what God requires and He wants to reject their best
- God confronts them instead with the need to take risks by giving Him their first

Here's how that works. To me Gideon misheard the angel's "*The Lord is with you.*" Perhaps he had been taught to hear such a thing in the plural – to hear "you all" and not YOU. But what if, actually, God had been speaking in the singular? Now I'm in all kinds of trouble if the Greek and Hebrew don't bear that out. I know too that, initially at least, I'll seem to be paddling upstream in favor of ministry monasticism, but bear with me. The evidence is that the nation wasn't ready to give God anything, but Gideon, bless his cotton fleece, in God's eyes he was nearly ready. This story is so famous; you'll be bored if I unpack it all, so here's the speed version:

> **God** (*cos the angel has morphed into God, told you he/she/it would*): You can save Israel
> **Gideon** (*still not hearing*): My clan is too puny and, not to put too fine a point on it, I'm only seventeen myself and never trained for battle what with half my life under oppression from marauding hordes.
> **God** (*turning up the celestial heat*): I WILL be with you.
> **Gideon** (*eyes finally opened*): If you are who I think you are, I'll need to bring you an offering (*because I listened in Sunday school all the same, and I know what "our fathers" said about you, because, secretly, it was important to me*).
> **God:** I'm not leaving (*despite what you said about me at the start of this conversation*).

Gideon goes in, prepares a young goat, reaches for a loaf and thinks hold on a minute, this is definitely a Passover kind of conversation. So he makes unleavened bread, the way God likes it, plus it's quicker, but that is part of the original point. Gideon, too, is slowly picking up that he needs to be "reading" his story in the (correct) context. Unleavened bread is how it was in the exodus, this I'm sure pleases Gideon's "exodus heart" seeking a long-awaited game changer.

Gideon finds the angel/man/android/who knows what's still there and makes the offering. God accepts this with fire and the angel rises up on it, all very scary. Gideon realizes he has seen God and expects – like every good Israelite – to die on the spot (especially having ragged on God quite a bit for all the 'not showing up and doing something').

God, on this occasion, doesn't smote, He says, 'Shalom' (wholeness), it's all fine, Gideon has no idea that this shalom is a prophecy. God sets Gideon a test which means it's time to go public with his faith. So rather than complain about the absence of God, it's time for Gideon to take some action to be His presence. Time to indict the absence of faithfulness in his own compromised nation, in his own compromised town, in his own compromised family. Time to listen to his own un-compromising heart and do something.

You know the story; he cuts down his father's altar to the infesting god Baal. He thus openly opposes his own family's complicity with idols (thankfully dad wasn't too sincere, it turns out). He then stands up bravely to the whole assembly when it is discovered that he dunnit. It is interesting though that Gideon chose to strike his victory for God under cover of darkness. Easier? You choose.

So Gideon, our man-boy, earns his fighting chops. They give him a new name, they call him Jerub-Baal (Baal will contend with him). They wait to see what goodies Baal has in store for this angry young dude. Belief in Baal to one side, they know it's one thing to sneak in and rip down a phallic symbol with the aid of night vision goggles – it's quite another still to put your head above the daylight parapet in the current political climate and keep that head on your shoulders for long. After all, they can hear the annual locust-fest gathering on the horizon. This little story isn't over yet.

And so our stage is set for a new storyline. The storyline of Jerub-Baal, God the innovator and the 'I am' moment. For that moment to come, God will have to allow Gideon to express his faith and his doubt the only way he knows how – by giving God his best. Gideon's people, who have all but forgotten what it means to do so, will also be allowed to try to give God "their best".

God doesn't want either of these bests, God wants the first.

So let's draw out if we can that 'principle of first'. After all, if I just keep barking at you "God wants the first", then I'm like a lot of people who write with gravitas in Christian books, repetition in the place of profundity. What did that really look like in this story? Have I got a case?

Gideon has been strangely changed by his victory over Baal and the villagers. Like Samson and others (Saul, David, Deborah, John and Jesus to name a few) this fills him with the Holy Spirit and turns him into a firebrand. He then summons four and a half whole clans to his disposal, some 32,000 men, and how they come! Interestingly though, in the face of his own epidemic of "church growth" Gideon lays a fleece for confirmation that the victory will be his. Where did that doubt come from? Had he taken a wrong turn, struck a discordant note? We don't know, all we are told is he doubts. Thankfully he is man/boy enough, to take that doubt back to God.

There's a problem with Gideon's storyline and, before this story is over, he is going to have to learn what it is and how to put it right. Gideon shows, even with concomitant periods of doubt that he wants to express his faith in God. He does this the only way he knows how – through a cushion of culture and expectation that leads him to try to attempt ministry monasticism. From the moment he sat in his winepress all by himself, he was doomed to try and give God "his best".

In the current situation how did he know what that best should look like? Well, history taught him for one thing. The rehearsed story and self-image of Israel taught him. The people are oppressed, God raises up a champion, the champion raises up an army, the army wins a mighty victory, job done...

Here is Gideon playing to that form, he has become the champion and there are thirty-two thousand reasons for him to feel vindicated. His momentary self-doubt has been squashed by a convincing supernatural wet blanket and he has faith that God is backing his campaign. Gideon asked God directly:

"If you will save Israel by my hand..."

...and God has said 'yes'. So now he can afford to have confidence in his calling. These thirty-two thousand men camped around him, this storyline – these are a living example of a faithful servant at his 'best'.

Although arranging the toilet facilities alone, doesn't bear thinking about.

There is then a tough conversation around the corner for Gideon. It is a conversation *precisely* about the storyline and these thirty-two thousand confidence-inspiring men. God shows up and ruins it all. He says, 'Look Gideon, I don't want this, this isn't what I have in mind. Give me decision-making control for a minute and let's see what we can do' – and it is 'we' because Gideon will be announcing the results of God's thinking.

And, importantly, Gideon does give Him control. Let's offer the people personalized prioritization says God. Let anybody who is frightened know that they can just desert the needs of the community and go home. Well that's totally mad for a start, it's a war we are having here, most of them will be frightened. Most of them are. Mass exodus, twenty-two thousand down. Still, ten thousand left, not the end of the world.

Then God says, 'Still not happy, take them to the river and I'll sift them further. I'll say who goes with you and who stays, I'll pick'. God picks only three hundred worthy souls. Three hundred! *One-hundredth* of the original size and force (of the congregation); a force now so paltry it has just two chances of pushing back the locust horde: no chance and fat chance. Gideon dutifully sends nine thousand seven hundred armed men back to their tents. His remaining three hundred are not stupid though, they get the field rations and the battle horns off the others. Importantly, not one of them suggests choosing a new leader instead of young Gideon, one that's less of a loony perhaps. He certainly must look nuts. Gideon's grasp of the situation must feel to have come somewhat "unhinged".

Dude, what just happened?

What happened is that God has saved Gideon from a ministry monasticism. What has also happened is that God has rejected the best that Israel has to offer. What has happened is that God has set a stage for His best and all that He really requires is that Gideon, and the people who have rejected personalized prioritization, get ready to take the almighty risk of trusting God by giving Him their first.

God, it is evident, expressly did not on this occasion want a great victory for Israel (with His help). Since that was very much on the cards here with thirty two thousand men, God rearranges those cards. This is hardly a conclusion of exegetical genius; God says as much right there in the text. Clearly God did not want Gideon's best and by extension (and inclusion) He did not want some of Israel's best either. He wanted to reject these. He was after something deeper.

We have to stop and ask why. Why does God let one-third of Israel's armed forces muster for battle if He had no intention of using them? Why send them away so theatrically and so deliberately? The implication seems to me to be that, in this, God wants the fact that He doesn't want the best Israel has to offer to be experienced by them. God didn't just want to reject the culture and expectation of the same old storyline; He wanted to publicly reject the culture and the expectation of the same old storyline.

Poor old Gideon though. He had, even with doubt, still expressed his real faith in God the only way he knew how – by giving God "his best". God doesn't want it. If I was Gideon, I'd be gutted.

Gideon can afford to be gutted, can't he? Didn't he listen to the angel? Didn't he risk a great deal in tearing down the altar? Hadn't he made his case plain to God, that he wanted to have a faith in the God of his fathers, in the God who rescued the nation from the oppressor? Hadn't he been empowered when God told him (twice) that he himself would be instrumental in creating that victory? Hadn't he done his (best) part?

Well, yes, obviously he had done his part. Thing is, Gideon can't conveniently invent post-modernism. He can't be seen as having a responsibility to "do" just *his* part; to give just his own definition of best to satisfy (and sanctify) the needs of his own individual faith journey. He can't be permitted to commit ministry monasticism. Gideon had a responsibility before God to "be" a part of what he said he cared so much about – the people. There was a necessary plurality to all this and God forces that hand on him here. So he is not let off the hook, he must experience "corporate" in the midst of his "personal". He needs to do this to get any kind of grip on a God who transcends both of them.

Being a part of Israel's experience still had something to teach Gideon himself and that would qualify his 'I am' moment when it came. He was Israel too. Part of him was plural.

The storyline that involved Israel trying to give God their best was derived from their knowledge of God to date, a cushion of culture and expectation. The trouble is that this expectation and culture were fundamentally backward looking into the very storyline that had created the current impasse. If Gideon had been listening more closely to the dialogue he himself had been having:

"go in the strength you have and save Israel", *"if you will save Israel by my hand"*

Would he have been able to see the insight, the innovation, coming?

Now there's another post-modern risk alert coming here before you read the next paragraphs. I am not, in any way, saying that this story was really only all about God's relationship with Gideon all the while. What I'm asking you to entertain is that this story was also about God's relationship with Gideon. Different thing.

This story is not just Gideon's "personal" journey; the experiences of "corporate" Israel are integral to it. I hope that point is made. However, and it's a mighty big however for those of us who believe that God is an innovator – corporate Israel was just about to learn something truly profound about God from *one* of its persons daring to break tradition and daring Israel to risk following him as he gives God his unalloyed *first*.

Gideon's personal storyline had been set up deliberately by God to clash so that something innovative would be possible (that's why, especially when we hate it, we have to go to church). God is about to do something amazing for Gideon (and for Israel). Before He can though, there is some business to do with the beleaguered Gideon. God has to help him deal with an apparent failure. The way God does this is to re-establish intimacy and purpose. He comes very close to Gideon again and gives him another personally *risky* choice – reading between the lines, you'd be forgiven for thinking that God, faced with Gideon in the way of the warrior, misses Gideon in the way of the winepress, it's almost like His power is made perfect in weakness... Anyway, God asks Gideon a question. Not just any question.

'Are you afraid to attack the camp now Gideon (sub-text, now that you have got only three hundred men left)?'

The answer is not recorded.

This is not a conversation about the 'mighty warrior' but about his doubt and fear. This is why the fleece encounter, although it's the most narratively appealing part of the Gideon story, is less interesting than this conversation. Just like the tumbling walls of Jericho are, actually, less interesting than the conversation over Joshua's sandals. Gideon is being given the chance (like Joshua before him) not to offer his best, but to unswervingly offer God an un-pre-defined *first*.

This story began with a confidence offering from Gideon to God. It becomes complete in a confidence offering from God to Gideon (and the three hundred). God doesn't want Gideon's ministry monastic best, because God wants Gideon to know that he has been found worthy of being involved in God's best. This will only come about when Gideon inspires everyone to give God the first.

If you are afraid about what to do now, says God, take your servant and, just the two of you, go spy out the land (echoes of Joshua and Caleb for me here, only send two). Go on, I want to let you into a secret. Gideon, who we can assume, therefore, IS afraid, goes. What we are then given in the unfolding story is a bizarre sequence of events which could neither be predicted from the current state of affairs or from past experience. Midianites start prophesying that *Gideon's sword* will overturn the camp.

And then Gideon finally gets it (supernaturally I would argue), this is his burning bush moment, his commander of the armies of the Lord has come moment, *"go in the strength you have..."* What was I thinking! God is willing to turn my *own strength* into something great for Israel. God is offering to do something amazing if Gideon will take the risky path and put his faith in God out there, just put it first, don't bother trying to transform it into that culturally expected "best".

In getting this point and then acting on it, Gideon becomes the usher, the announcer, the vanguard of the new thing the God of innovation has been trying to unveil, something new that God was trying to reveal about Himself.

You can't buy that if you tried with thirty two thousand men, but you might just make it truly famous with three hundred.

So, Gideon wakes them all up. Only loonies fight at night, how are you going to see a thing? So Gideon the inventor, inspired by God the innovator, on the spot bless him, creates the stealth torch^{TM}. All three hundred braves come out with a torch in a jar in one hand, a sword in the other, and Gideon says two great words to them, given where he has come from on this journey, they are amazing words really *"Watch me"*, he says. And then three even greater ones *"Follow my lead"*.

'Now you're getting it!' shouts God. The three hundred of them surround the camp and then, my favorite bit, blow the number of trumpets commensurate with an attack force thirty times their actual size (smart warriors, keep the trumpets to make a sound that, literally, can kill someone). There's a trumpet sound, there's a shout, and there's a new Jericho, there's a new Joshua, there's a new aspect to the fire of our God that burns from a broken jar. That jar is the mold of 'the story of God so far' - the failures caused by well meaning ministry monasticism, the compromises caused by personalized prioritization - and these are broken in this victory. That's the FIRST that God has been looking for. The best always tends to keep the game the same, the first always moves it on!

This victory will break all of the rules of history so far, of military combat indeed, of good counsel and of self-preservation. God becomes the rearguard of a lunatic risk. In a culture that was used to having Him up the front (as insurance). God is saying through Gideon, you go up front, 'give me *your* first' and see what faith in me achieves. *"A sword for the Lord..."*, amazing *"... and for Gideon"*, ... how cool is that? Moved the game on completely.

You know the story; they run in, suicide proportions notwith-standing, and God's spirit sweeps in behind them. He does not go before them, as in the days of old, He comes in behind, after faith and courage are wild and free, and He is whooping all the way *"a sword for Gideon"*. He giggles, because from that first encounter with a young man in a winepress, a sword (reward) for Gideon was part of what this was all about. One young harvest bringer – with wine as his context, finding the strength to save them all.

Faith and courage alive in experience, hanging on a precipice of "now" and released in a crazy, reckless surge of "I am", that's what strengthened and changed Israel forever.

God didn't want the best that Gideon had to offer at the head of a mighty army playing their traditional roles. God wanted Gideon. Jealously. He wanted the first of him, having found the boy *himself* a fitting offering for God. A suitable candidate for a place in God's purpose.

Bloody marvelous.

So what do you think? Do we have enough raw material yet? Can we start our hermeneutic of church right here? Would it be possible to "read church" through just this storyline in our bible? I think so.

Before we get to that, and the principles for church that might shake out, let's introduce a complimentary New Testament reading. Let's talk about a tattoo I'd like to get. I would emblazon Paul's Athens speech across my back, here's a highlight:

> *The God who made the world and everything in it is the Lord of heaven and earth and does not live in temples built by hands. And he is not served by human hands, as if he needed anything, because he himself gives all men life and breath and everything else. From one man he made every nation of men, that they should inhabit the whole earth; and he determined the times set for them and the exact places where they should live. God did this so that men might seek him and perhaps reach out for him and find him, though he is not far from each one of us. For in him we live and move and have our being.*

Actually, that would be a painful tattoo to get, perhaps I would just have a bit of it. Whilst that last line is the coolest, its sister line is the most interesting, the one that goes:

"And he is not served by human hands, as if he needed anything".

That so utterly cuts across everything you might conclude from the bulk of the Old Testament expectation, the life story of the man who first said it, the subsequent history of Christianity and the praxis of the church. That is a very liberating line in lots of ways. That line should be a paradigm breaker for the Church of Christ. God *doesn't need* anything from our service. We are not, even at our various "bests", going to be meeting a need which God has.

Now a warning flag goes up. I surely cannot be building my ecclesiology on one tiny atomized passage of the bible and making it serve as some kind of colossal mono-polar agenda. No, I'm not.

That's what sermonologues do. I'm not doing that.

What I am doing is asking modern Christians in a modern church a modern question: Should we be the ones to define the agenda for how we give our God our individual and corporate best? When we read for the answer in the bible this part of the bible allows the *suggestion* that God doesn't need anything from us. That might shape our thought, at certain times. God doesn't need us.

So, here's a Gadfly moment.

- Am I saying that meeting God in failure and fear is good and means you should be taking more risks?
- Am I saying that God has disallowed you from being (solely) individual, that, in calling you into church community, God has made you irrevocably plural?
- Am I saying that God doesn't want individuals or churches to pre-define what's best to give Him because it gets in the way of Him being able to include you in His best?

Well, yes that is exactly what I am saying.

That's the church I'm talking about.

Maybe you don't agree, maybe you think it is important for people to be inherently conservative about all this stuff. Maybe your God doesn't take risks ever, or giggle. Do you feel people need, in sobriety, to take the time to consider before God what He is calling them to (as individuals)? Can it take a fair while (years even!) to come, as Paul says, into full maturity? Here's the thing though, twist and turn all you like but the church that seems to be the result of that conversation is a conservative, individualistic church which can be chokingly dull and impotent. A Church like that needs stealth torch badly. Here's how to get one:

I said, way back when you thought Gideon's story was the tangent and not the subject of half a book all on his own, that there were ministry keepers (small 'm') out there who think they are doing the best for God. I pretty much suggested that over time this kind of best is in danger of becoming a strangulated hernia in the body of the church. It traps us all in the idea that God stays predictable from His past behavior.

I said the "busy nine to fives" are giving God the 'best of the rest' when all the other stuff is done and the decisions are made, fitting God into their priorities, making Him into an image of their priorities at times. I pretty much said that these people, in their expectation of church, are trapped by their own reluctance. Also, I said there are a lot of "married with families", struggling or otherwise, out there who ache to do things "for the best". I pretty much said that these people are trapped by a tendency to normalize their own need for approval.

These were pretty mean things to say, I know. I said at the beginning of the book that I would draw on my own experience of church though. Mean or not, I've seen these things at work in the church. You have too. They trouble me. Do they trouble us?

What if the *real* Gadfly moment then, was to be this:

What if – after all this damning commentary (my own

included), after those countless books, after innumerable beat-you-rite™ sermons – I said to the people in churches the one most significant thing they never want to hear? What if, in the middle of this whole interpolated you beat me up, I beat myself up, self-generating, self-serving, guilt-house critique somebody just said: Can we stop this conversation, it's boring...

Let's just stop...

...take a moment...

...and listen to that sound...

...the sound of the bubbles...

...the sound you get just after the champagne has been poured.

A hermeneutic of the church from Gideon helps because it would say: to change your storyline in God is a non-negotiable of His kingdom. God asks Gideon to re-imagine a story that is already a failure; he's threshing wheat in a winepress for goodness sake. We have a God who does not take Gideon *back to* the same script of failure and ask him to try harder with that SAME exhausted storyline. Even the loosest possible grasp on the significance of Jesus tells you He's not saying that to the church today.

If Gideon, after all these centuries in print, is showing us a thing, he is calling out to us that the champagne of the kingdom ferments because of the power of re-imagination. Without the re-imagining part, the calling of the church will always turn the wine flat. It will always become culture and expectation. That's why the gift of re-imagination seems to skip whole generations at a time. I wonder what happened to mine.

So, let's cut this millennia-old boring conversation about church being somewhere you meet the grade, do your best, or whatever you want to call it. Let's just pour the champagne. Pour sparkling 're-imagination' into the heart of your personal and your plural story. Begin by re-imagining your God who has to jettison thirty one thousand seven hundred perfectly good soldiers to get enough attention to bring Gideon's imagination up to the par of His own.

I'm trying to humbly suggest (I know it doesn't seem all that humble) that a good way to start that re-imagination journey is to take a seat in that winepress and thresh what you bring. Accept that your God doesn't have to be the God of your mothers and fathers' inherited values. He doesn't want you (or us) to set an agenda wherein you give your/we give our best as pre-defined in our religious cultural polemic or in harking back to the preaching of yesteryear, so often preached only yesterday. The God that draws close in the winepress wants the first of you. Jealously. It's ridiculously potent.

Re-imagining ministry, leadership and commitment

This re-imagination will ask us to have a whole new conversation now. So, sons and daughters of Jerub-Baal, re-imagine with me now we've got that pricey green bottle tipped on the delicate edge of that shiny little glass. What would the pathologies of the church we discussed at the beginning of this chapter look like if the players on those stages just took a sip of God's liquid re-imagination?

Let's allow Gideon's 'I am' moment; Paul's 'in him we live and move and have our being' moment, to help us to examine small 'm' ministry, church leadership and priority setting behaviors. You might as well, you've come this far...

Small 'm' ministry leadership

Ministry leaders you need to avoid ministry monasticism. Let's recognize that we are all called to build God's church and let's not supplant that with a commission to preserve it. Commit yourselves to the idea that God wants your ministry to be a source of (re)imagination. All who minister must agree to be change agents. All ministry, we must agree, can be fluid. That way you will be willing to let God make you into a vanguard, not rearguard. To be the God who puts a stealth torch in one hand –

to light the way in the uncertain – and a trumpet in the other – to make a big noise about what is revealed. Not to be the God who sits in heaven receiving the praise of the celebrant at a distance, but the God who comes in close behind to celebrate what you do for Him.

Why would He do this? Well, because Jesus has not given you the responsibility for a ministry, He has given you something better. A role in a dynamic, advancing kingdom. I have a friend who works in a successful High School which is considered radical. When asked about the reasons for its success he says "we don't wait till it's broken to fix it" or sometimes "if it ain't broke, we fix it anyway". The organization embraces innovation as a primary creative force for success and learning. So, ministry leaders, do you know what happens if you are found:

- Not coming over as a little obsessive about how things should be done "properly"?
- Refusing to invest this service with a personal story of 'faith actualization', but always expecting to release yourself into something new – and re-imagine your own gifting, or find a surprising new one?
- Refusing to allow yourself and your ministry to be essentially synonymous, but expecting to be accountable for keeping one eye on the task in hand and one eye over your shoulder looking for a successor to take over (modify, improve) your (developed) ministry?
- Welcoming being asked to step aside for a time: because you give the God of innovation some room and are found in Him expecting your ministry NOT to stay the same in any long term way?
- Not frustrating anyone in your congregation in the interests of your ministry but supporting a church leadership which only invests in short ministries of succession and designs this life cycle into them from the beginning?

Do you know what happens?

Me neither... I have no idea what happens!

I don't know where that will take you, how could I? What I do know is your ministry will never be an end in itself, a well worn pattern, or a harness for you to die in. It will be designed by (and for) the God of innovation and you will build His church, not seek to preserve it.

Does this sound good? Then the leadership of your church will have to take a leaf out of Gideon's re-imagination manual and accept really tough decisions about who should minister where, how and for how long. Some of these decisions might cause anxiety when they may even look like they *weaken* the whole show. If Gideon is unleashed like this in fact, they actually move the whole game on in a new way.

Three hundred men indeed, the Almighty's avin a larf He is...

Church leaders

Let's re-imagine some traditional 'non-negotiable areas'. You are organizing a resource primarily made up of people and that's a scarce resource right? Because of competing demands for time some of which are exacerbated by personalized prioritization? Fine. Try asking some of your people to go part-time.

Yes, I did say that. Ask some of your talented, hard-working people to give up a portion of their career and success indicators as a sacrifice to God. To go part-time and to give one day a week of their skills and abilities directly to the church.

Leaves time for tumbleweeds to roll – leaps up with a flame thrower and torches the buggers in mid tumble. It's not THAT MAD! How much do they really like work anyway? How important is work, actually, compared to the kingdom? What if such a radical re-imagining *created* new types of calling? What if the sacred-secular divide could really be a bridge?

If you convince five people to do this you have just landed one of the most multi-skilled, multi-tasking, highly energetic, full-time members of staff any church is ever likely to have. If you convince twenty-five, well, just imagine.

If we can't afford that approach then go to plan B. Take a look at your planning processes. Get some of your highly skilled project-manager types to give some of their professional consultancy time to 'church-as-organization' (not as its only identity, don't walk into that bear trap). Do stop for a moment though just to take a long, clear, hard, business-minded, strategic and helpful look at your seasonal planning. Task them with looking at why the church *always* feels tight on resources and to come back with an action plan for making it, well, not. Of course they have to do this for you without forcing a situation which cuts the vision cloth to suit the resource purse, that's not biblical.

Gideon's Hermeneutic suggests a paradigm which is this, make room for God to identify your church's *actual* resources (as He sees them) rather than accept that this is in any way self-evident. Let Him sift you down to that willing and effective "three hundred", whatever form that takes. Send the rest home/back to the tents. Yes, you heard me, no more sermons about 'no passengers'. Ditch all this 'everyone having a part to play' stuff. No more 'mustard seed' nonsense (go read it again, the point is not that the mustard seed is small and worthless and is allowed to constantly rehearse the storyline of its meekness, the point is that it rips up mountains in the end). End the annual rehearsal of fruitless encouragement, just send them home.

Once you have done that of course, to stop yourself looking stupid, you are going to need a battle strategy that focuses on the mighty (and supernatural) success of the three hundred that God gave you. That last part is very much your job and if that fills you with fear, good. God has a solution for that which only works in the midst of the risk. This is where stealth torches and trumpets will need to be identified (stop me if I am getting metaphysical). What I am saying to church leaderships is *why*, why burn energy on a lament for what an aimless thirty-two thousand do not seem able to achieve? Resource your three hundred and say to them, 'Watch me', 'Follow my lead'. How counter-cultural is that for our churches? How much flak will you get for that fundamentally un-pastoral thinking?

That's the point where you need to be brave and find your moment to *"go in the strength you have"*. When the flak hits, it is worth remembering that there did come a point when even Jesus (as a leader of a movement) preached a sermon that was intended to send most of His followers back home. Maybe you need to take a risk that God doesn't want your team to lead *a whole church* to the best that it can do. God might *not* have called that whole church any more than Jesus called all his disciples at any given point, or Gideon really needed all those soldiers. If you insist, by some inclusive theological agenda, that God must use all the troops then maybe you are trying to get the best out of what you have. To give God the best. This can become an impediment to effective involvement in what He is actually doing. He wants the first.

What if, in the church He has trusted you to lead, God has no interest in compromise or consensus but just wants to run behind a small wave of re-imaginers – giggling all the way? Why not make the choices that might pave the way for a few individuals to lead your community's 'I am' moment. To be brave enough to accept the mandate to be part of the best that God is about to do.

Just be brave enough to accept in fewer people and less resources. This is what it means to commit to giving Him the first. Maybe the time after that, it will be six hundred. Because people see a role for themselves in building an uncomfortable, risky church proposition rather than preserving a comfortable, dull one. Because they have seen what champagne does to a party.

"Commitment"

In The Princess Bride we find this exchange:

Vicini: *Inconceivable!*

Inigo: *You keep using that word, I do not think it means what you think it means.*

I wonder if we understand what we mean by "commitment". To the person in the second year of marriage onwards who wants quality time to be the performance indicator for their commitment to marriage. To the couple with young children who want raising them (unassisted) to be their paramount commitment. To the parents whose relationship with (commitment to) church rotates around whether it caters for their younger and teenage children adequately. To shouting-match families broken over conflicted commitment to church every Sunday. What can we say?

Well, that's a tougher shout. Isn't it? I mean, isn't this where the reality of modern life brings us up short? I'd say 'no'. Not if we are people of the book. Not if we let Gideon help us start to re-imagine our way out of these perennial challenges that will come to all churches. We have to let him thresh what we mean by "commitment", have we turned it into a best when it really should be a first? Re-imagining here has to arrive smack in the middle of our 'historo-traditonal' (made up word, I can't do Latin) model of the definition of commitments to 'family and church (family)'.

To the young (and not so young) married couples, is it inconceivable that marriage enhancing quality time together could come from serving the church as a couple? To put God first and your marriage second? Notice, I am not saying that you should do this *as individuals*. I'm saying you should do the "putting God first thing" *as a couple*. Hold your church leadership accountable for calling you as a pair, the pair that were "joined" before the assembly and before God. The pair that were not to be separated. Or was that bit just a load of ritual and a pretty frock?

To the families where children do come along, is it inconceivable that the church, which is many hundreds of years old and has had plenty of time to think about this, makes infrastructural arrangements to share the care with you? What if the life of the church (even to the extent of employing support staff) was committed to deliberately seeing child-raising (and parent releasing) as a ministry focus?

To the Fractious Families shouldn't we say here is a case in point where you should 'share life when it hurts – share life till it hurts'. Shouldn't we find creative ways to squeeze community love into those Sunday shouting matches? Ways to converse with (and let God engage with) edge-dwelling teens (or younger) who have rejected some combination of church and parent-as-church-as-control.

Couldn't we use what we learn to be a house of love? To release that love of God into our community? Love all those parents/adults represented in these groups – so that we don't cast them as victim or villain quite so easily. Shouldn't we want a re-imagination for them as well? Don't they get a glass of re-imagination too? If they do God might be asking you to hand them the glass. Do we ask God to help (force) us to engage with these families acutely because we see them struggle, or do we passively stay backed off from them and watch the crash at a safe distance? Do we subtly interrogate their situations (both children and adults) and when we have garnered enough start wearing out our (metaphorical) knees in prayer pleading with God to effect a change for all. Maybe asking Him whilst we are at it if there is something we should do?

I suppose I am daring to re-imagine that when this and other time-worn dialogue turns up again *in our churches* we could have a new way to read ourselves and our storyline that means we don't want to stay stuck in the SAME storyline, and that this would not just be for us. If we got our own storyline anywhere near right in these matters, we could change the storyline for those outside of our churches as well. We could dare to re-imagine that by modeling this "it takes a village to raise a child" wisdom we *actually become* a village wise enough to create structures that would help others who are not in our church, but who are, to stretch the metaphor, in our village.

To achieve all of this and more Gideon (and he's not alone in this) teaches us there has to be implication through radical action.

Sending some back to their tents (modern reading)

Point one: Got some grumpy adults in your church with no time for noisy children or poor parenting? Tell them to shut up. We need them to learn to offer all the kids who are happy to be in our churches, and patient with our stuff, as much 'place' and joy in the community throughout our service as they clearly have when they are running around at the end. We need these adults and these children to see a vision of Jesus that accepts unstructured, raucous praise from children, and to accept that He did this as an indictment of the adults it offended.

We need to stop lying about wanting to be cross generational in our Sunday services. I used to be on a church leadership, we always said this was a "very important" subject. We were lying. We needed to stop saying it, or start doing something real about it. We did neither. We needed a powerful re-imagination that we weren't brave enough for. We needed to get parents and adults before God to ask not what church can do for children, but what (honest) children can do for a church. Ask yourself, do you actually want children to come and sit quietly, to sing responsorial songs and listen to homilies and then go to something a bit like school? If the answer is 'no', then something pretty big needs to change, right?

Point two: Got some grumpy kids in your place that hate being there? Ask them not to come. Because their parents still want to come, you might need to set up some supervised activity for them to tide them over. Sure, there might be a revolt amongst the church kids if the naughty kids get to play video games and that looks much better than Sunday school. But that just raises a question about the authenticity of engagement at the Sunday school, which is just no bad thing.

If these are angry or sullen teens in your place who *really* don't want to be there? Show them to the door. Encourage their parents to set them free from duress and attendance. Could we, as a community, not create a structure where we really do "carry out", rather than reject, young people for whom the challenge of a life of faith has no relevance/acceptance? Do we really want them to have to struggle free through an escape hatch of their own making? Do we really want to re-watch that car crash as the parents tear themselves up and create rules like 'you have to come until you are sixteen'?

Why not make what is paralyzing, sour and rejecting into something enabling, sweet and affirming? Think of it like this, we won't baptize them until we are sure they are making the choice for themselves. What if we honor that wisdom and also let them make other faith decisions for themselves, including the rejection of faith? What if we don't hold them to ransom for inclusion predicated upon a belief structure we know they cannot (at the moment) accept and we do not, if we are totally honest, want them to fake?

We could just have a fond goodbye and show them that the door's hinges swing both ways. When that's done we go back inside and build a conspiracy of grace and fellowship around them. Set them a place at our meals (teenagers love food, it's a growth thing) and offer them encounters designed around their needs not our wants.

Point three: Got some grumpy parents in your place? Share the care. Create a fluid infrastructure because 'person-shaped' gaps are bound to be created. Our young men will be seen as ripe to learn early parenting skills from babysitting duties. Our singles, and those who don't have children themselves, can be given a *real* stake in the children of the community to which they belong. Or are they just to be your joy? This is not to replace you in, or rob you of, your parenting. It's just to help; to release a little bit of the pressure, to free up a little bit of quality time that you wouldn't mind giving because it was structured and planned to be free, not stolen.

If this mattered to us enough, we could set this up; we would get intertwined in each other's lives. Don't believe it would, or should, work? How do you explain what happens when death or major illness strikes a family in your church? You don't just sit and watch do you? Suppose for a moment that we really didn't need nearly that high a threshold for the avalanche of love this creates? Suppose it was our (budgeted) intention all the while to provide, in the very structure of what we do as a community, constant sources of support, respite, and wisdom training for families, parents and children/young people.

Be a community. That is what I am really saying, be the community of the three hundred who ditch ministry monasticism, who foreswear personalized prioritization. A community like this opens its eyes to the re-imagined victory that God wants. You'll be delighted to find Him running in giggling after you all the way.

A hermeneutic from Gideon

God's victory in Gideon's story only developed when God was allowed to send people away, to clear the stage. Are we brave enough to do so? The thing that gives me hope that all this could be different is what I am calling textual life. It's not that complex, it is just using the bible to mine for paradigm by trusting its God to be serious about what He put there. It's not just a hermeneutic in the end; it's seeking a way for the text to impart the life it promises. It's what we should be doing with this, let's get really, really good at it. Without that, Gideon is just an old story and a tonne of the rest of the bible too.

Yes, but is this 'first not best thing' real hermeneutic or just a good sermon?

That's a good point. Well done, you've picked up on this sermonologue idea rather well and you are holding me accountable for it. I think this principle is all over the bible. Let's take a quick thematic look and see if we can *really* read this principle of 'first not best' that I have invented.

Joshua: When Joshua is on his way into Jericho God gives him an instruction that the entire battle, the entire city and all that is in it is to be dedicated to God (a slaughter by any standard). The principle was that this is Joshua's first battle and God wants it as an offering. To make that point abundantly clear, God sets Joshua's not unimpressive army a ridiculous non-strategic task at the end of which a war trumpet will blow and they are all to give a shout. Then they will either hear something like sniggering or something seismic, you know the score.

Joshua was told, in no uncertain terms, that God wanted this first victory for Himself. Human skill and or dedication were never the defining features. In the middle of those purposes, God accepted Joshua's obedience – because Joshua gave Him the first. It cost Joshua to do this because as a consequence he looked, well, nuts.

Saul: For Saul's first major victory it was the same deal, God, likewise, wanted the lot dedicated to Him. Saul failed to do that (what is this sound of bleating in my ears?) and excused himself by saying 'I saved the best for God', or, alternatively, I've set aside the "best of the rest". He gets put in his place by Samuel, to paraphrase, 'God doesn't want the best'. Or, alternatively, 'you think you are giving the best when there are deeper issues of identity, authority and fear at stake here and God is not fooled, and neither are you.'

God did not accept the best of the rest from Saul, however

well endorsed Saul's actions were from a complicit group of beneficiaries. Saul tried to compromise and put himself in an acceptable light rather than meet the scorching demands of God. Saul tried to set the agenda and define what was best to give to God. He got no marks for crowd pleasing politics. When he did not give God the first he was asked for, he was summarily rejected.

Jephthah: When Jephthah tries to lead the people, he tries to get God to accept his best. He swears an oath that whatever meets him at his door upon his return from fighting God's enemies (thus securing a return for himself) he will dedicate to God by burning it in the fire. Idiot. You know how that one turns out. Rather than deal with the consequences of his sinful ideas of "best", he sacrifices his own daughter on the idolatrous altar of his own idea of true faith. There is no word at all from God in that. Why would there be?

Dipping in to Jesus for a moment, it's possible to see this same principle when He is being offered fealty. One says, *"I'll follow you"* and Jesus says only if it involves staying in nice houses. One says, *"I need to bury my father first"*, and Jesus says *"let the dead bury their own dead, you follow me"*. Jesus teaches in numerous ways that those who put job, marriage, tradition, possessions, family or life itself in a (not entirely unreasonable in the latter case) priority position are *"not worthy of me"*.

When a woman is inspired by a prophetic urge to douse Jesus with a year's wages, a metaphor – if ever there was one – concerning the reckless grace of the one she anoints, she is criticized by everyone else in the church. She is considered beautiful by Jesus, because putting Him first is more important than doing your best for the poor. He teaches a parable of the mother of all parties and of the people who miss out on it because they won't put Him first.

Throughout the bible, when crops are grown, animals bred,

children are born, when battles are fought and won, when gifts are offered God says, bring me the first. The reason? Because it says something about you:

- It says you don't consent to an individualism in your contribution to the church that allows you to define what's best around your own agenda
- It says that we will not be satisfied as a community to define by consensus a best to give God that is really a cultural definition and free from any real risk
- It accepts that our failure and particularly our risk might actually be a vital source of God's deepening relationship with us
- It says we will realign our thinking to be supporting God in His best by bringing Him our first

If the thought of giving stroppy kids a get out of jail free card from church worries you, think about my stroppy teenager sitting alone threshing wheat in a winepress for fear of what society had become. He was very deeply questioning his inherited beliefs and really not at all sure about his God. God was attracted by him, came and sat down, and challenged him to have a key role in the future of God's vision for his community. God was only able to do that by a conspiracy of grace and pain and, above all, risk that goaded Gideon into learning how to sacrificially give Him the first.

There's power to that reading of Gideon. God celebrates in that the calling of all Christians to come and be individuals who want to give God their (raw) genuine first, not their best. That risk acts *in the plural* and raises our imagination to the level of our God.

The proof that the fermenting power of re-imagination has been at work is evidenced in our community of bubbles rising to the top of what has now become a very expensive champagne.

Chapter 3

Authentic Friendship

Become my friend, give me your hand, put down other roles and masks, confide in me, accept my confidence in you, if you would risk that, then let's join spirits and make a start on something real.

Common in the complexity of our design, God has put into us a craving for intimacy. This is something the church ought to be famous for wrestling with. Of all the things about which we might have something significant to say, this one matters. Joy as community is supposed to be part of the church's identity, it comes in differing forms, of course it does. It has to reflect our differing emotional ranges for one thing, and the world is a big place.

I'm not having the greatest of times in churches at the moment it has to be said. By the time you read this, I think it will all be sorted out though. So I'm troubled to write about it in that case. Partly, because it seems cheap of me to potentially defame others to promote the righteousness of my own ideas. Partly because, as a Christian, it seems unforgiving to make a permanent record of 'the discord' played on an instrument which I know to be inherently tunable. Especially if in so doing, I seem to justify my part of the bum note this instrument currently plays.

Doesn't that just demonstrate that I lack insight into what I am doing wrong? I mean there's no point in writing a whole chapter about re-imagination setting us free from a paradigm of critique only to launch into that very critique in the very next chapter. Is there?

Here's a worry though. What if I am not doing *anything* wrong, as such, but that there is *something* wrong in general of which my experience is merely a symptom. That's what this chapter is going to be about. Ideas surrounding authentic friendship are a real tension for me personally. I think it is also one for the UK church at large, examining that we might find:

- When it comes to friendship in the church, we may have given in to a culture which compartmentalizes spirituality and humanity, we, therefore, find it difficult (and optional) to offer authentic, costly and vulnerable relationships to others in the church
- The bible offers us extreme models of friendship with God, with strangers and with each other: the most extreme of these, by definition, is the vulnerability, accountability and intimacy of Jesus Himself
- Jesus *commanded us* to follow Him in this 'way' – we may have ignored Him

It's a massive over-generalization, but when we go in search of a model of community in church, our radical preachers will often hearken to a first century – one that we know virtually nothing of – and talk about the shared possessions and sacrificial love of the first Christians. They may be bold enough to point out (to western democratic readers) that this was a flirtation with a proto-communism. It's not recommended though, it was fanatical and it next to completely fails. The New Testament letters are clear on that.

If we want to use the bible as a guide here, it is rather difficult. Jesus and His people inhabited this weird, 'otherly' world where He seems to have run some sort of short-lived political commune. We cannot know too well what this community was like or why, and that's sad. For one thing women were included in this, uncharacteristically for the time, possibly in new and interesting ways. The recorders, burdened by their culture, failed to record enough of that material for us to conclude how and to what effect. When it comes to what they did generally put on record, we are still left with an investigative journalist's challenge.

What little we do know next to completely fails to fit our situation in any case. Why did men, although they were married, spend more time with Jesus and each other than they did with their wives and children? If we are honest, we can't interpret first-century practices like this adequately for the twenty-first century. Especially since today we have normalized, in our culture and our churches, the precise reverse of some of the behaviors of Jesus and His people.

We all know our search for community is rhetorical and it won't scratch the surface of decisions and actions in the normal nuclear day on day. If we were serious about radically different ways to live, be and raise children which might form a nexus of Christian witness, we'd have done it by now. Let's talk, well, first, let's read:

Dear Jon

I saw you in church this morning and I wanted to come and speak to you and then I didn't do it. I'm not sure I know the half of what is happening for you or what you are going through right now but it just strikes me lately that, when I see you, I say to myself there's someone I don't really know, and I feel I'm the poorer for it.

A problem I think we face in the modern church is simply this: we may have found authentic friendship so hard we've made a Greek dilemma of it. The horns of the friendship dilemma are that we either over-ritualize how we relate, or over-spiritualize it. In the former, I'm going to argue that we run the risk of creating a community of association. In the latter, we risk creating a community of aspiration. In either case, we are impaled on inauthenticity.

The churches in my recent experiences are very real, very valuable, very 'lots of things' places. That's why I am writing this book. The principle for church that I would want to see established has been tested in the fires of my experience, of my pain even. Although no one is burning my fields and killing my children, so, let's keep the 'p' word in its proper global context.

The friend who sent me that e-mail did so out of a back story that we don't need to go into. What we catch in it is an essence of two men. These men can know each other fairly well over a decade and a half, go to Christian festivals together, write and perform drama together, attend each other's weddings and visit each other's hospital beds. In the final analysis, because we are both committed Christians, it's a shame that our friendship hasn't resulted in the real spiritual accountability that the e-mail poignantly mourns. It shows we do not *know* each other even when, in rarer moments, we might want to. That's one horn of the dilemma.

The opposite horn tends, in my experience, to come for you in the non-mainstream church. The 'alternative church' tends to have a culture that insists on high levels of spiritual accountability – because that goes with their "more serious" theology. I don't need to give you examples if you recognize what I am staying. What can happen is that people, especially the leaders in this tradition, want you to leap into a relationship of full accountability before there is a deep friendship, or sometimes any friendship, upon which to base it. The assumption is that the friendship will follow. That's a bad assumption.

Two horns of our authentic Christian friendship dilemma:

Friendship without spiritual accountability loses its way by becoming over-ritualized and collapses into association

Spiritual accountability, without friendship, risks the friendship never truly starting because it is over-spiritualized and collapses into an aspiration

This is a true dilemma. In church, in my real experience, we feel to be losing the art of authentic, accountable friendship. When this happens it gets into the fabric of the community character, how can it do anything else? It leads inexorably to variations of what I am calling community of association or community of aspiration. Let me try to explain more fully what I mean by those:

Community of association

How are you?
I'm fine, how are you?
I'm fine thanks.

I get up from my bed, I go downstairs in my house, I read my bible and pray to my God, I get in my car and I go to my church, I sit in something approaching my seat, I worship my God and hear what He has to say for my life, I have a cup of tea and a polite conversation or two, I get back in my car and go back to my house, I eat my lunch, I get back in my car, I go to the cinema and enjoy the film, I come home have a glass of wine, take a bath and take myself to my bed.

At every turn, I am in control – control of the location, control of the locomotion, control of the levels of self revelation and the personal enquiry I undertake. I am living in the twenty-first century 'wish dream' of a tight nuclear family which I transport between experiences in privacy; experiences within which we often only experience privacy. At church, people break into this to ask me how I am, I say that I am fine. I ask them how they are, they say that they are fine.

I have known these folk for a decade and a half, but I do not reveal my soul to them and I do not ask them to reveal theirs to me. I don't ask them how they are walking with God and if they are moving and growing more and more into His likeness, I don't expect them to ask me the same. I don't ask how their marriages are going, even when it is obvious that they are not going that well. I don't expect them to give an opinion on mine.

I don't ask them if they are struggling with parenting, even when it is obvious they are.

There's so much I don't ask, it's not considered polite. If these tricky things do need to be asked about, then that's the job of the professional minister and the pastoral team. Not my job.

How are you? I'm fine, how are you?
The traditional church doesn't actively preach this kind of individualism, quite the opposite. But, in the twenty-first century middle classes, in the UK at least, if church grapples with elemental community at all, it seems to conclude that this has to be largely a soft concept; a community in which people politely associate with one and other until things go wrong. So we default to a practice of association, is that so bad?

Well, yes, because the deeper reaches of authentic friendship, therefore, become quite rare. They only tend, in my observation and experience, to be brought out by crisis events. Is your husband dying? We'll power up our community into a crisis reaction mode which is really quite appealing. We will meet your children's needs, we'll cook you meals and carry you along, we'll go to all lengths practically, and in prayer. When the dust settles, we'll get back our individual journeys and expect you to do your individual same.

We are fine, how are you?
In association churches, we rarely eat together, we watch poor parenting and do not comment and share wisdom, we congregate in the most spectacular demographic imaginable and then do little with it. We retreat into stereotypes which fit just like masks stuck on with self-fulfilling prophetic glue. You are a teenager – I expect you to be bored. You are ninety – I expect you to be (oppressively) easily pleased by old hymns, children in tea towels at Christmas and to go on about your illnesses.

How ARE you?

Well that depends, doesn't it, on what you mean by the question:

- Is it my health you are interested in? Well, I'm disquieted by a lump in my testicle and I'm anxious as hell about the scan.
- Is it my sexuality? Well, I'm 'single and stuck' and not only do I feel your pity for me – like a corpse in the room – but actually, I wrestle for an appropriate expression of the sexual being God made me when that expression needs/must be solitary.
- Is it my emotional life? Well, I'm feeling increasingly at ease with myself, I've come to terms, despite the jokes, with losing my hair and, since I started investing more in them myself, I feel my friendships are improving.
- Is it my spiritual life? I've just spent a magnificent weekend fasting and praying and for the briefest of moments there I felt the veil was lifted and I could sense the pleasure of my creator coursing through my veins like fire, I have never been so alive, so vital, but I don't know what that means for my life back in the real world.
- Is it church you are referring to? Well, there I'm struggling, it just feels like Groundhog Day to me and half the time I'm sitting in judgment on people whose prayers seem as deep as a puddle and who just seem to chant static mystical incantations that leave me completely cold.
- Is it my relationship with you that you are asking about? I saw you blow your stack last week when someone tried to rearrange things to suit what they were trying to do. And that's not the first time is it? I'm afraid of your temper, everybody is.

Anyway, how are you?

Don't get me wrong, a community of association church is a *real* community. We do want to be together and we should be asking each other "how are you", we should care. I'm not questioning that. What I am questioning is whether our association might, in the final analysis, actually be driven more by what we need as individuals than by what our community could mean or achieve. This is because we do have needs as individuals, ironically, that require groups to meet them.

So we establish a (legitimate) group. On closer inspection it's only a loose group formed on a range of insubstantial associations. They are substantial enough to allow us to congregate, to make decisions together and to participate in common objectives. When it comes to really knowing one another, loving one another, being vulnerable and holding one another accountable though that is not going to happen, or it is going to be pretty rare.

Arguably, and I know this is coming off harsh but let me keep going, we are a community because we sing better together. We are community because we can pool finances and own a building. We are community because our children can be in clubs together. We are community because we have common theology, we like a particular form of ecclesiology and have a common point of identity differentiation from those around us. And, yes, there is nothing wrong, per se, with any of those things.

But deep concern, deep interference in one another's lives, cross-generational wisdom sharing, not just through the pain, but in correction (admonishment with all love), counter-cultural inclusion and profound intimacy, naa... that's not it at all. That requires something far greater than what we have. That requires an authenticity that no one seems to be modeling or preparing us for. Communities of association, however we wrestle within them, are politely counter-productive to authentic friendship. It might be bumped into from time to time, but it isn't the norm.

You do have to question our songs though, our psalms of longing. We are all standing there facing the front, singing momentarily with one voice, sometimes in a profoundly heart-wrenching way, crying out for intimacy. The shame is we put that back in the God box straight after rather than, as we are supposed to, gift it to one another. Afterwards, face to face with the ones who have just cried out for intimacy, we falter, and we are just politely interested.

You have to question our crisis response though. We transform dramatically into a very real and very deep concern in any crisis that lays bare our humanity, mortality or vulnerability. When one of our people dies or falls seriously ill, a formidable community will rally momentarily. We will all be joined in common suffering. The trouble with that is that it doesn't deepen us permanently; the shallow water calls us all too soon. In fact – harshness alert – that crisis-led intensity might actually be a partial reflection of our guilt. We over-react with love in a crisis because we are brought up short to realize that the real love we are now experiencing was not *already* there.

In association church communities we just seem to find authentic costly friendship too hard. It is easier to default to a ritualized position where we are content to know *of* one another, but we don't *know* one another.

You have to conclude, really knowing each other is not why we are together, because we are always asking "How are you", but we don't really want the answer.

A community of aspiration

It's never very helpful for churches to parody one another. This used to happen a lot between the traditional denominations whenever they got together. Maybe that was to sort of cover up how embarrassing it was that the church of Christ really is spectacularly "with schisms rent" as the hymnist says. If you hang out with cutting-edge churches though, you can't really help but notice they are a bit patronizing of their more traditional counterparts. After all, part of their identity is that they have set up "the meaningful alternative" to the ineffectual, tradition-bound church.

Their alternative, if we are honest, shares some of the traits of the association model but it tends to focus on a differentiating value set around expressions of the 'R' word. Real. Real spiritual growth, real worship, real walking with Jesus and of course, real community. There's also a lot of evidence of the desire for 'real community' in sermons, mission statements and in values on the website. Nothing wrong with any of that.

To keep earning its "R" rating, this tradition tends to talk about itself as stretching for authenticity a lot of the time. Perhaps this is a reaction to how insipid the association model can be. So, there is a big focus on outward physical, emotional and spiritual expression. People strive to "do business with one another and with God" and to do this underpinned by a perceived biblical premium on relationship with accountability.

Potentially in the cutting-edge church model, the people who lead it do seem to achieve an authentic version of "intense relating friendship" due to their sense of calling and their living by faith. This is double-edged though. They tend, not in a bad way, to be a tad more authoritarian in leadership. This is an odd consequence of increased freedom, but I suppose if you drive a fast car you need it to have better brakes. The result of these and other factors is that: although there is a greater premium on honesty and tough-talking; although there is a, largely consensual, more emotionally "challenging" atmosphere in these churches; although there is more heavy shepherding and although this is all seen as "doctrinal realism" – "real" still becomes cultural. This is my experience.

In placing too high (or too early) a premium on interpersonal spiritual accountability, the accountability *itself* starts masquerading as the biblical love it is aiming to produce. This is where the second horn of our dilemma might turn up, and the friendship might not.

Let me recognize what a tightrope of criticism I have been walking here in what seems a quite harshly written section that gently takes apart two church models. Let me also recognize that I am deliberately not doing that by relaying any actual experiences or any real examples. I hope this is a small bit of evidence that my wrestling is for the church, not against it.

However badly I've explained it here, what I am saying is that neither strategy seems (to me) to lead to searching, authentic, accountable, costly relationships. You can't have friendship by just practicing association the whole time and hoping that it will turn up. You can't have an aspiration to friendship by front-loading the process of getting to know each other with too super-spiritual an accountability as if that matters more.

So, all right, you've read eight and a half pages of my polemic on that but now you want to ask, not unreasonably, why have I set this particular bar so very high? Why am I asking for this kind of depth when I'm sort of suggesting that no one else appears to really want it, or be able to achieve it?

I'm sorry, it's an old chestnut really, but it's not me that is asking it's Jesus – and He is supposed to be in charge of the church.

Reading friendship through reading Jesus

Jesus not only demonstrated authenticity and accountability in His friendships but, as His last commandment on earth, He made it the mandate for His kingdom church. Churches are all required to show an extraordinarily deep and accountable love (modeled on His own). This is a love that, in and of itself He said, will be the identity of the church in this world and the seal of discipleship. This plea wasn't lost on the writers of the New Testament who picked this up and cried out at every turn for authenticity, take this:

> For the word of God is living and active. Sharper than any double-edged sword, it penetrates even to dividing soul and spirit, joints and marrow; it judges the thoughts and attitudes of the heart.

Nothing in all creation is hidden from God's sight. Everything is uncovered and laid bare before the eyes of him to whom we must give account.

You might say that's about spiritual accountability between people and God as expressed in personal religious experience and that this is different. Granted it is but, as this whole book is about trying to reject the notion that there can be a bifurcation between the expression of a person as spirituality and the expression of a person as a humanity, that's not really going to wash. In any case, you don't always want me to leap into periods of long exegesis so let's just say that if you disagree, 1 Corinthians 13 will hunt you down.

Despite that Corinthians passage being a convenient bit of poetry for weddings, it's actually not, on close inspection, really about marital or romantic love at all, it's about church love. You know it so well that I don't even have to quote it. Why do we need deep accountable, authentic, vulnerable friendship in the church? Easy, because it's Jesus' foundation for everything else and Paul agrees with Him.

So, if I am saying these two community archetypes evident in the modern church can sometimes fail, in differing ways with differing techniques, to develop authentic, accountable friendship, you know what I am going to say next, don't you? Is there a way to read for the principles of that friendship in scripture? Can we read it into the churches through their reading of the bible?

Oh yes.

Friendship is one of the strongest hermeneutics in our bible. So let me labor this a little bit longer. Let's just take the time to look at three examples of authentic, accountable relationship. I'd like to use these to highlight the "art" of getting that friendship done. These are revealed in Jonathan and David, David's mighty men, and Jesus and two disciples in particular. I'm conscious that these choices do reveal a male bias but as Ruth, Esther, Abigail, etc. would need whole chapters on their own, I'll have to risk the accusation of bias. In the cases I have chosen we do see the principles underpinning authentic accountable friendships which I think have something to say to the church. This is because they are examples which are typical of three forms of profound relationship needed by any church, these I will call:

- The one to one
- The many to one
- The one to many

Catchy huh?

Swap clothes: In the David story, back near its origin, an adolescent David has just killed Goliath. The current King, Saul (who was too frightened to do so) has given David an audience. This is not necessarily to congratulate him. Saul finds out who his father is and asks him to maybe find a bucket and clean the rug from all the ooze that's been dripping from Goliath's severed head in his hand the whole time. From that time, Saul kept him near, first as a pet, and then – as the shrewd king holding onto power – a threat.

The bible says that after Saul and David had finished the post-match analysis that Jonathan, Saul's son, became one in spirit with David and he loved him as himself. Saul gets David to move in. This pleases Jonathan who makes a covenant with David because he loved him as himself. Jonathan took off the robe he was wearing and all his battle kit and gave it to David. Not unsymbolic in itself. The two of them fell in love. No eyebrows need be raised at the back there, the bible is crystal clear on this matter; the two of them fell in love.

The story winds on, battles, victories, and the growing paranoid schizophrenia of Saul, who, it turns out, enjoys lovely evenings of music appreciation followed by a quaint little game called "I'll pin you to the wall!" David hotfoots out of it because he realizes what a mad king means when he says 'I'll make you a nice kebab'. God protects David by intervening. Even a murderous Saul can't help stripping off to prophesy in an ecstatic all-nighter which gives David time to escape.

David goes to Jonathan, his friend.

Your dad is trying to top me, says David. Not so says Jonathan, I'd know about it, he'd confide in me, you must have made a mistake. David says, look, on my life, literally, your dad is on to us, he knows what good mates we are and he wants to kill me on the quiet so as not to upset you, or get himself in trouble with you, but he's up for killing me soon as look at me.

Jonathan, who loves David, believes him over his father the king and then, in an emotional version of giving him the tunic the sword and so on, pledges to him *"whatever you want me to do, I'll do for you"*. This is edging minute by minute towards treason, and Jonathan cannot be unaware of that, or of his dad's temper come to that.

David says look, here's the test. When your dad asks why I am not at the feast tomorrow night, tell him I had to go to a big family festival in Bethlehem. If that's cool, I'll admit I've misread the whole pinning me to the wall episode. If he flips, I'm dead meat. And if he flips and you agree that I am in the wrong, that I am a threat; then I hold you to your covenant and you have to kill me, don't wimp out and let your father do it.

Jonathan says, he won't flip, and I am not in on it, don't you understand that I love you? If I get wind that my dad is up to no good then here's the deal, may God punish me if I don't take your side. If dad is that nuts, I hope all the blessing that God gave him (as king) passes to you (as king?). But you be God to me (as I know you can be?) and when the tables are turned, don't kill me yourself. And, whatever happens, don't get a bloodlust on my family, not even when every other enemy you have is dead in the gutter, do you get me?

So Jonathan, in a supreme act of treason, handed the crown to David and he did it in covenant love with David and with David's descendants (including Jesus then) that the enemies of the house of David would be called to account by God (including Satan then). He reaffirmed his (personal) love for David right there. Saul fails the test, Jonathan has to do the spear dodge shuffle himself and he is fierce with anger at his father. He contrives a signal to David, true to his covenant. They meet one last time and the bible says David bowed three times to Jonathan. Then they kissed each other and wept together – but David wept the most.

Because Jonathan was prepared to give up his kingdom and almost certainly his life for his beloved friend. David dressed in the clothes Jonathan gave him, David dressed himself in Jonathan's birthright which Jonathan did not covet, though it was his, preferring the way of love for his friend. David dressed himself intimately in Jonathan, who did not consider equality with the king something to be grasped, but humbled himself.

It doesn't go well for Saul, or for Jonathan. They die.

David writes a lament, including the words:

I grieve for you, Jonathan my brother;
You were very dear to me.
Your love for me was wonderful,
more wonderful than that of women.

Where do you start with a love story like this? It speaks volumes about the need, the imperative no less, for profound 'one to one' love between persons who are cognizant of the place of that love in a greater context. Jonathan and David, where are you in the church in the UK and beyond today?

Go to the well: There's another story of David, it goes like this: AAHHRRGGHHH, how crap is this!

Perhaps a touch more detail. David is now king, he has a band of mighty men who fight with him in his campaigns and also look after him in various ways such as bodyguard. On one campaign the Philistines came up to war against the new king David, there was an outpost in Bethlehem and David was held up in the stronghold. Thirsting, he cries out, if only someone would get me a drink of water from the well in Bethlehem. It's the frustration talking; he doesn't mean it to be taken literally.

Three of his mightiest mighty men take him at his word and decide, without taking him literally, that they will take him literally. It is intentional you see, not foolish. They set off (presumably armed to the teeth and carrying a bucket) break through the Philistine lines, draw water from the well and bring it back to David. He turns the water into an offering to God, seeing the water, metaphorically, as the blood of the men who risked their lives for him. He didn't feel worthy of their gift, he knew God was worthy and it was a safer bet to give it to Him.

Thing is, how cool were those mighty men! All it took from their leader was that he said the word and they risked their very lives for him. This was integral to how they saw their identity. Notice, they risked their lives not in a legitimate battle – as they had done so many times before standing in lentil fields and what have you. Not on a high risk mission actually given to them by their lord. It was on a desire to rally the spirits of their friend. On a desire to give him confidence in what could be achieved for the love of him. All right, on a desire to kick some Philistine heads in as well, but that aside, there is a tremendous underscore of sacrificial love in their act. They went to that well for him because they loved him.

What they demonstrated is 'many to one' love. They loved their leader as a group of people who were committed to him deeply and intimately and were, therefore, willing to risk everything for him. Maybe they were show-offs as well, but that's forgivable. Jesus' own mighty men were trying to channel this level of love and fearlessness. After all, every one of them said at some point they'd die for Him. Some of them said it twice. Truth of the situation was it was a pretty hard ask for them to stay awake for Him.

There is no judgment to be found in how right or how sane David's cries for water were. That's not the point of the story. The point is he honestly laid bare his frustration at events, and his mighty men went off on a love project to give him confidence in them, and in himself with them by his side. Which church members' meetings do you know that have this sort of love as their guiding principle?

David is (rightly) shocked by their love and turns it hastily back to God because he can't control it, he's a bit overwhelmed, he has learned something profound about how he is loved, and not by being told it either. Both sides of this relationship have pushed into very deep water here and David, quite rightly, considers this to have been a sacred exchange. How cool would it be if this authentic, accountable, costly friendship was one of our sacraments? How could you not love that idea?

Can we really aim that high? Too right we can, but it takes a certain value to be placed on selflessness. That value, that selflessness clearly has to draw from a deep well of love as its center, and be validated in the riskiness of the actions of the many to the one.

Unbelief and hot fish: Pop quiz: Name two disciples who get bad press in modern preaching?

Answer: Thomas – The doubter. Peter – The one who denied.

Why is that? Mainly, it's bravado. If you ask a switched on Sunday school child what is Thomas famous for, she will say he is a really useful engine. When you reboot the question she will say he doubted Jesus. If you ask a child nearby what Peter is famous for there may be more possibilities (asking Jesus to depart from him because of his sin, failing to walk on water or being called Satan might all spring to the more astute mind) but the granddaddy is still going to be the triple denial.

Let's rewind and unwind these notable stories and put them in a fuller context. Thomas did not always doubt, I hope you know this, or is he a cardboard cut-out in your theology? We, who smugly judge him in idiom and sermon for his doubt, are not really in a good position to so do. If you'd seen your hope die as horribly and with such finality as he had seen his and you did not yet know that the power of the resurrection was a defining quality of God's Messiah, then, surely, you'd doubt too. So, if we leave post-traumatic Thomas to one side, we get a very different man.

Jesus is heading to raise Lazarus from the dead, but the last time He was in that neck of the woods they tried to kill Him, something that the disciples are quick to remind Him. Jesus says something cryptic about walking in daylight whilst there's time and that means He's going back. He also says something more worryingly cryptic about "joining" Lazarus, who is, er, dead. Presumably the protagonists might get a better run up to it and actually kill Jesus this time. When have you ever heard a sermon on what Thomas says next? I'm guessing never. I've only heard one in 25 years (thank you Brian Raitt).

When the cost of following Jesus is inflating at a pace and death is a possibility here, Thomas faces all of his disciple buddies and says:

"Let us also go, that we may die with him".

Take a second to savor it. Who rallies the disciples for martyrdom? Thomas. Sure, he bottled it with the rest of them when the chips were very much down, but he had bravado enough to get them to that level before he bottled it. Thomas' view of himself was that he was so sure of his faith in Jesus he is willing to risk death.

74

When it comes to Peter, why do we never ask the really interesting question that should be obvious. Did Peter know that he was risking his life by hanging around too close to the action at Jesus' trial? Of course he did, he was playing chicken with himself. Sure, he bottled it big time, but where were the rest of the twelve (and the thousands) at this point? If he bottled it at least he did so like Thomas, from the nervous edge of nearly giving his life. He had bravado enough to get it to that level.

How does Jesus actually treat these two men? Well, it depends on your theology. A theology of correction will give you a slightly exasperated Jesus. A theology of connection will give you something else entirely.

Doubting Thomas says, I'm not believing it until I can place my hand in his side. If you were to show me a new living Jesus, he says, that won't be enough, I need to touch the very one I saw die. Jesus connects with that and, as you have heard preached many times, so values Thomas that He makes a special appearance just for him. Jesus, we have to assume, might have known what He was doing when He chose to appear to the disciples without Thomas.

The special appearance for Thomas is not any old 'sorry I missed you', therefore. It's a *doubt-valuing* invitation which is tailored even in the choice of words to let the recipient realize he is *known*: *"come place your hand in my side"*. It's a proofing kind of relating that Jesus does here. It is *validating of* the one who *wanted* to come and die with Him. To demonstrate to him that a special trip is not so much bother really for the one who loved Him like that.

Peter also says, I'd die for you (actually they all do). Peter, in his bravado, gets to go to the edge of that and watch his inner coward in action; word and deed thoroughly define him. Three times. A heavenly number of times. It would have been better if Jesus had taken Peter at his (more authentic?) word when they had that miraculous catch of fish way back in the day:

"Go away from me Lord; I am a sinful man".

If you accept that Jesus is actually connecting with, not correcting, Thomas by reminding him of his own words and this is very valuing, then look at what He does for Peter. Peter, the more complex relationship maybe, is treated similarly. Jesus meets him (and Thomas for that matter) when Peter is once again fishing – when he has rebooted his former identity presumably being scarcely proud of what the new one had brought him.

That new identity had begun with a miraculous catch of fish and the words *"follow me"* and to be fair, follow he had. When it got near the end, Peter famously says:

"Why can't I follow you now? I will lay down my life for you".

He'd got close to it, but he couldn't really come through on that promise and Jesus knew it.

The old identity sees Peter back in the boat and, here's the valuing thing, they have a miraculous catch of fish (again). Peter realizes who causes such things and dives in to swim to the risen Jesus, whom he has already met, so why is this visit so special that he can't wait for the boat to land? I'd suggest it's because he has instantly resonated with what Jesus is up to. This visit, like Thomas's before, is personal, it is for Peter. It's Jesus' resonant intimacy.

So, Jesus and Peter have a private conversation, only Jesus doesn't call him Peter, He calls him Simon, son of John. Peter the rock is on hold until Jesus reinstates Simon, son of John. He does this by requiring a triple enunciation of love to undo a triple denial (something Peter surely twigged along with every preacher since time immemorial). He may even, I am recently told, wrestle with Peter in this conversation in the choice of the term for "love". Peter prefers a manly brotherhood and Jesus is courting a deeper thing.

So where do the fish come in? Well, they are the reminder of the prophetic context of their relationship. The fish are part joke, part prophecy, part underlining the heritage of their relationship. It is valuing the original encounter to which it refers, that mattered, and it still matters. So when Jesus stages a re-enactment of it in a new version, it's a heavily pregnant encounter. It is love language, and Peter gets this. Then Jesus offers Peter a glimpse of his own death (the context of their break up). When the full weight of all that they mean to each other is in view like this, Jesus then reinstates their relationship from first principles.

Jesus doesn't just reinstate through love, He reinstates through 'role'. Jesus offers Peter the same miraculous fisherman role (reinstated) and the same resonant command (re-stated) *"follow me"*. And now Peter, bless him, can, and now he will.

Two millennia of piety have perhaps so stereotyped Thomas and Peter (and many others) that they have robbed us of just what a love story these relationships were. Jesus differentiates when He loves, Jesus resonates when He loves, Jesus gets up and comes to you in the very place where you can't come to Him because He loves and His love will not leave us as orphans.

Are we able to pick up that mantle? Of the recorded acts of the resurrected Jesus precisely none of them is about something other than relationship of the one with the many He loves. Can we find an expression for a one-to-many love like this in His church?

Let's try, shall we? In fact let's re-read these three different examples of different kinds of love back into the potential life of the church of association and of aspiration, where will it lead?

One-to-one love in the church: Ministers, leaders, it starts with you. Why wouldn't it? You need one-to-one love like Jonathan and David in your ministry and you need to teach and model it to your people. I'm not sure what they teach you at college about "clinical distance" being needed to pastor or the "dangers of bias" being introduced from having close relationships with one of your members but let me say this, it's utter nonsense. It does not stack up with what the Old Testament, the New Testament letters or with what Jesus says about leadership.

It is, in fact, a late modern authoritarianism which endangers church leaders of working in a desert of proximal love and thus becoming all the more easily disenfranchised from their people as a result. It turns pastors into psychologists, something they are, in my experience, neither qualified nor called to be. You don't "do ministry to" people. Anyway, enough, you see what I am saying.

Where are the unabashedly potent one-to-one love relationships fueling God's kingdom leadership now? Where are the men (who remain in the majority as leaders) who are unashamed to love each other so much that they will covenant with the one they love? Who (men and women) is giving up all personal rights so that a beloved one might prosper? How many ministers have such a Jonathan/Joanna nearby? How many future leaders feel themselves to be wearing someone else's clothes? If there's a reason why this story is in the bible, it's because it pleases God when we get our kit off for each other.

In all the churches, and not just towards leaders either, we are being called in the scriptures to believe and behave in a way that means we can love as 'a one' to another. This is to their great benefit and deeply praises the nature of our maker.

Many to one in the church: Members, friends it starts with us. Does the story of David's mighty men, or even Jesus' slightly less mighty disciples show us a paradigm for church? Is that sort of "many to one love" something that the church needs? I'd say yes and not solely because most Christian churches are around a size and governance where the majority of the pressure is on one leader. Every member in those churches clearly has an expectation of, and a stake in, that person. Sometimes that expectation is big and important. Sometimes it's petty. Sometimes the stake matches the expectation, other times not.

Here's where many to one love has to flow. If we do not see it as inappropriate that so *many* people are permitted to demand so many differing things from that *one* person – something they find all too easy to articulate in a range of ways – then there are clear implications. Our theology and our practice has to set us into a form of relationship with that one person, a form where we seek to love the person as "a many". Fueled by a reading like that of the mighty men and David, that relationship comes with a profound calling to love and sacrifice. 'The many' should feel that they would be willing to lay down their lives for 'the one'. They should feel this *as a many*, not as individuals.

This is a plural kind of love. It is not just the sum of the individual loves taken in unison. It is not optional. In loving like this, the many will have a profound effect by drawing 'the one' much nearer to God. This is what happens to David in this story and it strengthens him deeply. 'The many' *can decide* to do this, we see David's mighty men achieve it in this story. Their decision releases the sacramental force of loving, sacrificing friendship. It shows the real value of authentic, accountable, costly friendship.

After all, how many churches think that having the one who leads them drawn as near to God as possible is a bad idea? It is one of the quintessential things the many *really* need from her/him, despite what they might say they want. It will fuel the leader to put up with being 'the one', especially when things are not going well. How many church Ministers and leaders bathe daily in this sort of behavioral evidence of confidence in their value? How many church congregations have this as an article of covenant for their memberships? The answer is probably not none, it is probably only a few.

In all the churches, and not just towards its obvious leaders either, we are being called in the scriptures to believe and behave in a way that means we can be 'the many' who believe that they can love 'the one' profoundly – as a many. It should be integral to how we see our identity.

One to many love in the church: You might feel my system is creaking – a bit of a good phrase in search of a good idea. After all isn't "one to many" love just going to be the sum of all the "one to ones"? No, it isn't. Let me say it more clearly, *everybody* in the church needs to have relationships which are:

- One-to-one: Close, dear, powerful and accountable love between individuals.
- Many to one: Deliberate, heartfelt and sacrificial love from a group to an individual, very often the leader or leaders.

I think we can get our heads around those. However, to be the distinct community of love designed in Jesus' model we face a greater challenge of what we do with both of those in the need to show plural love. We need the distinct love of the 'one to the many'. The examples of Thomas *and* Peter have risked clouding the issue a little, I give you that. They appear to be perfectly good examples of Jesus showing 'one to one' love. That's because they are that, but He drew that individual love from a deeper well.

To see this more clearly we need to take a deeper look at how Jesus maintained the power of the intimate, valuing, love relationship He had with *a group*. The answer is "slowly". He did it using a "trajectory of transparency". Here's how that might work.

Let's just all look at Jesus in the bible without any theological or political intent (hard to do, I know). The model of plural friendship (and therefore of church) that I can see from Him is really quite beautiful. A masterclass in fact. Let me creatively paraphrase 'one to many' relationship from Jesus through the eyes of a gospel, in short, it goes like this:

It begins with curiosity: "Behold the lamb who takes away the sin of the world". Into your zeitgeist someone introduces a meta-concept. A thought-leader says 'that guy, now he is someone worthwhile'. If you are two switched-on young guys looking for a mentor, you might well be interested.

Curiosity leads to overture: You are so interested that you open the relationship and say 'Master, where are you staying'? Jesus is offered your interest in Him, with a suggestion of company.

It progresses with invitation into knowledge: 'Come, follow me, and you will see'. What they will see is not made very clear but these are hidden in the politics of attraction and meaning-fulness.

It moves towards relationship: It does this in a classic, theologically enormous sound, literally global signal of emotional investment with lowest risk and highest possible benefit – Let's have dinner together. Dinner reveals character. As well as being, well, dinner.

It develops companionship: I am going on this journey, would you like to accompany me? Now here is a commitment, but hey, it's only a bus ticket short of being broken at any time and a road trip is a road trip, all good.

It grows into shared beliefs: As they went along, he taught them many things. Convincing things, it turns out. He begins to affect them. In so doing, he reveals a medium-cost part of himself. Because they might not like this more fully revealed Jesus and, if they don't, that might turn the early attraction into a later repulsion. At one point He does challenge them on this. He asks whether his last sermon makes them want to leave, it doesn't. So He sees a little bit of risk in that Himself.

It becomes mission: They begin to agitate together because, do you know what, it can't all be about putting the world to rights over a roast duck and a glass of Pinot Noir now, can it? This agitation is not always comfortable for the disciples. They, and it is becoming a "they" which can be felt and consented to, begin to stand for something. The disciples start copying the master with mainly affirming results.

It opens the eyes of wonder: At the miracles, all were amazed, and those close by more so, 'well I didn't know he could do that, who is this that the wind and waves obey him?' There really is nothing up his sleeve, I saw him getting dressed this morning.

That creates a longing for depth: At first this is based on their mission, their values, some kind of round-up of their common bond. Philip says, 'Jesus show us the father and that will be enough'. Jesus says 'Philip, don't you know me after I have been with you for so long?' Well, that's provocative. Taken to the next level it's also a challenge to know Him better.

Depth moves into emotional intimacy: They are associated with one another and proud to know it (all the more sad when they have to make that intimacy a first casualty when it all goes pear shaped). For now though, at key festivals, in the middle of debates and dinner parties, it becomes pretty much a given that they will be together. Eat, talk, act, face threats together, what's this bus ticket in my pocket; I won't be needing that.

Intimacy begets love which contains physicality: Unbelievably a semi-naked Jesus touches and washes them, an act that they will later describe as the way in which He showed them the full extent of his love. An act, which He describes likewise. If their memories are working well enough, they might catch a hint of Jesus modeling it on the full extent of a repentant prostitute's love for Him. He takes the initiative, sure they have been accountable, sure He is the leader of the operation and the heart of it too. Sure they have been getting a load of knock-on benefit from knowing Him, but He has driven it. Then, in a potentially very uncomfortable moment, He reaches out for intimacy with them.

Love grows reciprocal enough to withstand accountability: Jesus can indict them in Gethsemane for being bad friends who'd rather doze off than care for Him in great need, and they can be ashamed, speechless even, but there is no sense that the relationship is somehow, for this, in trouble.

They share anguish: Jesus warned them that they would desert Him, and they do.

They develop an unbreakable bond: Love is as strong as death, the bible says; greater love has no one than to lay down his life for his friends, Jesus says; the disciples became convinced of this and several of them, we know, became exceptional women and men who lived and died believing Him and believing in Him.

Watch Jesus in this though, He does not merely model a Gestalt love made up of lots of post-modern individual relationships. At the end of His trajectory of transparency He leaves a plural mandate for the church and says:

> *My command is this: Love each other as I have loved you. Greater love has no one than this: to lay down one's life for one's friends. You are my friends if you do what I command. I no longer call you servants, because a servant does not know his master's business. Instead, I have called you friends.*

You see, God and Adam and Eve, they were friends...

Now read that bible quote again. Notice Jesus is speaking in 'one to many' terms. To me this intimacy and accountability is where you have to assume Jesus was heading all along. He clearly placed enormous stock by it. He took His time building a trajectory of transparency so that He could declare His shocking love. He bruised His followers to their core with this. He fought back their protests with the strongest of protests Himself, saying that without this sort of love they could have no part in Him.

In this, He would make it powerfully clear what kind of relationships He needed in His church. They were to be the plural kind that precisely reflected His 'one to many' model of love for His people and for His world; the kind that He could symbolize with finality in an act like willingly accepting crucifixion.

Has the church internalized this at all? How many ministers allow themselves to view their relationship with their people in these terms and seek this 'one to many' that still has the personal intimacy like that of Jesus? Or do they stick to a safer, professional version? How many members of churches likewise feel charged by Jesus to love their whole church and give themselves up for her? To love the world and do likewise? This is what we are for. I give you the New Testament letters if you disagree.

Jesus' love for church and world is very wonderful because it is:

- Founded on the existential power of the 'one to one'
- Requiring of the solidarity and sacrifice of the 'many to one'
- Causative of a church and society revolution of 'one to many'

These three forms of love are the ones which Jesus, supported by the textual life of the bible, *requires of us*, His church.

So, here's a Gadfly moment then:

- Am I saying that intense 'one to one' love in church is non-negotiable exactly because it is cognizant of the greater context of the significance God wants from the church?
- Am I saying it is a requirement of the people of a church to find a 'many to one love' for their leaders and each other which conspires to be an inspirational and sacramental confidence?
- Am I saying that church leaders must be in 'one to many' love with the church as strong as the strongest of 'one to one' loves and undiluted by culture or expectation?
- Am I saying, thus fueled and inspired, the whole church will express a 'many to many' love it is called to for the world?

Yes, that is exactly what I am saying.

So, why didn't I just say that? Well, because we can't 'say' this into existence, we have to read this into the church. We have to seek textual life in our bible within which we feel it is God who underscores these imperatives. When we read and see Jesus raising the bar we will be convinced that neither communities of association with nor communities of aspiration will be enough. We will want to be friends, authentic, accountable, vulnerable, loving and dying for each other. Like Him.

Let's ask ourselves church goers, to whichever kind of church it doesn't matter, are we as congregations afraid perhaps of the messiness of the intensity which Jesus has modeled for us here? Is that why we prefer the apparent counter culture that says politely serving each other is a higher ideal, and gloss over the bit when Jesus says servant relationships are *inferior to* authentic accountable friendships?

Let's ask ourselves, church leaders, are we afraid of the vulnerability which Jesus calls us to? Do we provide doctrinal and spiritual hurdles to this and hide behind teams and professions which validate our separation? Are we expecting not to love the people of the church in any sort of visceral way and yet claim they are the ones whom Jesus calls us to sacrifice ourselves for? What would that sacrifice really mean?

Let me ask myself. Will I prevent, by my very honesty and transparency, people from holding these attitudes to me? Will I come to church to share inner life in dealings, feelings and relationships? Even if I am hung up at times, will I let this create forgiving maturing, authentic relationships? Will I look for friendships that are for the journey?

If all of us in the church will but aim to give ourselves more to each other in these ways it will change the face of church. It is in giving in the way that Jesus patently gave, and in the way entire books of the bible center on and celebrate, that we will feel God's pleasure. God showed us (and told us) this sort of relating is His joy. Jesus said this makes His joy *complete*.

I'd just like to suggest – in case you are missing it or I haven't really made it all that clear after twenty-four pages of your patience – that the church through its authentic, vulnerable, friendship people is the mediator of the world covenant of Jesus. In practicing such friendship *as our community ethos* we reflect the *possible* world Jesus had in mind when He died for *the existing one*.

If we catch this spirit, those outside the church take note of us and start to say:

'Hey, look at them! What are they doing?'

...and God will say:

'Too right look at them, they are building a champagne fountain, that's what they are doing'.

Summing Up the First Three Chapters

This seems like a good place just to stop and take stock. Let's take a short hard look at what I've tried to say so far:

In chapter one: we opened up the overall debate that often the Jesus of the church is too small. That's because we have a poverty of ambition that makes us clumsy with the text making us all too keen to absorb it into our pre-defined cultural models. We looked at an example of what I mean at all when I speak of a hermeneutic of Jesus. We demonstrated how this showed that we need to allow Him to be bigger and more threatening. This is why we can (and should) seek to explain stories and sayings within a hermeneutic that make Him huge, cosmic even. The result is that He becomes more powerfully intimate. He stops being a figure.

In chapter two: we pushed into stranger waters where we said that in the reading of intimate personal stories left to us in the bible – like the one where God related to young Gideon – we see how God is out to capture the trajectory of your life. This is in order to steer it away from the culturally determined storyline. Away from the pre-defined, presumptuous even, idea that we can independently assert that God is pleased if we give Him our best. This becomes, after all, a culturally pre-determined storyline itself the minute it is given any credence. We wrestled, as Gideon did, that God doesn't need our best in the church, He wants the church to rise up to the height of a calling wherein we become a part of His best. Gideon ably demonstrates that God wants us to experience this as a member of a plural entity, not just as an individual.

In chapter three: we have just hit the blue-water, with David and the mighty men, Jonathan and David, and Jesus and the disciples. We unpacked the critical hermeneutic of authentic, accountable, costly, sacrificial friendship. In particular we asked why, when our text places so much emphasis on Jesus calling His disciples into friendship and intimacy – which is perfected in sacrificial love – the church seems, at times, to have made such a polite hash of entering this calling. All this, despite His express instruction that this was to be the banner tied to the mast of all of His discipleship communities before all the world. We differentiated that three kinds of this sacrificial love were needed for Churches to function distinctly in this world. These were "one to one", "one to many" and "many to one". Taken in total these turn the church into the ultimate expression of God's love for the world, "a many to a many".

In all three chapters we have concluded that greater personal risk, again counter culturally, lies at the heart of a hermeneutic of church through a hermeneutic of Jesus.

If that's where we have been, then this might be a good point to ask, where are we going?

In chapter four: I want to introduce what can happen when we are found to be getting our hermeneutic of church wrong by turning our reading of God, the bible and Jesus into something omni-inclusive and unwilling to cause offense. We will examine how there is no inclusion into Christianity without condition. We will conclude that there are necessary exclusions therefore. Jesus himself excluded any who would not pay His cost of inclusion or who wished to haggle over it. We will see that the ultimate challenge of Jesus is not that we are the ones who choose Him but that He chooses us.

In chapter five: We will try to understand if there was some kind of overall controlling hermeneutic on the lips of Jesus for the church. We will conclude that His passion was that it be a place of sustenance and not counsel. A sustenance which, first to last, was about extending the kingdom forcefully in the world. This will call into direct question any a priori value we might attach to a church which defines itself via a singularly pastoral ethos. Essentially, we will see that love without risk is not at all like Jesus' love.

In chapter six: We seek after and find a hermeneutic of relationship with God which shows He is keen to meet us at the very edge of our being rather than at the center. This fact will call for greater personal and corporate risk-taking and allow God to push us to that edge only to find a new country of the soul where He is both more threatening and more intimate.

Hope that is going to be interesting....

A Reading of Jesus 1:
Introducing the Half-told Kingdom

The subtitle of this book is "reading church through reading Jesus". At key points along the way then, I want to just stop and try and read about Jesus and His view of what He called "the kingdom of God". As you get to the closing chapters of this book you'll hopefully see that it starts to focus on how Jesus wanted that kingdom of God to be expressed through the church. So, I will periodically try to "read Jesus" with you for the identity of that church. That way, those parts make more sense when we get there. Here's a first try:

If it's hermeneutics we are after, in our search for "a reading of Jesus" we'll need to keep going back to one particular kind of text. Jesus' text. The kingdom stories He told and the proclamations He made about it. If we want any hermeneutic to speak of the church it has to be this one. We need to look more seriously at the kingdom stories Jesus told to have a hope of unlocking how He intends the kingdom to function, rather than as a content base for children's talks. It's not that I don't like children's talks, it's just that they can make us over-familiar with the parables in a way which might partially trivialize them if we are not careful to balance them out with some more serious exegesis.

Jesus was *the* authority on the gravity of the advent of the kingdom. As well as His teasing parables *about* it, we also need to try to fully understand His proclamations *of* it – because through them He said He was giving the church the keys to this kingdom. Whilst we are at it we will need to understand, as best we can, Jesus' *kingdom praxis*, His embodiment of it if you like, but we'll get to that later. It's just worth noting, for all those who want the church to be so very literally "bible-based", that in all three cases (parables, proclamations, praxis) a pretty profound tension between Jesus and the rest of the New Testament will hove into view. That's why you need your brain on to read this book; these things are a wrestling matter.

As a first step, let's take a look at the parables of the kingdom which Jesus told and start by taking these very seriously indeed. To give them their proper place as Jesus' great inauguration of the kingdom. We are going to discover that, among other things, they testify to a kingdom redefined by transformative patience, a justice leveling grace and, somewhat unsettlingly, a coming destruction. These will create a fluid and organic (champagne) cocktail of ideas of kingdom (and King) – one that had not been easily predictable before the advent of Jesus.

The church is then asked to drink it.

Parables of kingdom come

When we think about the direct kingdom teaching of Jesus, direct is the right word. In His parables, Jesus was as dynamic and provocative as He was in His ministry and prophetic practice. His kingdom stories are the narrative equivalents of the cleansing of the temple. For some people they caused deep thought and rejoicing, for others deep upset. All of this was deliberate provocation. Jesus set up a back-catalogue of wisdom tales that He clearly expected people to remember and pass on. Paradoxically, He said that one purpose of this practice was to obscure the truth of the kingdom for a time, or rather, for the timing of the implications of His actions. To unpack these parables fully, therefore, we will always have to take Him at His word and somehow try to fuse their possible meanings with Jesus' subsequent actions. They don't stand alone; they have to become complete in Jesus. Before we get to that, we have to unpack the stories themselves.

Jesus expressly told stories that He claimed revealed God in His kingdom on earth and how we should understand that. The first thing that should strike us when we look closely at most of them is that Jesus only half-told them. It's a particular habit of

His in the kingdom parables to leave the endings somewhat vague to say the least – a hung imperative. I find the mandate for the church that we can read from that fact alone, wholly fascinating therefore. There feels to be a need to read Jesus *out of* His stories and into ours (and by this stage you must know how much of my agenda lies there). Clearly for my purposes, I don't want the church to resort to pure allegory here, that would be/has been a mess. It might not seem that new to you, but what I want to point out is the fervor of Jesus' expectation. That is staggering: *Jesus invites us to experience Him as the King of the half-told story...*

There are around 121 *mentions* of kingdom (singular) across the four gospels:

- John has the least of these – with only 4 across only two conversations (Nicodemus and Pilate, hmm, interesting). For John, Jesus didn't talk directly about the kingdom.
- Mark and Luke have 63 between them (20 and 43).
- Matthew has 67 all on his own.

I realize that this analysis is driving a bus through Source Criticism, but I don't really care. Stripping that analysis down yet further for *stories* of the kingdom (not just its mention) there are, give or take a split hair or two, 19 stories on offer.

- Mark has 2
- Luke has (the same) 2
- Of these 4, precisely none are not covered, usually in more detail, by Matthew.

So, we can conclude that Matthew is the kingdom story keeper. The following is a selective list. Since you already know them, I'll paraphrase heavily. Notice, as an opening gambit, only two of these stories are not what I would call "half-told".

13:1 The parable of the farmer who sows seed somewhat sloppily (I'm cheating already, this parable doesn't use the word kingdom at all, but it is so obviously part of the set that I have brushed over that minor detail). The places where the seed falls denote the effect of the 'word of life' on the world, or, if you are of an esoteric frame of mind, on the individual parallel states of a person's heart.

This one is complete. We can understand how it ends.

13:47 A net is cast, fish are caught, good ones kept, bad ones thrown away. Be a good fish.

This one is complete. We understand how it ends.

13:24 A man sows good seed and an enemy, bad; the man's servants want to pull up the weeds. The man says no let them both grow till harvest.

This is incomplete, the ending is hung. Is it saying something pretty profound about the judgment of God and the function of saving grace?

13:31 A mustard seed that a man plants becomes a huge tree and all the birds come and nest in it. Way beyond the scope of this book to unpack so much Old Testament prophetic eschatology, but works on the Sunday school level of a little faith can go a long way as well.

This is incomplete, where will these birds come from, who are they, how will they know there is a mustard tree in Israel?

13:33 A woman puts a little yeast in the dough. The kingdom works all the way through that which is not kingdom, and transforms it.

This is incomplete, does the yeast work, does she bake the bread, who eats it, was it good bread?

13:34 A guy finds treasure buried in a field, buries it again and buys the field to get the treasure. Is this theft? Anyway, work out what's important in life and make the field of your endeavor surround it.

This is incomplete. What does the original landowner do when he finds out that the guy only bought the field for a tonne of treasure. What does the guy do with this treasure, does he put his feet up or found a farmers' charity?

13:45 A guy is well into pearls but finds one so incomparable that he sells all the others, so he can own just this one. What is it that is of such singular value to you if not God? Everything you are should serve that.

This is incomplete. What does he have to live on, now that he has sold everything? Does the pearl now satisfy him, or will another more desirable one come along? Does he let people see his pearl (maybe with an exit through the gift shop)?

18:23 A king wants to settle debts. A debtor can't pay and begs for mercy. The king is merciful. The debtor attacks one of his own debtors and doesn't show him any mercy. It does not go well with the first debtor. It's about forgiveness flowing out of you, stupid, and about the king who has the authority to throw you in prison and torture you (not a popular theme).

This is incomplete. What happens to the rest of the king's debtors, does word get round that if you can't pay he'll let you off, do many more start begging him for mercy? What happens to the unforgiving debtor, does he survive his torture and the loss of all he has and repay, or is he just unable to repay and is tortured forever?

20:1 A landowner employs day laborers in his vineyard and keeps going back to the marketplace where he finds people still needing employment. He generously takes all comers and gives them the same reward irrespective of the work done. This upsets some people. He tells them to shut it.

This is incomplete. What happens in the pub that night; is there a brawl? What happens the next day, do the workers unionize and force terms on the landowner? Does word get out that he is a soft touch and people begin to take him for a fool, only turning out in the marketplace sometime after lunch? Do the day laborers who were treated generously repay his generosity with harder work and greater dedication?

Even in this high-speed sweep of Jesus' kingdom stories we can conclude two things already. The first is that He expressly intended for these stories to function as narrative truth, not literal. When He says a woman lost a coin, nobody says what was her name or bring her out here so she can tell the story from her perspective. People rejoice in the story and that it is a story. Jesus uses it to say something truthful and liberating, doesn't He? The woman who lost the coin is not real, but she is true.

The second is that in telling all these 'not real but true' stories, Jesus kept back secrets. Part of the truth He is trying to covey then lies not in the surface content of His clever little stories, but in the hung imperative of them. This is a hung imperative that will only really be qualified by the subsequent actions of Jesus. The full sweep of His meaning would have to become a hybrid of His 'narrative truths' and His observable actions. In fact, I'd go further and include the observable actions of His church, but let's not get ahead of ourselves.

To me this has to be why quite so many of Jesus' kingdom stories have this 'half-told' nature. He was going to complete them later and even that was not going to be what we would expect. He was going to call His church to complete them further, in fact, eternally. In this way Jesus' stories are swept up into contributing to and pointing at His *own* collected and controlling story. In so doing, He was, therefore, giving the church His hermeneutic.

Let's explore that assertion first by engaging with three of the stories themselves. Each will introduce one of Jesus' kingdom paradigms. They are saying something about 'transformative patience', the 'justice of leveling grace' and 'the coming destruction'.

The wheat and tares (my paraphrase): A farmer had a field and he sowed it with good seed. Along came an enemy and he sowed it with weeds. The enemy doesn't want to move the boundary, he doesn't want to steal the crop; he wants to make it difficult and unfruitful to use the land as it was intended. As the land is neutral to what is sown, it's the implications of what is sown that interest him.

After some time passes, the servants of the farmer said "hey, those look like weeds, didn't you sow good seed in this field? Shall we go and rip em up?" The farmer says "no, let them grow together until the harvest, when the harvest comes get the weeds in first, tie them in bundles and burn them, then get the crops in".

This is one of the truly great half-told stories of the kingdom. Jesus lays down all these elements of metaphor for us to ponder and then He expressly doesn't give us the punchline. Now, you are entirely in your rights to say 'hold on a second, didn't Jesus explain that parable later?' Yes, yes He did, but even then He still left it half-told. This serves to illustrate what I mean by that catchy little expression. Here's a paraphrase of what He said:

The field is the world, the farmer is God and you are the seeds, the enemy is the devil and the weeds are his work, the servants are angels and the harvest is the end of the argument. When the kingdom comes the angels will pull up all the weeds and burn them.

'See' you say, 'how can that be half-told?'

Well, Jesus, in the telling *and* in the explanation, is deliberately blurring something. It's the distinction between who is 'wheat' and who is 'tares', with a twinkle in His eye, no doubt. This is a parable of a *fluid, organic* kingdom He is bringing. It is not a wholly static story, it's dynamic. We are invited to fill in the end ourselves.

The scientists among us thought they could helpfully do so. Seeking to simultaneously embellish and pin Jesus down, they retrofitted some botanical thinking to buttress the literal meaning (massive assumption here that Jesus wanted it to have a literal understanding). 'Weeds and crops, at certain stages in development', they say, 'might look the same. You have to wait for them to grow a bit for the differences to emerge, so as not to inadvertently pull up your crop.' Cheers guys.

I'm sure Jesus would be pleased that people are listening, but isn't this a bit Calvinist if you think about it? Sure, maybe in real life you can't tell which ones are the weeds yet, but the ones that *are* weeds will stay weeds in that reading of the story. They start weeds and end weeds and you can pull them up in a minute, and burn them. That doesn't really give the story much kingdom chops does it?

There are three protests against this line of (rational) reasoning. The first is that it is sloppy comprehension. The agro-workers in the story can tell which are the weeds, the whole moral of the story is predicated on that. The second is that to over-literalize it like this does damage to Jesus' reputation as a story weaver. If the wheat and the tares means to point out that there are good people and bad people then Jesus must have been having a bad day.

Why was Jesus so stuck for material that He tells a little ditty like that when half the Psalms and a third of the Proverbs (that people know already) bend over backwards to point out this reality? The world is populated by good people and bad people, and the bad people are gonna get theirs when the revolution comes. Why tell it? It doesn't work, it's not edifying.

The third objection to botany (or biology when it comes for fish with an evolutionarily pointless proclivity to eat shiny objects, or physiology when one little sailor on a whaling vessel is swept into a whale for real and found alive at its demise) is that Jesus isn't telling us stories to do with facts, He is inviting us into meaning. The story is not meant to be clearly understood, He tells the disciples as much, not to be clearly understood is *why* He is teaching in parables.

It is in trying to understand what is hidden that inspiration (nudged by the Holy Spirit) comes. That's why so many of the parables, in and of themselves even as content pieces, are stories about what is hidden. The story keeps the form of its own meaning; would you expect anything less from a master story-teller? Sometimes what can be revealed, particularly in a community appropriation of the meaning, leads to radical belief and action.

When it comes to the wheat and the weeds, we are directed (by Jesus) to look at the (kingdom) sense of it, not the reason in it. Jesus says that the farmer says *"let them grow together until the harvest"*. This is a parable (in my reading) about the transformative patience of God. So God doesn't go "aha! a weed, let us rip it up and burn it!" He goes, "hmm, another weed, let's leave it for a bit". Why does He do that? A weed's a weed, right?

By that token, a man possessed by a legion of demons would be beyond hope, and people who can't be cured by medical science would stay sick, and if Eve and Adam junior are dead when Jesus gets there, they stay dead, right? Jesus loves the half-told stories which open up innovation through impossibility, because God is a God of innovation. He doesn't just keep banging away with the same failing story.

As kingdom people, what we really need to get our heads around is that God often seems to delight in using the impossible to draw attention to His authority to innovate. So it goes in this story, it's only an interesting story because weeds can *become* wheat.

If left (by grace) long enough in the presence of wheat (and the blessings it receives) the weeds are given to wonder about another destiny beyond their nature, that destiny, and not their natural one, might befall them. Jesus is saying that He has read all those Psalms and Proverbs about "the wicked". He is saying so has God. Between them they do realize there's a problem with evil and holiness, so they effect a revolutionary solution to the problem of evil – transformation into holiness, not condemnation. What are by nature weeds, somehow, *by spending time in the company of the wheat*, become wheat. That 'somehow', as Jesus alone knows at this point, is going to be spectacularly costly and hard to bear.

There is a cost to this.

The generous landowner (my paraphrase): There is this landowner who uses the market as a source of day laborers for his fields. As others have pointed out this might not be a benevolent practice. Landowners who employ seasonal labor on a daily basis don't have worker's rights or the livelihood of worker's families beyond the next sunset top of mind. They also save a tonne of money by not having enough permanent employees to run their businesses. They probably don't even have a pension scheme. Jesus' landowner, however, keeps going out of his way to go back to the marketplace all through the day and even into the evening and he *over-employs* these vulnerable workers. Even as dusk appears, he finds there are day laborers living without hope of work. He keeps on saying, to their surprise and relief, there is still some time to go and work in my field. When no more work is necessary or possible, all come in and all are rewarded.

The laborers who were first employed, the ones who worked all day, see even the most recently appointed workers receiving the same whole day's rate. They get somewhat grumpy and the farmer tells them straight. We agreed what was fair, you accepted what was fair and it is still fair. What's really ticking you off is that these workers earn the rate for so little work and you had to do the expected amount. You want my grace to them to effect a scale which would favor you as more important. What's really getting you is that I am generous and some will always benefit more than others. You are feeling hard done by, even though all have benefited. Get a grip.

This story leaves a state of affairs which transcends our earthly idea of fair, neutralizes it in fact. There is a greater authority than "fair" or even, dare I say it, "human right". The landowner is the only one who has the authority to institute complex systems of "fair" in this scenario (like a detailed ethical-legal Decalogue perhaps?). Instead he proves to be a great leveler. He shocks them all with the simplicity of his justice of leveling grace. There is only one rate for working in my field. If your friends want to benefit from it, then tell them to be available in the marketplace when I walk by.

There is now only one rate.

The unfruitful tree: Jesus tells a parable on the delicate subject of death and judgment. In the NIV this is tactfully termed "repent or perish". It doesn't mention the kingdom, not in words. Like others that do though, it starts with a landowner (and we all know who that is) who has a fig tree (a key symbol of Israel). The landowner keeps coming to this portentously symbolic tree looking to get some fruit off it. Like the landowner in the workers' parable, *He keeps coming.*

It's not a pretty tree – it's a working tree. Every time the landowner looks for fruit, no dice. So He calls the gardener (a new player on the scene) 'I keep looking for fruit on this fruit tree and I don't see any, cut it down, why should it use up the soil?' This tree is not doing, nor is it going to do, what it's for, so it can't just sit here and sponge benefits from the system when it doesn't return some profit. Kill it. This landowner is the antithesis to the one in the wheat and the tares. In Jesus' story he has another side to his character then, an angry side.

The gardener (intermediary) immediately places himself between the wrath of the landowner and the tree. 'You're right, of course you are, I'll do as you say, but hey, maybe it's a bit root bound, forgotten how to tree properly, why don't I give it some structural work, dig it out, loosen it up, put on some fertilizer that sort of thing? Let's give it one more season, if still no fruit after that, I agree, we chop it down. What say you?'

This is a pregnant story. We assume, rightly in my view, that connoted in the compassion of the gardener is an understanding that he knows the landowner wants the tree to be good but just can't see how that will happen under the present circumstances. Connoted in the gardener's plea is that the landowner trusts the gardener with his property. The owner owns it, but the gardener tends it. Together they constitute the authority of owning *and* the compassion of loving.

We assume the landowner gives the year's stay of execution. He, based on a plea for mercy by an intermediary and not by the reaction of the stupid tree to its impending demise, says to the gardener 'ok you know trees, but this better work'. Less easily so, in what is really a rather more edgy parable, there's still that transformative patience being testified to.

Suppose the gardener turns to the tree and says 'there, I've bought you a year, I've saved you short-term, now let's work together on this because, trust me, your time is up, fruit is the only thing that will save you. I've bought you time, I'll give you care, but only you can produce fruit you were made for. Get back to what you were made for.'

Back at the time of the telling of this parable, in case they are not listening correctly, Jesus turns its temperature way up high and says (like he does in the wheat and the tares), the axe (judgment and destruction) is not just at the foot of this one metaphorical tree, it is at the foot of every real tree, all of them. Every one of them that doesn't produce fruit will be cut down and burned.

There is a coming destruction.

The wow factor in the parable of the weeds is the revelation that Jesus is instituting a kingdom where growing beside His good people will turn some of those weeds into wheat. This is His cue for the church. Here's the innovation, says Jesus to the church, the world *changes* at our presence. So go into (all) the world, lead an onslaught on it, and I will come running in behind giggling all the way. The inherent evil of this world subsides, transforms even, at your presence. If the conditions are right, says Jesus, the world will change and this is to happen before the harvest. So take a mandate to go and make the conditions right.

One consequence is clearly that a church so inspired would not see itself as just called to stand in testimony over this world. It would see itself as being called to make an intimate difference to its DNA. Perhaps this is even one weed at a time. This change will not come about by proselytizing or, worse still, protesting. This will come about by the overwhelming power of God's transformative patience expressed through the overwhelming practice of our mercy as we grow alongside this world. Mercy that Jesus frequently (and occasionally angrily) spoke of God "desiring" from His people.

Just like Gideon's story, God doesn't want an offering, He wants us to become a part of what God is doing. Jesus is, in His half-told Kingdom, instigating a church He *expects* to change the world.

The amazing corollary of the parable of the generous landowner is brought by a Jesus who said at His death *"it is finished"*. It would be pages' worth to speculate what He meant by "it". For my purposes, He could well have been saying "there is now only one rate". God has revealed Himself as a leveler, not a legalist. We've got ourselves tied up over that for centuries. The grumpy workers didn't write Amazing Grace, the surprised ones did. Jesus says in this parable, listen up people and stay surprised, this is powerful, reckless stuff and you are to unleash it on this world.

For the praxis of the church then, there is a mandate for 'excited and surprised'. How energizing would it be if we really did get this recklessly? This is what Jesus is asking in this parable.

The incredible invitation from the parable of the unfruitful tree is to see that we are being invited into something else as well; the permission to seek to overturn the portentous ending. We are *invited* to ask, 'will this end badly?' Jesus wants to infect His church with such a question. We need to push the parable off the end of His reading. Will the tree produce fruit? Will we? That's a mighty open-ended heuristic we have been left with here. Have you risked that Jesus is calling you to accept a role from this parable. If I accept "tree" that's one imperative, sure, but what would happen if I chose "gardener". What if God were saying 'I dare you, go on, choose gardener'.

These stories were half-told by Jesus because there is a need for the end to arrive. Christians (and the church) have to decide whether Jesus, in such stories, is handing us a fate (paging Mr. Calvin, Mr. Knox is waiting for you in the departure lounge) or handing us a role in their ending. Perhaps most edgy of all, is He, in fact, giving us the power to *change* their ending?

In such a brief tour I have only set out a small stall here; one that shows how things might be about transformative patience, the justice of leveling grace and the necessary reaction to the coming destruction. You might think that's not much more than a sermon in disguise (you might be right). This little stall after all, just points out that Jesus said 'complete and incomplete' things about the kingdom. He says the kingdom has a supernatural potential over and against its apparent size and worth. He says the kingdom transforms the world in which it grows. He says that it is a 'now and not yet kingdom' and there is work to do, even if dusk appears to be approaching. He says the kingdom only has one rate of pay.

He also says the kingdom brings a terrible wrath for those on the wrong side of it. We have to take all of this very seriously and facing up to this last point leads us to a difficult topic...

Chapter 4

Singing Songs of Exclusion

I can't sing

I can't sing
Which is a shame we all agree
Some more than others
If they are singing next to me
There seems a sad confusion there
As if the fact that you can sing
And I cannot
Is not God given

I can't sing
But circumstance and desire both conspire
To deepen my dismay
Because I long to sing
Just like you
I want the tunes you make so naturally
To be attributed to me
It's not as if
I'm deluded, lost or malcontent
To nefariously defame the perfect voice of grace
Or with more effort
Would not throw off your tune

I can't sing
And you know it
And we have a little joke
You and I
Nothing malicious

But it eases your pain
You who did not that I'm aware
Graft for purchase or practice
Your voice
You whom God has blessed
Can at least laugh with me
and that's a passing harmony ·
For you

I can't sing
And that's a shame I'd agree
Given the songs I've written
When the song I want to sing
Is a child for my arms
Who will never come
When the song I want to sing
Is a lover for my own
Who will never warm my breast
Who will never dent my bed
When the percussion in my head
Is not your gentle stealth
Of stable mental health
But the omnipresent rattle
Of pills that still my brain
A back-beat of obsession and searing mental pain
That's a hymn sheet for the lost
And if you are singing next to me
My source of confusion
Is the song you sing so naturally
Is my song,
Of exclusion.

I can't sing
And I know it

But in my head won't you see
There's a choir

Christianity, if you overlook the factual epistemology of the term and its associated back story of prophecy, started with an angel making a proclamation. A baby had been born in inauspicious circumstance and His advent results in peace on earth between God and all men. Sounds pretty inclusive then, job done. Only it's not job done because who to include and who to exclude have been a real struggle for the church ever since, why wouldn't they be? This will be a tricky chapter to write, and maybe a trickier one to read. It will seem to point at the dark little underbelly of the church. Rejection. Here goes:

- Jesus neither claimed, nor it appeared intended, to bring "peace on earth" by any Christmas carol definition of that term
- Jesus' teaching and practice juxtaposes a paradigm shifting agenda of inclusion with a value inverting agenda of exclusion
- The church patterned on Him needs to recognize this and have inward and outward behaviors which are legitimately rejecting
- This practice of rejection in the Church actually authenticates the inclusion patterns Jesus required from His kingdom community

For the church, rejection cannot be an underbelly. No matter what all those people out there, and a good chunk of those people in here, might think, rejection is actually a required character trait of the Christian church. Any reading of the bible shows us that our rejecting is not a failing or an error on our part. This is precisely because we worship a God who wants us to exclude, a God who definitely rejects, He has a long track record:

- For God so loved Adam and Eve that for one little bit of self-centeredness He slung them from His presence knowing that this set the world on the murderous trajectory it would take without Him.
- For God so loved humanity, that He was willing to drown almost every inhabitant of the earth (or the near Middle East) and put more effort into saving the dumb animals than listening to the drowning screams of those He created in His image, and their babies.
- For God so loved Moses, one of His only friends in that world at the time, that because of one capricious moment (after all the pressure God heaped onto that man's shoulders) God denied him the meaning of his life in his dying moments.
- For God so loved the nations, that on repeated occasions He instructed His holy people that whole races were simply to be annihilated.
- For God so loved sinners, that He created laws that involve several cases where persons should be stoned to death.

Need I go on? The church is brave enough to leave those laws in the bible, although not often brave enough to read them in public celebration. Thank God that Jesus repealed them – but He wouldn't have had to if they weren't there. The church is brave enough not to sanitize our back story and clean up this apparently embarrassing history. We leave it out there in the open, but that doesn't mean we understand it. We just stubbornly claim this is an all-loving God.

Theologians are left to come up with theories aplenty to argue the darker parts of God's story away, and they come up with some pretty weird theories at that. The thing is, if we want to read the church through the bible, the bible tells us we have to accept a God who rejects. Or, to put it in His own words, a God who says:

...I will have mercy on whom I have mercy, compassion on whom I have compassion ...When the time comes to judge, I will judge.

Now, you might say 'ah but Jesus changed all this didn't He?' It was all part of God's plan for the world. The revelation of Jesus would bring peace on earth to counter all this. So we can consign such an Old Testament God to the record books and roll out a newer model. It's a clean slate for us and for God too.

Well, that very much depends on how you hear the Christmas angel at Jesus' birth, and at every Nativity thereafter. Is he/she/it *actually* saying there will be *"peace on earth to all men"* (and women too, it's just clumsy to mess with the lyrics the whole time). Is that what the baby Jesus, when He grew up, went on to symbolize and offer? Or is the angel actually heralding *"peace on earth to all men* on whom *His favor rests"*. Could you not read that to mean that some are excluded as well as included? This is arguably less of a sloppy hermeneutic when we draw close to what the man the baby grew into actually said and did. Or why He was murdered, now that we come to it.

Take one example. The peace-bringing baby grew up into the man Jesus, who tells parables to indicate what God's kingdom is like. He says it is like a great wedding feast (the mother of all parties). He makes it abundantly clear, however, that certain people are definitely invited to this party, others may even be compelled to come, but some are not invited and will, if they try to attend, be thrown out in the darkness. Doesn't that scream "terms apply"? Anyway, it's not as if it was only in hazy parables that Jesus spoke of exclusion:

Not everyone who says to me, 'Lord, Lord' will enter the kingdom of heaven, but only he who does the will of my Father who is in heaven. Many will say to me on that day, 'Lord, Lord did we not prophesy in your name, and in your name drive out demons and perform many miracles?' Then I will tell them plainly, 'I never knew you. Away from me, you evildoers!'

You may say, well we applaud Jesus rejecting a religious formulation of assumed piety. We put checks and balances in place into our messages and our communities to make sure that our people won't fall foul of this condition. So Jesus comes back at us:

> *Do not suppose that I have come to bring peace to the earth. I did not come to bring peace, but a sword. For I have come to turn*
>   *'a man against his father,*
>   *a daughter against her mother,*
>   *a daughter-in-law against her mother-in-law – a man's enemies will be the members of his own household.'*
>
>   *Anyone who loves his father or mother more than me is not worthy of me; anyone who loves his son or daughter more than me is not worthy of me; and anyone who does not take his cross and follow me is not worthy of me. Whoever finds his life will lose it, and whoever loses his life for my sake will find it.*

Any exegesis of the prophetic intent of Jesus (notice He is quoting) in using this passage aside, it still feels pretty harsh and exclusive. It still seems to say conditions apply. You might feel you can cope with this too. We don't need the 'gentle Jesus meek and mild'. This sort of challenge is what makes Christianity a muscular religion, right? We can go for the burn – no pain no gain. Of course if there is blood on the floor in trying to get round allegorical or literal utterances of the incarnate Christ in the modern church, it's a Tarantino movie when the church tries to tackle the risen one:

> *I know your deeds, that you are neither cold nor hot. I wish you were either one or the other! So, because you are lukewarm – neither hot nor cold – I am about to spit you out of my mouth.*

So, if you do not want to hear that the beloved Christmas angel is offering a lesser peace, a peace with conditions attached, then just don't read Jesus' "sword of division" speech because either it didn't happen (floodgates at the ready), or it is a very strange rant. If the Christmas angel isn't offering a conditional peace, then blank out the majority of the Old Testament references to God's judgment – even the nuanced, and very New Testament-feeling ones in Ezekiel 18 that seem to square the sin – punishment circle for a moment. If terms don't apply, then bin the New Testament letters, they don't make sense. And for goodness sake try your best to keep your Jesus Nativity sized.

The bigger Jesus is blunt. He denies in public that He has come to bring peace on this earth. He says He's come to set it on fire and soon. There is a (pan-biblical) song that supports this and the church is called to sing it. Humming along in a noncommittal kind of a way is not an option. So, the trick then has to be not to deny that song is there but to learn the right words. The song of God's exclusion has a refrain – that there are *necessary measures* one must take if we want to *choose to* be admitted into His son(g) of inclusion.

Terms apply.

If we don't own a "song of exclusion" we might say we are the church of Jesus, but actually we are something else. So a chapter covering this tricky subject of exclusion is a necessary risk for a book like this. It is a necessary biblical contextual backdrop to my hermeneutic of church. The Angel, the teaching of Jesus, the New Testament letters and the track record of God shot through the Old Testament record are all pointing to the fact that consequential inclusion *and* exclusion are central to Christian faith. We should not try to evade our responsibilities in this hardest of matters.

If the church is not supposed to sing a song of unconditional inclusion but one of conditional exclusion, how are we to sing it? You guessed it; it's a three-pointer, yay!

1. The outward-facing church has to keep its nerve and exclude people without presuming to play God and without failing to honor His son.
2. The inward-facing church has to recognize that it is, often by default, singing the wrong songs of exclusion to its own people.
3. The modern church has a right to its identity within the song of exclusion that Jesus Himself sings.

Buckle up.

Finding the nerve to exclude

Right, there is on this subject of exclusion one huge area. In writing on it, in actually putting down the words, I am going to look like a bigot in freefall. So I'll do it first and I'll do it quickly. Whenever I bang on about the hope I have in Jesus to unsuspecting fellow humans they are often wont to politely apply the "what about" clause. What about Muslims, Hindus, Buddhists, Jews, Unitarians, Christadelphians, Mormons, Jehovah's Witnesses, Aboriginals, Californians, Druids, the philanthropic woman who lives next door to my mother... what about them?

What about, whatever form it takes, seeks to offer a philosophical shortcut to suggest that the whole conversation on the challenge of Jesus and of faith is steeped in relativity and, although it is vaguely interesting, it cannot be understood. What follows is that this conversation should really stop soon with the admission, on my part, that I am only one among many faith propositions. All of them should be treated with respect for their relative pros and cons.

Thus the what about clause undercuts the entire claim of the gospel of Jesus Christ on the life of a human being by doing two things. First it assumes an unimpeachable moral high ground which condemns any exclusion as wrong. Second, by a comparative sleight of hand, it says that Jesus cannot be the searing truth of God for the world. This is plainly true because when the whatabouter compares Him to the many other searing truths evidently on offer, and compares the acumen of Christian faith with other faiths, there is no evidence that ours is the more admissible truth. What the whatabouter is usually ever so politely getting at is that, in the face of so many other truths, I must be a bigot in freefall if I suggest that mine is the only truth. Come on, see the evidence; see the sense.

The whatabouter finds a sneaky post-modern fire escape that just says whatever works for you is fine and whatever works for me should be too – rarely stopping to underscore the total lack of substance of anything "working" from their side. They never say 'what about me?' Because that is the question this obfuscation is designed to distract from.

I often say to my whatabouting friends, it's interesting that you raise Hinduism, Judaism, Islam and so on. I find these challenging myself. Tell me, what have you read about them recently? Have you, as I have, bothered to go to night school and be instructed in the ways of these faith propositions from individuals who practice them? Shall we have an edifying conversation where we compare the images of God in the bible with those in the Koran?

I never get very far because the answer, ever so politely for the most part, goes on to reveal that the whatabouter wants to raise these other faiths (and non faiths) as an objection, in principle, to faith itself. This is rarely an informed objection, because the average whatabouter doesn't know what they are talking about. It's a game. If a whatabouter does want to give themself a veneer of considered spirituality, they will feign an interest in Buddhism. If they had the time to pursue a faith, which they don't, that one seems to appeal. Well it would wouldn't it? It is a faith proposition almost purposed designed for philosophical lightweights to shoplift gravitas. I tell them about a Buddhist I know of (and admire) who spent a year living in a cave to improve his meditation skills. That doesn't go over well.

So, I said I'd be quick. Three questions:

1. Do Christians believe that every other faith proposition in the world is wrong? Yes they do.
2. Do Christians reject the idea that there are many possible ways to God and the important thing is not so much the route as the journey? Yes they do.
3. Do Christians reject all of the people of all of the faiths in the world and consign them to hell? What do you think?

I mean come on; if our song of exclusion was that trivial we would be carpet baggers. A song like that wouldn't come close to explaining the sacrificial history of Christianity and the, frankly muscular, faith proposition wherein our central figure dies an agonizing death on behalf of the whole world.

When the outward-facing church keeps its nerve and does exclude people without presuming to play God, it is because we are called by Jesus to do so believing it to be a paradoxical proposition of inclusion. We are doing it to honor God's son. We are doing it believing that excluding people is loving them because it gives them an authentic Jesus. It also gives Jesus the headroom He needs to offer to include them into Himself. When we get it right we exclude on eschatological, not human, grounds. We exclude temporarily but we never want the person or group concerned to be excluded permanently from the community we are experiencing with God and its existential consequences. In truth it is because we have *already* excluded ourselves to the same ends that we do not overlook the unacceptability of anyone to God just to save on embarrassment. Here's how that works:

Christians are not so self-obsessed as to have overlooked our own unacceptability to God. Christianity requires its supplicants to first, and completely, undergo a rejection from God and from

Jesus. It is a core article of faith. That proposition – taken from the lips of Jesus – is so serious to us that we recognize it by following a rite of symbolized death and burial to show that we mean business. Thankfully, registering our savior's experience and intention for us, we also undergo a symbolic resurrection straight after that. We perform this death and burial rite with water so that it also connotes a washing to cleanse us. This cleansing is understood to be from that which makes us worthy of rejection. We also connote a kind of re-birth in the same narrative which is why the term "born-again Christian" was popular once.

There's half a book waiting to be written on the many other parts of our theology and praxis which underscore this essential part of the Christian faith structure and psyche, but I'll spare you that. Rites such as baptism assert that Jesus first rejects us in order to accept us. He rejects us to cleanse and save us. After that He reforms us by an ongoing transactional rejection of our outstanding faults and sins. So, when we reject those who are yet to face up to the imperative of salvation, we are not actually suggesting any standard be applied to them that we did not first apply to ourselves.

There is a more powerful reason why we must accept the rejecting side of Jesus when it comes to other faith and non-faith alternatives. As an individual Christian I can only experience conversion (an extreme moral and spiritual turnaround in intention and status before God) through clothing myself with a Jesus who Himself experienced what it meant to be "despised and rejected". This is central. To go on to suggest that God was only using one of his many stage names when He called me to that – dictated by my geographic and cultural disposition – wholly undermines the power, and the effect, of what happened to Jesus and what has consequentially happened to me.

Christianity offers, therefore, as its central defining character-istic, a critique of all other faiths (and I use the term 'faith' positively here, some of these people have faith as strong as mine) by asserting that the life, death and resurrection of Jesus makes Him the one who has embodied the rejection of all of humanity by God and the only savior of this world's inhabitants and the farthest cosmos.

That's a pretty exclusive claim. We assert, therefore, that God *and* Jesus reject. We claim to have experienced this personally and lived. We are not permitted to share the death of Jesus with other saviors. That's what puts the fundamentalism in Christianity, despite what you see on the news.

We have to sing this song, to be who we are: faith in "Jesus savior of the world" defines us. Take it or leave it. Jesus wrote the lyrics to that song in blood. It is a song of exclusion sung by Him as His own funeral rite. Then afterwards (because we believe there was an afterwards) He sings another hard song. This one He sings to His church. He says *to us* if, after this, you try to believe in *some* of me, I'll spit you from my mouth.

If the church ever commits the sin of including all (because we are not brave enough to exclude any on Jesus' own terms), if we let them come to that great wedding feast inappropriately clothed, that's not going to go down well with the father of the groom, or with the person themselves after that. In fact, if we read the bible's warnings to heart, it's not going to go down well for us, this failure to sound the trumpet clearly. So, again, we preach and accept a Jesus in Christianity who is not emblematic, but one who has declared the searching implications of faith in Him when He says:

> *Do not suppose that I have come to bring peace on the earth. I did*
> *not come to bring peace, but a sword. For I have come to turn*
> > *a man against his father,*
> > *a daughter against her mother,*
> > *a daughter-in-law against her mother-in-law –*
> > *a man's enemies will be the members of his own household.*

Anyone who loves his father or mother more than me is not worthy of me; anyone who loves his son or daughter more than me is not worthy of me; and anyone who does not take his cross and follow me is not worthy of me. Whoever finds his life will lose it, and whoever loses his life for my sake will find it.

He who receives you receives me, and he who receives me receives the one who sent me.

This tells us He has not come to bring peace on earth as we would define it, or even as we might wish for it. He has come to divide human community in all of its strongest possible relationships right down the middle. He then says the reason that this painful division – this song of exclusion – is a critical part of our message to this world, is because of what *other people can receive* if we sing it. They receive an authentic Jesus. If they receive Him in this way then they also receive the one who sent Him. His words, not mine. This elevates the purpose of our exclusion to really being an expression of God's passionate inclusion of the world. Put simply the church, to be the church, is required by God to hold its nerve.

Momma always said "life is like a box of chocolates..."

Right, if all of that seems a little airy fairy then let's bring things back to earth with a thud and talk about the internal-facing church. Here I want to say that the inward-facing church has to recognize that it is, often by default, singing the wrong songs of exclusion to its own people. This is a place where people might be all the more familiar with a practical, rather than esoteric, inclusion and exclusion debate. Let's talk about what we Christians do to each other inside our own stuff.

This section on exclusion, what we might call the "wrong song" section, is going to cover three topics. It's a three-pointer nested in a three-pointer, sneaky. These will briefly deal with significant sub-sets of the whole inclusion/exclusion debate:

mental health, procreation and sexuality. In each case I'm trying to say something different from what you have already heard.

Wish me luck.

When we talked about authentic friendship I suggested that Jesus' trajectory of relationship with His disciples was much, in pattern, like a real relationship ought to be. That there was a necessary courtship at the start of this of which Jesus appears to have been cognizant. There's probably a whole load of sermons just on how each of the disciples falls in love with Jesus – whether it's the infatuation of Nathanial, the obsession of Judas, or the rugby-boy camaraderie of the young James and John.

The church I attended when I started writing this book had courtship down to a tee. It was the most welcoming church I had ever been to. Genuinely welcoming people are at the door showing balanced levels of interest in newcomers. Sweet middle-aged guys politely introduce other people and offer me a nearby seat. Young men in their early twenties – who have better things to do chilling with friends and finding life-partners – cross the room to meet me and enquire after my well-being. And so it goes on, like I say it's the most welcoming church I have ever been to. Nobody had trained them, it was in their DNA. I might argue that it was a gift of the Spirit.

This sort of skill at courtship is important for our churches. It slowly unveils the benefits of inclusion and the possible depth of relationship to come. Deeper relationship, of course, comes with greater implications and higher costs. Courtship is good but it is always designed to be surpassed when you broaden and deepen your relating, when you show the real cost of you and accept the real cost of others. It is in moving from courtship to relationship and getting that wrong that we in the church sing the wrong song of exclusion. We also get it wrong when we do *not* move from courtship to relationship at all.

So, to tease out the implications of that statement a bit, let's talk about exclusion in the context of another church and how it dealt with mental health. That church will be nameless, of course. This was a flawed church, like they all are, and the flaws are a matter of perspective. They were doing their best. They were successful, wealthy and they were blazing a trail at that point in the early 1990s when there was a genuine sense of spiritual revival in all traditions in the UK – the one that paved the way for the impact of the Toronto Blessing, the rise of Alpha, the founding of New Frontiers, the breakaway success of the alternative Church and even the UK version of the 'mega-church'. Whatever you think of any of these things, they were/are signs of life and a passion for growth and change.

Almost all of these movements, a subject for another book entirely by a more well-qualified author, were typified by a greater overt kingdom passion than the traditio-mainstream had managed to maintain (I say "overt" because it would be a sin to write off the traditional church given that Jesus himself said the majority of the kingdom was done in secret). This particular church wanted some 'cutting edge' action. They were trying to be a bit radical, to be, as one sermon I remember from the time suggested, a 'box of chocolates' church – everyone was a different flavor, but each was needed to complete the array that defines 'box of chocolates' over a packet of sweets (or presumably nuts for that matter).

Let's call him Bob. Bob was one of those people who was attracted to church but not attractive to church. Bob was odd. The source of Bob's oddness was not clear. He wasn't, strictly speaking, mentally ill with a diagnosed condition, but he was a bit strange. Like many such people, Bob was not a particularly attractive person in dress or demeanor. Talking to Bob was not so easy, but he wanted to talk to you. Bob had learned, possibly over an association with many churches in his time, to speak "church" and so all the right spiritual words came out of him but they were copies, they weren't real.

The middle class church does struggle with friendship, I have said this already. An indicator of that struggle is our parlor games approach to fun. We are a bit middle class and a bit lame, sorry. A car treasure hunt was a pretty radical idea, and we were supposed to bring "non-believing friends". So I brought Kevin.

Upon arrival at the treasure hunt we were greeted with a steward in a day-glo vest in the car park. We were in an up-beat mood and we had the windows open so we overheard the conversation – actually we overheard Bob overhearing the conversation – since he was standing right there. The people in the car in front were asked if they had room for Bob, who had come to the treasure hunt, unsurprisingly, alone and without a car. The people in the front didn't want him in their car and kind of said so in a fairly straightforward manner.

Kevin, my non-believing visitor friend, graciously offered for Bob to come with us, although our car was already quite full. Having Bob for those couple of hours was not easy and I'd love to say that a long thoughtful relationship blossomed from there, but it didn't.

Also in a day-glo vest that day was Craig, another person with more obvious mental and personal problems than Bob's. He had also come, alone and carless, to be a part of the family fun. Now if finding a rent-a-friend for Bob had proved hard, Craig's case was impossible. My friend Ian, who was deeply embarrassed himself that no place at all could be found for Craig, ended up giving him the day-glo jacket and promoting him to "Steward". I loved Ian that day, not for his trying to make the best of a bad situation, but for his personal sense of loss that the church could not find room for Craig. That unspoken lament, deep in Ian's spirit that day, that neither Craig nor Bob could themselves earn or deserve a room at the inn. "*The poor you will always have with you*". Or to put it another way, every box of chocolates has a couple of coffee creams.

Notice a few things I am not doing and not saying. The thing I am not doing is using the church as a punchbag. I've deliberately chosen "mild" stories of exclusion here because, as I said at the outset, I am not writing this to beat up the church. There are deeper, harder examples – you probably know a few yourself – but we don't need them here. We need to simply help establish a principle. The thing I am not saying is that it is easy for a person (myself very much included) or a church, to have affecting relationships with people on the fringes of society or well-being, it's not. I'm not saying that every saint in a church can have the compassion of Christ for the outcast, or the willingness to bear the cost of meeting their hungry needs, they can't. I am not suggesting that I have a formidable track record in this area. I do not.

Here's a mini Gadfly moment then:

- Am I saying we need a bit more humility in the church in this area to base our love rhetoric on our actual track record?
- Am I saying that, when it comes to the lonely, to people with (overt) disability and mental health issues, our song of exclusion is often a paradoxical one. Is it to pretend that we are even capable of inclusion?
- Am I saying this is not good enough and that I am not good enough?

That's exactly what I am saying, yes.

Jesus, our template in this, did embrace in His time, those that were called the demon possessed (not that I am suggesting for a minute that mental health issues are demonic in origin, the bible pre-dates the DSM and it doesn't really have a classification language for severe paranoid schizophrenia, or bipolar depressive anxiety for that matter). For Jesus embracing those on this particular edge was a part of His capability and His calling. I'm not saying it was easy, but I am saying He was obviously very good at it. It needs to be part of our capability and calling and that will take work for us to want to be good at this, to be obviously good.

Just because we are currently no good at this doesn't mean we are off the hook for trying, because that is singing a rejection song. I think churches should find the training, the time and the compassion to *design* this kind of difficult inclusion into their ministries. We need to recognize from the outset how hard it is to do. Far from being calculating and loveless, that is the most lovely thing we could do. Such a decision to love, if it avoids patronization, may honor God more than to *"love those who can love you back"*. Such a decision to love might just change one key verse of our song.

It's not even as if a policy of planned inclusion is revolutionary to our community psyche. We practice a shadow of that 'desire to include' regularly. Every time we have that conversation about "children" or "the elderly" at the church meeting. We do want to write a new song for ourselves. So, let's agree on the tune at least. Let's agree that we often struggle to include. Let's not beat ourselves up about it and then carry on singing the wrong song. Let's just make it important, however falteringly, to learn a new one and see what that's like – chances are it will sound pretty tuneless to begin with.

That new verse in our song might also have one other beautiful collateral effect. It might just validate, at last, the 'under the radar ministry' of all those people in our churches who do have a track record in trying to love and accept those on the fringes. The people who, it might be noted, often do so from a familiarity with the fringe themselves.

If it is important to us, we will be able to see what God can do. We will do this because, as John Bell so passionately says, the fringe people are beloved creatures of one and the same God as ours. You know Samson, in all probability, was suffering from paranoid schizophrenia, God still gave him a purpose for his car crash existence.

I did meet Bob again some years later in another church. His story moved on, he was (largely thanks to my friend Neil) seeing modest success at being accepted and valued by a church – one of my favorites in all the world, in case you think I don't like any of them. He was still Bob though.

Unto us a child is given

So, we have identified the first verse of the Church's "internal" wrong song and that has got us quite far already, but let's push it into the mainstream. Let's talk about another internal group the church can exclude. They are an altogether more elusive and private group. I might just label them "non-procreators". Since I know you will be pleased to hear about my mistakes, here's another snippet of my story:

Helen and John pretty much knew from the outset of their marriage that 'the child question' would be a difficult one, physiologically speaking. For the early years, that was not going to be a problem, since they were becoming professionals they were holidaying, learning to ski and they were enjoying what it is to be married and have each other. They were also serving the church diligently, in case you think they were just a couple of yuppies.

John was 28 when they married; Helen, a slip of a girl at 24. Late perhaps for Christians, but not late in general. The church, where Helen had being going since she was 3, rejoiced and all was good. In the passage of time Helen's older brother and his wife had a little girl, and then another. In the passage of time a great many people of a certain age had a certain number of children. Helen and John did not.

When they had turned to face what they knew would be difficult, their instincts about that were pretty on the money. On the money for five hard years. It's not hard to count them now, but it was hard to endure them. Undignified treatments, ethical anxiety about what more radical treatments might lead to, disappointments, upset, despair and, in the middle of it, of course, a certain hope.

Here's the mistake, we told no one in the church, no one at all, barring God, no one knew about the problem and its associated pain, no one knew about the slender hope, not even Helen's parents or mine. We thought it was enough to endure without pity. We were wrong. It was harder to endure without the pity, we know that now.

But why did we choose to keep it secret? Well, damn near everything in this book so far ought to clue you into that little conundrum. We struggled to have a big enough Jesus to cope. We were trying 'our best' in the middle of this car crash to our joint faith in a God who could not answer so simple a prayer, who did not know the plans He had for us, or the desires of our hearts. We lacked, even within our own close family, a commitment to authentic, accountable, costly friendship. We were also part of a community that very much didn't have a song of inclusion for this because it was so busy singing an alternative song (about celebrating babies) at the top of its lungs.

Keeping it secret was a mistake. Telling everyone felt like it would be an even bigger one, and in some ways, it would have been.

Let's talk.

Sensitively, we need to let some of the pressure out of this story. I say sensitively and, as you read on, you are going to know why. Daisy, our only child (and a gift of God), is now 9. So we did, at the end of it all, have a child. That doesn't take away from the fact that we learned deeply (and over years) how it feels, in the modern church in the UK, not to be able to have one. If you are reading this and you do not know if you will have a child, I am sorry. Please don't hate us for being another one of those infertility stories that ends with a child. If many infertility stories do end with children, I know from experience that it is of no comfort in any way to hear that. You know it too. Our story ended in a child for our arms, goodness knows, I hope yours does too.

Here's the thing, Church is a little bit obsessed with a normative model of family. However, the church maybe needs to grapple more fully, and more overtly, with just how excluding that is; excluding both to the single and to the childless. Where I am not just repeating what many other fine commentators have said on that is to say that the church's understanding of this needs to be visceral, not cerebral. We have to learn to mourn with those who mourn from those who mourn. We have to do this in a complex way so that we actually get the wrenching gut ache that they do. We have to learn to sit, like Job's comforters, appalled together. And, unlike Job's comforters, we have to learn to keep our bloody mouths shut.

Childlessness is visceral. It is to do with the very viscera of you, you have to take the mysticism of its antithesis and put that through the biggest mincer in the butcher's shop. It doesn't stop for a second to grind bone as well, just like the psalmist says. If you ask Helen and I whether our church experience was a painful part of childlessness, we'll tell you straight, Sunday morning 11:00 a.m. was a reservoir of pain. But we should have told someone you shout ...I know that now!

Who would you have us tell and, more importantly, how would you have us tell them? You'd be forgiven for thinking the only language about children on offer in a church was a fertility rite of passage. It begins at the wedding for goodness sake, it's integral to the blessing, it continues with knowing glances, it goes through cooing and joking every time you are holding a baby niece. It degenerates into a Kafka-like nightmare where a small number of women of a certain age and fecundity line up in a corridor of shame holding pocket watches and tutting.

When they have run out of innuendo they just repeatedly ask you "isn't it about time you thought of having children". The "about" is my favorite blade in that sentence. "Isn't it about time you thought" – we've thought of nothing else for five years.

The thing is, to treat us this way, to be so cack-handed as to truly give us a signal that it's like Logan's Run in the church. In case you are too young for that reference, this is to say that to be beyond a certain age (without children in my version) is to be of no further value. To let the weight of expectation that the primary method we will utilize to fill the kingdom – since we can't seem to convince a disenfranchised and disinterested world in Jesus – is to literally make the Christians ourselves, and if you won't play your part, well...

For Helen and I to be so cack-handed as to implode into the nuclear family myth, to be so individualistic as to think this was only our business; that this, however painful, was not the very material of what it is to belong to a church community in the first place. To mourn alone and therefore miss the Jesus-kissed blessing in that was our mistake.

Here's a mini Gadfly moment then:

- Am I saying that a church with no sensitivity to childlessness gives the non parents a signal, not just about their utility in the community, but about their inherent value as persons?
- Am I saying that childless couples who cannot find the grace to bear their story in community reject the value of that community by seeing it as a set of relationships with limits?

Yes, that's exactly what I am saying.

If, to the one, we say you are of a lesser value if you don't acquiesce to our cultural norms and contribute children to the community. If, to the other, we say you are of a lesser value because, when the deepest most pain-seared thing I can go through in my life to date is happening, I'm not going to tell you. Then that is two songs of exclusion for the price of one, a battle of the bands.

But to share love, to love as we have been loved, is to get over these tired categories. Just as the church is supposed to seek to worship God on the basis of His attributes alone, we could seek to include people in our midst as beloved of that God. To always value them on the basis of His attributes alone.

When it comes to childlessness the church really needs a new song for that. It's a complex harmony, what with it being one part lament one part love song... (just like the psalms and half the rest of the bible then).

The One in Ten

When it comes to exclusion, one of the most vexing questions for the church is love within a gender, and I don't mean greeting each other with a holy kiss either. What have we not already read on this subject? What pocket theory have we not already decided to adopt? What aphorism will we not trot out in a bold group discussion? To write on the Christian subject of same gender attraction, let alone same gender consummated attraction, is to look down a long, well-lit corridor festooned with bear traps of all shapes and sizes and, knowing every one of them is on a hair trigger, switch the lights off and run.

And run we must, the Church, the whole thing, stands or falls (for me) on its fidelity with what that bible says, intones, leads to, suggests and screams. If we need to be drawn to certain kinds of exclusion that's because the bible and Jesus, however paradoxically as I have said already, call for that exclusion to be part of the DNA of our love. So we can't shy away from this. So even when our book says:

> Do you not know that the wicked will not inherit the kingdom of God? Do not be deceived: Neither the sexually immoral nor idolaters nor adulterers nor male prostitutes nor homosexual offenders nor thieves nor the greedy nor drunkards nor slanderers nor swindlers will inherit the kingdom of God.

...we sit up and take notice of the world of pain this is going to cause us when we want to convince this world that we aim to love it.

On same gender attraction and same gender love a couple of things seem clear at the outset. First, these are real within the church and without. Second, the church, which does, on the whole, think outward expression of such love and attraction is wrong, doesn't always have a ready and compassionate answer for what to do.

The debate of late, and I will only touch on it because I don't have an answer either, seems to have moved into a relativistic and linguistic phase. We are told that proportionately the mentions of same gender sexual activity in the bible are staggeringly few. Using a combination of statistics and context we can argue, therefore, that "gossip", for example, is an obsessive subject in the bible, and yet we don't get as steamed up about that at all. So, same gender sexuality is not a subject that troubles the bible as much as we think it does us. It certainly doesn't turn up (explicitly) in Jesus' world for Him to give us a steer.

If you really want to read our pain on this subject, then it is fascinating that same gender attraction is a bit like that other gender based conflict – the role of women – in that it spins on a single word. For the latter the word is *"authority"*, for the former the word is "natural", or "abomination" depending on which side of the compassion line you are comfortable.

That comfort seems to be where the new wave of linguistics is trying to bring us, which feels quite noble. So, of the few biblical mentions of same gender sexual practice we are told, when linguistic weapons are marshaled, most, if not all, of the references can be explained culturally. There are prohibitions on sexualized worship practice, prohibitions on prostitution and prohibitions on domination, or outright rape, between men which might, in line with the norms of the first century, be military or predatory in nature.

Linguistic weapons, of course, can be marshaled in many ways. They refute the Immaculate Conception, the virgin birth, the miracles of Jesus, His claims to be the son of God and so on. They can give us a completely new Jesus in completely new gospels which don't physically exist, they can give us at least two gods in the Old Testament and, at last count, four different kinds of Old Testament author which, when split, as they should be so the argument goes, fragment the unity of the messages of the bible irrevocably.

Linguistics can cripple systematic theology at a stroke by completely unseating the authors of biblical letters, or disconnecting them from contentious lines in their own texts. They can re-establish whole religions and cults and interpolate them into a Christianity which, for centuries, we have seen as a unity. In fact, they can even bifurcate sentences in the New Testament to the point where their meaning is indiscernible to all but a scholastic few. A few whose writings sometimes seem to betray no interest at all in the claims of the bible, or of Jesus on the life of a person outside of their intellect.

So, it's good stuff, this linguistics, but it comes with a health warning. We remain roundly convinced for the most part that God has chosen the 'reading of a text' as one of His primary methods of communication with humanity. Any of the more radical applications of linguistics, or literary criticism, tells us that this simple enough act is impossible. So just arguing about the actual words is always a dangerously incomplete approach. You need a hermeneutic, even for this; especially for this.

Thankfully we press on, because, God be praised, "comprehension and de-construction" do not have the monopoly on our relationship with this staggering library of resistance we call the good book. We need ways to read it which are more than purely intellectual; we need ways which are more existential. On this vexing subject it is "way" that concerns me. I know I'm quoting John Bell a lot, but I challenge you to find a finer oral theologian in the UK today who grasps the adventure of Jesus. He comes to our aid here because his epitaph might readily read:

> "Jesus never said He was the answer, He said He was The Way".

So we could rise to this challenge – to stop reading for an answer to this and start reading for a way. There is a way *in this* to have a reading of church. It is to that way, in an unsatisfactorily incomplete manner, I want to point you.

Let's be clear at the outset:

One, if same gender consummated love is a sin, the bible is clear that persons concerned in sinning – like any sinners over any sins (which is all of us then) – will face their maker intact and be able to throw themselves on the love of Jesus, the great leveler, and the power of His once for all sacrifice for all sin.

Two, if as an overt practice churches cannot condone same gender attraction and consummation then this is not as some kind of spectacular exception, it is in good company. The bible is massively clear that there is a huge range of other practices that we shouldn't condone. If we don't have a problem making these things lovingly plain, we can make this lovingly plain too.

Three, if you want to be fanatical in your dedication to the teaching of the bible on the sanctity of one-man-one-woman-marriage (something that large chunks of it actually sit very loose to indeed) then go ahead and limit love in that way. My reading (and that of the whole Catholic Church) is – as it is on the lips of Jesus *and* of Paul – the higher calling of love is not to marry (a person) at all.

Stop for a moment and see what a great leveler that is because the same gender oriented, the opposite gender oriented, the single and the married are actually given one and the same calling. A calling which is *sexuality independent*, which places spirituality, not sexuality, as the cardinal determinant of life and being in God. What a blessed relief. The intensity of that spiritual calling is also something to which the bible (again) assigns many more column inches to than same gender sexual activity – if we are going to play the statistics card. Strangely, the imagery of that calling is marriage, but clearly this is a deeper definition of that term than we ever care to imagine.

Four, I can't say anything wise on this topic. So I'm not looking to wrestle for an answer, I want to wrestle instead with *one* core idea. This is that all of us in the church, irrespective of sexual orientation, have potentially commandeered Jesus' definition of love to suit our own agenda. The best suggestion I can come up with is that we have to give it back. If we do that it will change the balance of responsibility within and the nature of this debate. So here goes:

To be human is, definitively, to be a sexual being (actually it is a sub-set of our physicality, but let's not split hairs) and all that evolutionary biology tosh to one side, there seems to be a reason for this sexuality and the reason is transcendence, transcendence into love. That is in the design of our intensely experiential bodies; that is in the design of our God. To play smoke and mirrors to suppress or, worse still, make this defining characteristic of our beings go away or be unimportant is a sin. Doubly so if, in the church, we bifurcate the human race into one bit that we believe needs to do so quite intensely and another that doesn't have to at all.

There's more though, there are other 'definitively human' considerations. We are definitively psychological beings: we think, we write, we read, we discuss, we live a lifelong journey with the voices in our heads – the speech of which we share with one another because, despite what Descartes had to offer us, we cannot think alone. There seems to be a reason for that and the reason is transcendence, transcendence into love. Loving each other borne on the wings of a shared mental life is another gift of our thinking creator and not, as we have been hoodwinked to understand, Plato.

We are definitively spiritual beings and I'm not going to waste ink telling you why I think that is, nothing has ever been more startlingly obvious to the human race than this. The reason that we are spiritual is transcendence, transcendence into love. Love is the very thing we are meant to be spiritual about because love is not of the earth, love is spiritual.

The story of Jesus tells us that not only did He recognize and validate all these loves but that, in His revolutionary view He was drawing them up into a quintessence. He was going to redefine for us how love could become *"greater love"*. Holy love indeed. He said this greater love is what we must aspire to if we are to follow Him (a single guy remember). Given the gravity of the incarnation we know that it is *as human-multi-faceted-beings* then, that we are called by Him into this. Each part of our being is asked to play a role in transcendence into what Jesus called greater love. That's a big deal and the problems start, as I said already, when we accept His *mandate* to greater love but not His *definition* of it.

It is a first corollary of our existence as a being who is sexual, psychological and spiritual all at the same time that no *one part* of our being, therefore, is allowed to define love *more intensely*. For the purposes of this debate I have to point the finger firmly at those who want to elevate sexuality so that it occupies that definitive place. Neither sexuality, emotionality nor even perhaps spirituality can claim the definitive supremacy in "our hearts" that means that they would *on their own* express or bring us into the love Jesus calls us to in His life. His greater love is always a matter for their sum.

In fact it is very much because our sexuality and our emotionality are cast in a being who is capable of spirituality that we will always be internally pulling to be more, even, than just this *sum* of our impulses. That's what transcendence effectively means, a going beyond. One quick look at human philosophy, or literature, or even soap opera and video games if you must, over the centuries makes that pretty obvious.

But wait. This gets bigger still, the calling to transcendence. Jesus, when He came to give us a faith which He said can transcend all of our (imperfection riddled) impulse, didn't just do that so we could aspire to a greater love for Him or even each other. He gave it to us so we can experience communion with each other and with God. The higher reaches of theology will point to that communion, in its quintessence, as the one which God the Father, God the son and God the Spirit enjoy by nature. We are called to join in. Join in to something greater.

So, to be fully human, fully made in God's image, is not to long for loving relationships that satisfy one or other of the aspects of our being, but to seek a communion that satisfies them all. This communion, the bible exhorts us, is to be expressed and experienced in and through the presence of God and with all of our being.

One easy further corollary of that 'called existence' then is the church might have to stop putting too much emphasis on the spiritual side of things the whole time of course. The church needs to make a clearer statement that Jesus requires *more* of a person than what any one of our "definitive characteristics" alone has to offer. Jesus requires what all of them have to offer. The church has to start requiring in its dialogues (about sexuality or anything else), and in its praxis, that its own persons be called to an accountability which is as whole *beings* therefore.

Why should this come as a surprise? When someone says to Jesus 'what's the greatest commandment?' (remembering that the commandments were, at that time, *the* calling into communion with God) He simply says what they always knew:

'Love the Lord your God with all your heart and all your soul and all your mind and with all your strength.' The second is this: 'Love your neighbor as yourself'. There is no commandment greater than these.

In Matthew's account, Jesus even goes as far as to say that all the law and the prophets – so practically everything of relevance to the Jewish worldview of God then – hangs on these. What is it we are to love God with? Well, it's our totality, our being. Please notice that Jesus doesn't leave out 'strength' either. Er, that will be what we do with our bodies then...

So, let me make one further observation before I tackle the responsibilities around love and sexuality in the context of church community which I think fall squarely out of even these incomplete ideas. The observation is this. No one says hold on a second Jesus, that's two commandments, we only asked you for one. If they had I'm sure He would have said 'actually mate it's three'.

Jesus' answer on the question of the greatest commandment from God to humans is not just saying the totality of what we are as beings must elevate itself into a loving communion with its maker. That wasn't nearly good enough. He is proper sneaky. He introduces three distinct existential challenges through which all human beings must be right with God:

'Love the Lord your God with all your heart with all your mind and with all your strength, and love your neighbor as yourself.'

If you read that statement in reverse, Jesus calls for three loves:

Love yourself; Love your neighbor; Love your God

Love yourself: We need to accept that this command of Jesus speaks of the necessity, not exclusively but maybe especially when it comes to the inner life of sexuality, to be 'in communion with' the whole of our self. We need a language for that. Jesus calls us to love ourselves. He says this is a pre-conditioning definition for how you are to love others. God the vast healer, in the call to love, is actually calling us into community *with our own being*, because community with Him was not the only thing that was estranged in Eden.

This is precisely on the lips of Jesus Himself, why same-gender attraction cannot be externalized in the person and be rejected and, by extension, nor can it be rejected in the church. In both, it needs to be internalized and accepted. Now if that sounds incendiary, it is because you are running away with semantics. Let me explain.

Here's a snippet of my story:

Helen, my wife, makes an assessment that I am roughly one quarter gay. I agree. This does not disturb or upset our marriage. Here's some of the historical logic of that statistic:

I grew up a sensitive "highly strung" individual in Paisley on the west coast of Scotland, the industrial west, the poor west. I'm a post-war baby boomer born in a prefab to a couple of fairly damaged parents (not their fault – the damaged part, not the having a kid part). From an early age I wrote poetry and loved science, and, because Harry Potter hadn't been invented then and Enid Blyton might as well have been writing in Dutch, my preference was D.H. Lawrence. I did it for show; I don't like him even now.

The product of an emotionally troubled household, I had an over-bearing mother (who herself had survived an incredibly abusive childhood) and a functioning alcoholic father (who, likewise, had done the same). They had no concept of what they were dealing with in me, something that had pretty negative outcomes sometimes. I was also bullied at school, actually, I was bullied pretty much everywhere.

The product is a sensitive, emotionally-connected, spiritual, poetry-writing, cries-at-films-man-boy with a firm interest in interior design, nice shoes and a couple of degrees in Psychology – who still goes to the gym and can't walk past a mirror to save his life. Thankfully for me, I don't look after my hair all that well, can't dance for toffee and have scant interest in the musical theater.

There are two other reasons that I know I am sort of partly gay. One is practical experience of same gender attraction in my late teens and early twenties. The other is that, from time to time, although rarely these days, I can still find people of my own gender attractive in more than just a potential friend sense.

Jesus tells me to love myself. Which absolutely means that I must love this about myself and I must let him love it too. Unto death.

I must love this about myself, because in that there is a key and the calling to loving it about others. Jesus' key to *"Love your neighbor as yourself"* is to transcend self-loathing. I must converse with my creator openly about whom it is I seem to be, so that I can long for whom it is that I am, the thing that He is interested in, the thing He made and loves and completes. That has to be my song of inclusion. Of myself.

I have to push the whole of myself, not an offering out of myself, but the whole of it, into the folds of His garments. His love covers.

Love your neighbor: The Christian church community is the worldwide owner of this commandment. To obey it we must become the ultimate expression of the way in which the many 'selves' of a church can draw into a holistic body reflecting Jesus' compassion for (everyone in) the world. This responsibility means the church has to be the ultimate communion. No pressure then.

That communion is not something as aesthetic as a gathering of "people with a personal saving relationship with Jesus Christ". That community is not something as individualistic as a collection of family relationships or marriages either – despite our best modern efforts to elevate these pretenders to that throne on a Christian society-wide level. That communion is God's whole church. It cannot be a set of discrete love relationships in Gestalt; it has to be a thin place where love has been elevated into something holy; a community sacrament in fact.

Jesus gave us a definition of "greater love". We need to aspire to be the sort of community where that greater love is one of our sacraments. It has to be more than an idea to us. As an integral part of that love therefore we must *wrestle* with same gender attraction. We start by avoiding the standard pitfall of turning our own practices into a "normative love" from which we judge it. That will not create the greater love Jesus spoke of. It will create an orthodox monoculture which will always trivialize our approach before it has begun. We don't want tolerance or empathy because if that is all we look for we are doomed. Anyone can see that's just looking for comfort. That is a pathetic substitute for Jesus' greater love. There's just no sacrifice in it.

The sacrament of plural (greater) love is something we need to respond with as a community of whole persons. So, for our next step, we need to break into the damaging 'either or' language of this debate and open up a new language which is more nuanced, more subtle and more of an honest reflection of the starting point of our shared humanity before God. The way to do this is to keep Jesus' definition of greater love at the front of everything we do here. Easy right?

Men (in particular but not exclusively), it is over to you to sing this song. I know the church is brimming with sensitive, educated, emotional and spiritual men who are called by Jesus to practice the communion of greater love. We must be men who might, in the right moment, therefore, also own a certain story (a certain song) that does include a recognition in ourselves that attraction to our own gender is a possibility, or indeed an experience. I don't say this as a hypothesis. I am a scientist and I have tested this concept over many years of sensitive conversation and found it almost always to be true. What kind of a possibility would honesty over this open up? Well, a wondrous one.

If we, of all peoples, will own life's realities – remembering that sexuality is only a part of what we are, not the whole – and speak frankly and honestly about what that is, what makes it up, where the struggles are and how they feel. If we will own this as an explicit part of our community identity (not a secret one) and share life like that, then we stand the chance of rising to Jesus' call to authentic costly friendship *in community*. The sort of community within which persons of same gender orientation, who very often seem to me to bear these same hallmarks writ large, might not feel so ostracized or excluded.

In case you are missing me, I really do not think we should be ostracizing or excluding same gender oriented people on this basis. That is what I mean by the wrong song of exclusion. Just to be clear. Now if you are still finding this incendiary you need to stop a while. There is more to say, but consider this: all that I am saying so far is that the church people have to seek transcendence into love to be the ultimate community God requires on earth and to be found to be made up of those who are ardently "fully human". The church which tries to do this without a language of compassion and acceptance *as* its heart is not church at all.

What I am also saying is one key to this is found in Jesus' sneaky third command, love yourself. As beings we need to reconcile that aspiration first in our own individual hearts. To give the church a chance – of transcendence into love – we need, as intimate persons before Him, to come to our God with the whole of who we are as persons, no compromises. Love self to love neighbor as self, and then we will, according to Jesus, be capable of "*Love God*". But that's a whole other book.

So, at the halfway point, here's a mini Gadfly moment.

- Am I saying that Christians need to own and share the capacity for same gender attraction within ourselves if it is there?
- Am I saying, even when it is not, Christians need to openly discuss this matter in the life of the church without precondition?

- Am I saying the best we can achieve is a conundrum and
  we need to accept people as beloved of God even if this
  means the whole debate must go on without resolution?

Yes, that's exactly what I am saying.

So, how do we get started on that?

Well, there are (at least) two more things I think we have to
do. First, I need to say this again, we have to use the right definition of love in this debate, the one Jesus actually gave us, not an
interpretation of it. Second, we will have to accept that a whole
series of 'ifs and maybes' is about the best this debate is ever
going to get.

The right definition of love

Jesus was a single man who claimed that marriage has no place
in the kingdom come. He called us in His life and particularly
His death to what He termed "a greater love". We perhaps strive
to understand this in the church by properly elevating it to a
sacramental status, but when we do we forget something. The
greater love to which Jesus calls Christians is, necessarily, plural.
He wants us to lay down our lives for our friends – plural.

As a Christian, therefore, (same or opposite gender attracted)
the true root of any agenda of love you have which is imitating
or responding to Jesus has to be plural. Your capacity for love
and your experience of its intensity needs to be judged in the
plural because this is the active context that Jesus gave it. In the
debate on same gender attraction I'm not sure that we are paying
enough attention to that. When we talk about any human love,
and when we are stressed by whether same gender sexuality is
all right or not, the unwitting benchmark is not actually Jesus'
definition of love at all. Rather it is a modern socially constructed
definition of justice. Justice for "a couple", for their love.

Ironically for the church, in absent-minded acceptance of
that social construction, we acquiesce to an unchallenged,

individualistic cultural process that we don't find in Jesus or in the bible. In short we receive and accept an *individualized* definition of "greater love", one that Jesus did not give us. We consent to defining love's greatest exemplar as the case where an individual seeks intimate, passionate and private approval from another individual. Then we mainly argue about right and wrong within that context. This is a mistake.

For the church to launch a debate which only speaks about 'correct or incorrect' love in a 'partnering context' is to surreptitiously consummate an illegitimate orthodoxy. That orthodoxy underwrites the idea that "greater love" can be redefined by our experience of justice as couples. Justice is expressed as the right to consummate (approved) love for another single being when that other being is not God. The belief that it is this which exemplifies "greater love" is inherited from our culture not from Jesus.

When that belief goes unchecked it becomes a constraint on the debate on same gender love and, more importantly on Jesus' calling for love to be the definitive characteristic of the kingdom church. So, the plural love He called us to proves so difficult that we collapse it into our own image not His. We thus artificially construe and accept a culturally serendipitous quintessence for love. We elevate individual love and marriage to a higher place of importance than Jesus models or allows. We romanticize our interpretation of Jesus' call to love into ideas of interpersonal relationship focusing it on 'the one' we would all die for, not the many He called us all to die for in fact. Thus we have a plain diminution of the quintessence of love which Jesus actually left us with.

If we don't set Jesus' plural love as our higher intention, particularly when we talk about opposite gender attraction and love; if the focus is not laying down our lives for each other in community – particularly when we debate same gender attraction and love, then we are in danger of placing love into a far smaller context than Jesus did. Too small a context in fact.

So what's my conclusion so far from this? Well, gay or straight or undecided, your calling from God is not to find life's true love for yourself and seek approval in that. Gay or straight or undecided, your calling – in the Christian context – is to love God's people and lay down your life for them as Jesus instructed.

If this is your desire then the question of whether you are capable of being in love with someone else, or deserving of the chance to be so, is to be judged by your actions in the community of love that Jesus inaugurated. Gay or straight or undecided, one action that must be defining for us, therefore, is our acceptance of community *with each other during this debate.*

That acceptance is an expression of Jesus' (greater) love. We (all) accept, as He instructed, that there is a necessary plurality to our existence that does not trivialize, but does transcend, our sexual orientations.

Accepting that there is a higher justice in rising to Jesus' calling to greater plural and sacrificial love will transform *our song* of inclusion. We will sing the song which Jesus Himself sang to us whilst we were sinners and which He still calls us to sing to each other as definitive of His kingdom. We will sing it however troublingly complex and nuanced the lyrics need be.

When we sing it, accepting His definition of greater love, we move that definition away from the interpersonal space it has been crammed into as a result of huge forces in our culture. When we do that something amazing will happen to the debate on same gender sexuality in the church. The debate begins to accept that there will not need to be a resolution or a stand-off here, there will need to be love here.

Wrestling with ifs and maybes: A whole series of 'ifs' now hove into view. If I am alert to that statistic, that one in ten, however faulty it really is; If I am alert to my own spirit; If I am alert to the spirits of other sensitive men and women who will be honest in their dealings with themselves and each other and those whom they influence; If I am to be alert to the enculturation of an increasingly normative status for same gender attraction...

...then I cannot sit in front of ten young people and tell them passionately "Jesus wants your all", when, for a very small proportion of a particular proclivity, the church I am sitting in whilst I say it underwrites a subtext that says there is one (at this point seemingly central) bit of their particular individual 'all' that He certainly does not want. I cannot give them, even by omission, the impression that Jesus will not talk openly to them about same gender attraction and the church will not talk about it either – other than to utter the predictable rehash of the prohibitive orthodoxy.

I cannot passively force such young people as Jesus died for, to journey alone and in silence east of Eden *by default*. That offends me. That Jesus is too small. So part of the way we need to tackle same gender attraction in our reading of church is – and I have said this is an incomplete suggestion – by learning to practice acceptance without approval. Where I think this becomes innovation and not patronization is that we have to practice it on *both sides* of this debate.

So, if you are more than a quarter gay and a Christian, acceptance without approval has implications for you. First, please don't let this single aspect of your being become definitive *for us*. Don't let this *part* of who you are be the defining politic of your *whole* relationship with God's church. Crazy as it might seem, given the air time we level at this subject, your sexuality is but one of the lenses through which you must see *and accept* the church, even if you can't approve of its position on your sexuality. There are many other lenses.

What seeking acceptance without approval is going to require you to do is to stop drawing that "line in the sand" for your own acceptance. Do not set our approval of your sexuality as a precondition for loving the church and its people, *especially* when you know it cannot easily be given. Instead accept a simple calling common to us all. To not be hovering at the fire exit of the community.

You have something unique to bring. The treatment of your sexuality, however powerful this is, is only one of the reasons you might have for wanting to leave; it need not be THE reason. Yet, in this particular case, that seems to be what we have made it. It's a trick of the devil that defines the internal conditions anyone sets for themselves to prove that they *cannot* belong to God's church. These become the conditions where you can, without reference to a Jesus who calls us to see Him as represented in the love of the community of God, write your own song of exclusion. More than that you practically force everyone else to sing it to you, even if, out of the heart of what we hope for in our own faltering love of Christ, we can't even recognize the tune. Sadly the converse is often true of course. Let us be fair. You may find in some churches that it is practically the opening hymn.

I said this acceptance without approval had to come from both sides. So, what seeking acceptance without approval is going to require *the church* to do is to stop conveniently recognizing that "line in the sand" as an escape clause from facing up to the need to accept people of same sex orientation. Of course the church also has to stop drawing its own line in the sand itself. If you are a church wrestling with your existence on this issue from the other side of either line, do not make a lack of compassion – born out of incomprehension and fear that you are doing nothing about – be the silent default position. Jesus has called you to more than this.

We in the church need to find for people who are same gender oriented the same acceptance without approval that we would give today to lifelong Christians choosing to cohabit. It's the same acceptance without approval that we would give to a single Christian choosing to be sexually active with others in any case.

We would love and accept them, but we would not be able to fully approve of their choices. We need to recognize that we are not actually asking, in behavioral terms, anything more of the same gender attracted Christian than we are asking of the many persons in our churches who remain single.

What acceptance without approval is going to be then is a grand and loving compromise. No one is going to totally win the debate or lose it on those terms.

We need to recognize of course that this will not help us with the external debate on this position. In fact it will generate a profound protest. In the mainstream of this issue, acceptance by the church is not considered enough, approval is required.

We can't.

To follow everyone else's lead. To allow a socially constructed justice agenda to be the sole determinant. To stop wrestling with this and just completely cave in like that, fundamentally unravels the identity of the bible-based church.

Sure, for centuries the drive to be bible-based has led to prejudice and injustices aplenty, and still does. However, faulty though we are, to aspire to be *faithful* to the bible (but especially to Jesus therein) is what defines His church. This remains true irrespective of how misguided we turn out to be in the practice. If *any group* strips us of that, because of what defines them, then you take everything else down with it.

Convenient as that fact (consciously understood or otherwise) seems to many churches to create a shield against this debate, we are not off the hook just because the bible does not approve of some homosexual practices. Actually, we are more on the hook for that.

The same bible calls us passionately to aspire to a greater calling than believing in its sayings and setting up rules of exclusion and self-preservation because of them. On this debate the greater call would want to *first* recognize what a sacrifice acceptance *of us* actually is for the one in ten.

When a person (beloved of God) knows how conflicted and upset the bible-following church will *always feel* about this issue, and yet seeks intimacy and community with us all the same, this should be recognized as exemplary of the vulnerable and self-giving love Jesus spoke of. That should release so profound a compassion in us that we would immediately temper the rhetoric of rejection long enough to seek to be authentic people who prove to be capable of loving this sacrificially in return.

When we take these two groups combined, we become a church made up of *whole* people who will all (irrespective of orientation) stop and find in ourselves there is a higher, self-sacrificing love in the call to love God's community – the church. That love would not tolerate a line in the sand from one side that asks for approval and from the other that moots uncomprehending condemnation. It would want to wrestle at the impasse, even if this wrestling was constant.

So, in my incomplete, near rambling, hermeneutic what I am saying is that God calls us to love in a way where both sides need to remove the lines in the sand. If we seek to do that these three things remain:

First, although we are definitively sexual beings, although this is *truly important* in the design of our God, we are always called to be more than the sum of our impulses, that's what makes humans beautiful. We worship a God who calls us to allow Him to transcend our definitions. That transcendence generates God's community, a community which speaks a language of vulnerability and openness and has a richness of compassion and acceptance as its very heart.

Second, I'm here to tell you, gay or straight or not yet decided, Jesus does want all of you. That is a life-long intimacy that makes Him the arbiter of your behaviors, the owner of your bodies and the master of your wills.

Third, as a Christian (same or opposite gender attracted), love is a reality which is called out of you principally into the world

145

which Jesus loved and died for. This world particularly includes the intense venue for honing this ability which is His church. His church of which He is "the lover". His church whom He depicts Himself as, one day, marrying.

So, when Jesus said, to *all* of us, a greater love has no one than to lay down his life for his friends (plural) there is no getting round how this must be primarily and particularly true in His church. There is no doubt that same gender sexuality is a proving ground of authenticity in God for all parties as a consequence. If we can't get it right in the church what chance have we got in His world? So, the church is a training ground for *all of us*, irrespective of orientation, to be the laying down of our lives for the love of the community of God. We need to get that right.

Consider in the end then if – for all of us on the many sides of this issue – when we sing a song of exclusion, it is the wrong one. One which endangers us of focusing on our own passions, our own limited definitions of justice and on a definition of love that is simply eclipsing the one Jesus gave us as his greatest commission. His commission to (passionate) community love.

Maybe, gay or straight or in between, that's the poverty of ambition on all of our parts...

...unfair, I know, but I can't say anything wise. I truly wish I could.

Harmonizing with Jesus' Song of Exclusion

Jesus, at the center of His ministry, more clearly than we perhaps credit Him with, sings a song of exclusion. It starts with Judas and it ends with a part of you.

Why didn't Jesus heal Judas' heart? Why did He allow him access and intimacy and, unlike almost all the other disciples who get air time, not change him irrevocably? Why does the bible go out of its way, on the lips of Jesus and in subsequent sayings, to pillory this misguided man and exclude him from the mission of Jesus to save the world? Why was there no room at the inn for

Judas? Why wasn't Jesus' love very wonderful in this case? Why did it lack the power to save? Well, as I have said already, God rejects. You have to get your head round that or, like the proverbial one-legged duck, your Christianity will swim in a circle.

Judas, plain and simple, is recruited in the foreknowledge that he is the freedom of fallen humanity in the face of the advent of Jesus. Judas is Adam. He is there to do battle with the claims of the new Adam, Christ. He uses the same weapons that the old Adam did, to put self (on behalf of selves) before God. If we are to believe historical reconstruction, he stands for old Israel. Judas comes to do battle with the will of God in the claims of the new Israel, Jesus. Judas will want to bend Jesus' identity to serve Israel's Jihad, to force Jesus, as Jesus Himself detected that others might want to, to become king by taking down Rome. He needs Jesus to take down the world, and leave Israel standing victorious as the only city of her God independently of her righteousness. Judas sings the now corrupted song of Israel's exclusivity. It is a sublime and painful irony that Jesus does not keep this identity at arm's reach outside of His perfect little new community. He welcomes it with full honors.

In the course of time naturally Judas also comes to stand for part of me, the struggle between myself and God in Jesus. The struggle between God and people. In microcosm we all bear his mark. Part of me is infected by Judas and I don't know why, but I do know and experience how.

All of that is before we even give any air time at all to the idea that your soul has a competitor for its affections. He goes by various names but let's just call him, as Jesus does, the enemy. In various ways Judas listened to the enemy, let the enemy enter him, and was rejected for it. God excluded him, Jesus excluded him, people excluded him. Judas, in the end, even excluded himself. He stands writ large on the story of God's rescue plan for the world as the justification of the need for that story to be an external intervention. The need for that story is to always end in a death. For Judas, death in captivity was always the end. For Jesus, death without captivity let him lead, as the bible says, the captives in His train. Just not Judas. Just like Eve, just like Adam, Judas' is a memorial song of God's right to exclusion.

That song says you have to do the right thing. Grace is not so much free as open. You have to walk in, it won't come and get you. The parable of the lost sheep is no succor here. The pen is open, you can leave. It is the will of God that not one of them be lost, but it is not the will of God that there be no wolves, not the will of God that all of them be saved irrespective. To say so is a mockery of Jesus. Because Jesus, like His father, excludes. Here are some examples:

Take the rich young ruler who pitches up and tries to show off in front of the crowd by taking on this heavyweight Rabbi. What must I do to inherit eternal life? He asks a question like a Barrister does, already knowing the answer. He struts up to Jesus and says what about me, how do I enter the kingdom. The bible says that Jesus loved him, like He does all young misguided men he meets, this isn't Judas, this is something else. Then Jesus exposes his egocentrism and says, 'you already know the answer to that question smarty pants'. The young man says, but if the answer that I know is the answer then I am already in the kingdom and it has been too easy. Jesus says, then one more thing you lack. The young man skim reads the Torah again in his head, was there something so obvious I could have missed? Jesus says, go sell your possessions, give the money to the poor and come and follow me, be the thirteenth disciple (well, the twelfth since one of them is doomed anyway). The man goes away sad.

Now, this story has been done to death, so, I don't need to flog it here except to point out the one thing we sometimes miss. Jesus doesn't whisper this rejection in his ear and tell him to come back when he's had a long think. Jesus brutally puts him down in front of all his peers, twice. First, when He rejects him. Second, as the young man is walking away, Jesus uses him as a publicly enacted parable. Jesus says, sadly, how hard it is for the wealthy to get into the kingdom. Just in case they weren't listening, He makes a standing joke of the point: It's easier for a camel to go through the eye of a needle than for a rich man (like this one walking away) to get into the kingdom.

If you are rich, you probably won't get into the kingdom. Jesus, in a living way, fulfills the prophetic song His mother sang at His conception. He has turned the rich away empty. He rejects them. Of course Joanna's cash is funding the mission the whole time, ironically and amusingly from a pay packet that Herod fills. So it's not the rich per se, whew.

When Jesus rejects this young guy who is surely a worthwhile addition to the gang (young, wealthy, perhaps attractive?) the other disciples are shocked, and so should we be. Like the parable of the prodigal son, Jesus leaves the dénouement unspoken; we don't know what happens to this young man. At that moment, Jesus has rejected him from the kingdom. The way of grace is open. Its door is an acceptance; there is a condition in this case. Terms apply.

When Jesus rescues the woman caught in adultery from being stoned to death it is an act of justice and righteousness. Particularly because the misogynists who wanted to brutally murder the woman had not, as the law commands, brought out the man with whom she did so to face the same fate. Presumably his identity was known, otherwise how do they know she committed adultery? When Jesus rescues her it's plain grace, "where are your accusers?" "If they won't condemn you then neither will I". All very inclusive. *"Now go, and leave your life of sin"*. The way is open, but she still had a choice to walk in.

When Jesus "heals" the man by the pool it's contentious. Does He take pity on a poor cripple and give him the keys to the kingdom? Does He heck. He finds him again later and he says, now that I have made you well, stop sinning before something worse happens to you than being crippled. The way is open, but not without a recognition of the God who sees and the concomitant cost of entry. The man doesn't like that one bit and goes off and dobs Jesus in to the authorities, the Jesus who freed him from four decades of infirmity.

Jesus says don't join the army if you haven't considered the possible cost of that (i.e. death) – His only military metaphor. He says don't build a tower unless you are sure you are going to finish it – surely Babel imagery? Jesus says that the guests who were invited to the original great banquet, the people of Israel, made the usual excuses. I've just got married, I've just made an investment, I've just expanded my productivity. Every one of them is rejected, in one version quite brutally.

Jesus rejects in real life and in His parables, enacted or otherwise. The gospel writers seem to want to throw in a selective summary. So people say to him, I'll follow you wherever you go, and Jesus says not if that won't be comfortable. Count me in, they say, but let me go and say goodbye to my family, and Jesus says, for one thing I am not Elijah (the Old Testament story the "go and say goodbye" deliberately references) and for another no one who puts his hand to the plough in this gig and looks back is fit for it (not even if you think you have got a bit of Elisha about you – coming back). People say, I'll follow you, just let me go and bury the dead. Jesus says, let the dead bury their own dead. There's not space to describe how counter cultural that is, it was, frankly, shocking. If you are not following me, says Jesus, breathing or otherwise, you are dead.

We can't run to Paul for comfort, he sings a harmony with Jesus, he says the same thing, he offers the same stark rejection. Death – life. John won't help you either for him it's light – darkness and people prefer darkness. So that is what they are going to get and God is going to give it to them. He is going to enable humanity once and for all at this point in history to completely reject Him, and how.

The people, of course, for whom Jesus stores up His most scathing rejection are the people who will be so incensed as to murder Him as this rejection. Like John the Baptist before Him, Jesus does not hold back on these "vipers", a deliberate reference to Eden, to the desert, to the reason the snake must be lifted up in the desert (Nicodemus, get back to your books, you slacker). Of these vipers, Jesus says hugely disparaging things. Here is an unstructured sample:

- You speak the natural language of your father, the devil;
- You are liars;
- You and your ancestors are murderers;
- You look good on the outside but inside you are cursed with death and corruption; You rob, you steal, you kill and then put on lengthy prayers and make big offerings to demonstrate that God condones you;
- You are sons of hell and everyone you touch is infected by you.

That's just a taster. With Jesus it's for the religious, those who speak in the name of God, who pertain to follow and represent Him that He reserves his next to total condemnation. He sums it up to His disciples :

Many will say to me on that day (the day of the great feast) *Lord did we not prophesy and in your name cast out demons and perform miracles and I will say away from me you evildoers, I never knew you.*

The way is open, but to paraphrase Jesus, it's a very narrow entrance actually and not many people are able to find it, make sure you do. Grace only operates as free once you have accepted it. To accept it you have to be willing to let it transform you. It is only free if you will let Jesus know you, before that, it has potentially insurmountable conditions, depending on what there is to know.

And Jesus doesn't let any of us off from these conditions. He says as plain as plain can be, you know what sin is, you know when you do it, it's taking you to eternal separation from God, cut off whatever bit of yourself is causing it, better to be maimed and at the bosom of God than destroyed. He says, when your child asks you for something good, you don't give them something bad, so you, though you are evil, know how to give good gifts to your children.

You are evil.

Jesus rejects. Jesus says, I haven't come to bring peace on (this) earth; I've come to set it on fire.

Now, as you and I both know, there is a flipside to these and all the other harsh sayings of Jesus where He rejects people and things. His kingdom parables and his actions of the kingdom are as replete with unlikely inclusions as they are with rejections. Of course we should find that is very comforting. Lepers say, if you are willing, you can make me clean and Jesus touches them. He is not infected, shalom is passed from Him to them. Chronically menstruating women, in an act that may be more bold than we allow, take hold of him in public, to call God to account for suffering, He is not made unclean, shalom is passed to them. Demon-possessed madmen, Dead girls, Canaanite women, Roman Centurions all present themselves. All that they stand for has already been rejected and judged as corrupt by this present Israel. They stand in front of the new Israel (and His unlikely twelve tribes) and find acceptance, credit for faith, admiration, life flows from Him to all of them.

When the whole Israel project looks to be back on track and a great and glorious prophetic procession is motoring into Jerusalem with unstoppable (revolutionary?) energy, one little blind man shouts out, never mind all that kingdom of David stuff, what about the son of David having mercy on me? Jesus draws the whole thing to a halt, heals, accepts, includes, smiles and then He goes to tear down the temple.

We can, and should rationalize that Jesus' rejections, like that of the temple itself, are often in fact "a cleansing" of that which is rejected (so there's an odd hope note in all of it). Many's the preacher, many's the church that has cooked up an oppressive Jesus by focusing on His rejecting side at the cost of His including side. The including is the more significant, of course it is, or we wouldn't be here listening to these preachers in the first place conferring a value on them that they damn well better live up to. The rejecting is not capricious, it has a purpose. Paradoxically, the rejecting sometimes leads to the including. Paul assigns pages of his thought to just that. It is a central paradigm of Christianity and one, as I have already said, by which we take license to be (and comfort in) excluding people.

If you want any better evidence of how paradoxical this all is, look at the final interpersonal act in the life of Jesus Christ of Nazareth – His short conversation with the Israeli freedom fighter hanging next to Him. To him Jesus offers inclusion (without cost!) simply for asking. To the Israeli who actually deserves what the innocent Jesus hanging beside him is getting. Judas and Jesus hang side by side. Adam says to Jesus, when your kingdom comes, will you remember me? Jesus says to Eve, my kingdom has come for you, now let's go home.

That micro inclusion, set into the context of the macro inclusion of the death of God's son on our behalf, speaks of an including God and requires that the whole world does not have enough books to contain that act. But it doesn't mean that Jesus didn't exclude, albeit in a song of exclusion which has a very complex harmony. So, we in the church are not free to cherry pick the Jesus we want to represent. We are called to harmonize with this song of exclusion at full volume. That means that there *are* things within our own hearts, within our communities and within our societies that we will willingly let Him set on fire, that we will allow Him to reject. Likewise, the grace-note in all three is that, sometimes, we will just have to hang there bleeding and watch helplessly as He pours on perfume and tears.

Summing up the song of exclusion

This has been the longest, and possibly toughest, chapter in the book so far. You perhaps deserve a small medal for all the twists and turns it has taken. Let me try to sum up what I think I have been saying a little more simply. You are the champagne of the kingdom of God. You are a signal that the wedding feast of the Lamb, God's fulfillment of the human race, is upon the world. This is an exclusive claim and it contains a rejection of certain things. In being that Champagne, however, the Church can, and frequently does, sing the wrong song of exclusion when:

- We set preconditions on functioning and fitness for acceptance
- We elevate marriage, fidelity or fertility over people's worth
- We won't talk openly about how limiting sexuality and sexual morality are as the defining argument for our humanity and love
- We don't hold the Christians of the churches to the full account of modeling the sacrificial love of our founder
- We preach a half-Jesus who never rejected anyone

Also, perhaps most bruising for those who want to comment on us, we sing the wrong song of exclusion when we sing it to ourselves. When we sing along at the campfire of the global village that an accommodating syncretism is probably fine, or at least less embarrassing for us. Champagne gets its name because of where it comes from. It cannot be from anywhere else. To be authentic Champagne, the Church has to sing the right song of exclusion. This song declares that Jesus calls us to be so exclusively faithful to Him that we may even reach the point where a person *"loses his/her life for my sake."*

I think it is crucial that when we are mulling over the losing our lives part of this statement that we don't let it eclipse the *"for my sake"* part of the sacrifice. When Jesus says this is *"for my sake"* you can read it two ways. One, I sacrificed my life for Jesus' sake. That reading points to my martyr-like bravery. I sacrificed or even died for the sake of Jesus and what He means to me. Although that is probably fine as a reading of Jesus here, I don't like it. It does not seem to me that He is calling us to validate personal faith through suffering or courting some kind of persecution. I prefer to read *"for my sake"* as a call to the true church to make sacrifices for the sake of *the mission* of Jesus on the earth. The church's martyrs (literal and metaphorical) are there to back up the frankly staggering claims Jesus made over all the earth.

This simply cannot be done if we fudge the issue of exclusion in a convenient agenda of soft love that wants to include everyone and every point of view without implication. You get the kingdom done for His sake when you don't allow any other value system to absorb or accommodate you and your Lord. When you sing a song of rejection over them. One that Jesus calls you to sing.

If we let other people live in a compromise because we 'relativize' the uncomfortably exclusive claims of Christianity ourselves, we are actually standing in the way of Jesus' mission. We are preventing the relationship He wants to offer this world. That seems to me to be what *"for my sake"* is actually referring to. Jesus is not offering a personal salvation to the post-modern individual for their private edification. That Jesus is too small. He is challenging all people that on earth do dwell to come home. An offer He has charged us with representing with our very lives if necessary.

In your exclusion of all other loves and all other possibilities you demonstrate the power of faith in Jesus as a savior. In your stubborn adherence to His claims on you, other people will be placed in a position to also receive the offer you have accepted. To receive Jesus and the one who sent Him. This operates for "His sake" not when it celebrates your impressive faith, but when it always leaves open the possibility of the same *faith for others*.

It comes to this. For Christians to be singing something like the right song of exclusion (of Judas, of sin, evil, you, me, other faiths) is really a part of Jesus' intention to have us hold open (from the inside) the way of inclusion into Him – just like allowing His son to be brutally murdered by the world is how God saves the world.

If that seems too massive a cost on your reason, your heart, your soul or your strength remember...

Champagne is expensive.

Chapter 5

Jesus Conceived the Church as
a Place of Sustenance, Not of Counsel

In this short chapter what I want to say is simple. The church was conceived by Jesus as a place of sustenance not of counsel. The way that Jesus, ever the figurative genius, helps us to understand this in my hermeneutic is found in His attitude to food. Jesus liked His dinner.

We find Him frequently at table, whether having His feet washed with tears, His head anointed with perfume, being accused of proto-feminism, being accused of unclean practices, being accused of feasting when He should be fasting, liberating sons of Abraham who'd fallen in love with money, including the sick in His ministry, suggesting that being dead is hungry work, indicting religious dining clubs for poor hospitality, instructing His betrayer to get on with things, suggesting He was made of bread Himself, heading towards instigating the most significant sacrament of the church to come.

Even after the resurrection, He is often given to us as an eating savior, someone who liked His breakfast and His dinner and to whom the eschatological renewal of all things is a big fat Jewish wedding (feast), if you get me. There's at least a sermon series, if not another whole book, on:

"Jesus: Good with food".

The story that I want to base this part of my hermeneutic upon is the feeding of the five thousand. It is in my view a manifesto piece, first for the disciples, next for the church. Since it is also a Sunday school classic, you could probably recite it from memory. As you grew up you would probably have become aware that this is one of the miracles of Jesus which is hotly contested by the rationalists who want to wish it away. This debate is made all the more fun by the fact that it turns up in every gospel (Mat 6, Mk 6, Lk 9, Jn 6) and in one of them it turns up twice.

The positioning of this story in the gospel narratives is also of interest. What it is before and after in each is very telling. In Matthew, Luke and John it appears immediately before Jesus walks on water. In Mark it appears before the transfiguration. Those facts speak volumes on its importance to the gospel writers right there.

What it appears after, likewise, is telling : Matthew and Mark place it after the beheading of John the Baptist; Luke places it after Jesus sends His twelve disciples on a mission and they return stunned at what they have done; and John puts it after a highly controversial healing and increasingly vociferous challenges of Jesus' authority. Whatever else we might make of this miracle, it is in a pivotal place in the unfolding definition of Jesus' kingdom.

In Matthew, Mark and Luke, the miracle takes roughly the same form which is as follows:

Jesus wants to take the disciples on a retreat (either because they are working too hard, or because they have just completed their first mission).

The crowds put the word out as to where He is and five thousand men, as well as many women and children promptly turn up.

Jesus cancels the retreat due to His compassion on the people who seem to Him to be "harassed" and teaches them many things and/or heals their sick.

As evening approaches the disciples ask Jesus to call time on His ministry activities since the people will need to get out and find bed and breakfast.

Jesus says "they don't have to go away, you give them something to eat".

One, some, or all of the disciples are gobsmacked since it would take half a year's wages to accomplish this feeding.

Jesus either enquires, or the disciples volunteer, how much food there is to be had. The stark truth is that there are actually only five loaves and two fish – in the synoptic gospels there is no beneficent young donor.

Jesus might say something like "bring them to me" or He might say something like "what are you waiting for then", get the people to sit down in groups.

Jesus looks up to heaven, gives thanks, starts the distribution effort and, miraculously, these meager portions feed up to ten thousand people.

The disciples tidy things away and find that there are twelve basketfuls of leftovers.

That's one basket for each tribe of Israel then, hmm, interesting. In John's gospel there are, as there always are with John, distinct differences and points of emphasis. Let's look at his version in full and then see if I can indeed make a case for the necessary identity of God's church from what it might be able to reveal about Jesus.

Sometime after this, Jesus crossed to the far shore of the Sea of Galilee (that is, the Sea of Tiberias), and a great crowd of people followed him because they saw the signs he had performed by healing the sick. Then Jesus went up on a mountainside and sat down with his disciples. The Jewish Passover Festival was near.

When Jesus looked up and saw a great crowd coming towards him, he said to Philip, "Where shall we buy bread for these people to eat?" He asked this only to test him, for he already had in mind what he was going to do.

Philip answered him, "It would take more than half a year's wages to buy enough bread for each one to have a bite!"

Another of his disciples, Andrew, Simon Peter's brother, spoke up, "Here is a boy with five small barley loaves and two small fish, but how far will they go among so many?"

Jesus said, "Have the people sit down." There was plenty of grass in that place, and they sat down (about five thousand men were there). Jesus then took the loaves, gave thanks, and distributed to those who were seated as much as they wanted. He did the same with the fish.

When they had all had enough to eat, he said to his disciples, "Gather the pieces that are left over. Let nothing be wasted." So they gathered them and filled twelve baskets with the pieces of the five barley loaves left over by those who had eaten.

After the people saw the sign Jesus performed, they began to say, "Surely this is the Prophet who is to come into the world." Jesus, knowing that they intended to come and make him king by force, withdrew again to a mountain by himself.

You have heard many a sermon and many a kids' talk on this miracle, so I don't want to labor the conventions. Suffice it to say, a shed load of people turn up in the latter half of Jesus' ministry looking for something with a bit more energy than usual. They don't come on this day with any expectation that they would be fed by Jesus. That's done entirely at His initiative. So the question has to be why.

Argument has raged for centuries as to whether Jesus actually multiplied this food or people simply followed His example and shared what they had. My view? He actually multiplied it. My reason? All of Jesus' miracles are "crafted controversy" and this particular controversy is, as my chapter title suggests, absolutely pivotal for the identity of the church. Here's how.

Jesus' innovation in feeding this huge crowd allows Him to play the prophet card again. Jesus has already been using codified language (for those who have ears to hear it) to show that He is a prophet. For example He says at one point:

"no one who puts his hand to the plough and looks back is fit for service in the kingdom"

This isn't just a funny idiom, it is a deliberate evocation of the Elijah – Elisha story. Elisha was called by Elijah when he was ploughing with twelve yoke of oxen no less. At his calling he bids Elijah give him permission to say goodbye to his father and mother. He then slaughters the oxen and burns the ploughs. So he, for one, won't be looking back. Jesus references this story to do a bit of rabbinical hinting that one greater than both Elijah and Elisha has come.

Can that be right though? Does Jesus *hint* His way through His ministry like this? Well, what if we were to find elsewhere in the Old Testament a small number of barley loaves was used in the hands of God's prophet to feed a disproportionate number of people? If we saw that something like that was the case, we'd be on safer ground to suggest that Jesus, in praxis as well as speech, is deliberately cross referencing. That He is *deliberately* tapping into the collective narrative psyche.

Funny thing is, that's exactly what we do find. Elisha comes into view again. He is given some barley loaves. Significantly these mark the end of a famine since they are made from the new barley. There are enough there to feed ten people. He turns them into food for a hundred, prophesying as he does that it is:

"the word of the Lord... that they shall eat... and have some left over".

That has got to pique your interest, hermeneutically speaking.

It has to be piqued because in every version of Jesus' reenactment of this miracle that is exactly what happens, but it happens on a spectacular scale – not least because it is multiplied fiftyfold. That is why it is *not* a surprise, in John's version of these events, that some people see this particular feeding as evidence enough that Jesus is *"a prophet come into the world."* So, already, it's more than just a "feeding", it has too much Old Testament prophetic DNA to ignore.

Now, that is not going to convince you to build a whole treatise on the identity and calling of the church to be a place of sustenance and not counsel. I know that. You need more right? Much more.

Well, what if in His own sweet way when Jesus spoke, as He frequently did, of 'hunger' and of 'feeding' in the context of His mission it could be shown to have the same double-edged meaning? What would such a huge feeding miracle bring to the party if that were the case? In the synoptic gospels it is the disciples who point out that the people are/will be hungry. In John we see Jesus ask Philip (a disciple whose hope of Jesus being the Messiah has already been stated):

"where will we buy bread for this multitude?"

"Multitude", good word Jesus. It is always 'if' in the hermeneutic game, but what *if* Jesus was testing him? What if He was using this event to deliberately reference something else? What if there was another (critical) Jewish meta-narrative hidden in His statement with Messianic overtones? That would be good, right? Well, there is because Moses, the prophet, fed the multitude with bread in the desert. Moses – a very big hitter for everyone in the audience – did, on at least two recorded occasions, demonstrate to a recalcitrant people that 'God is with us' by means of super-natural feedings. Moses brought 'bread from heaven'. Was Jesus referencing that? Was He evoking it and, by implication, what it symbolized? I think He was.

Now, if you leap up in Sunday school protest and say, no, the feeding of the five thousand is a micro-miracle, because it is to do with an interaction between Jesus and a small boy and the cosmic significance of that small boy's generosity. Then maybe you have been sitting in the Sunday school too long. I agree that, from the perspective of the boy, Jesus' treatment of him is deeply significant and charged with love. However, Jesus will very soon teach on the implications of this miracle with nary a little child in sight.

What we might also own, as my favorite oral theologian has pointed out, is that there is a great deal of potential humor in this story. Andrew – seeing that rueful look in Jesus' eye when He asks super-serious Philip about feeding a multitude – might just join in on the joke. So he says here is a small boy with a picnic Jesus, perhaps we can nick that? That's a cleaner explanation than accepting the sort of pious stupidity Andrew would have otherwise needed to be showing.

In any case, the Sunday School may have failed to mention that it was Andrew, and not the boy, who offered Jesus the food. Sorry to burn your crayon drawings in the inconvenient fire of the facts.

So, back to Jesus in the role of Moses. Here He is feeding this multitude in the wilderness where, as even the slow-witted disciples have pointed out, there is no possibility of food. That's an exodus narrative. It's a narrative in which God is leading a reluctant people for the benefit of a future people. It's one in which, against the backdrop of the oppression of Israel by a world superpower, God's prophet and servant (one who was born during the slaughter of innocent Israeli infants) has been sent with the heavenly authority to set the people free. The required calling card of that authority? Bread from heaven.

So, is my hermeneutic jigsaw becoming more convincing? Are there any other pieces lying around the Jesus narrative that might support such a reading of Him do you think?

Yes there are.

Jesus used "hunger and thirst" language very figuratively. He said, blessed are those who hunger and thirst for righteousness. He said to the woman at the well, if she were but to recognize Him, she would never thirst again. When the disciples urge a tired Jesus to take something to eat He replies that He has *food they know not of*". They wonder if that means someone slipped

Him a sandwich. So He says His food is to do the will of the one who sent Him.

He shouted out, at the great feast, if anyone thirsts let him come to me. In His instructions to Peter to commission the church of the resurrection He says that Peter must "feed" the lambs and the sheep. In the revelation Jesus is reported as offering food and drink without cost for all who come. Last but not least, and central of course to this whole book, is that Jesus describes the coming of His kingdom as a great wedding feast for the unlike-liest of participants.

All of these feedings are indicative of a spiritualized reality in all cases. So Jesus does have a track record for using 'thirst and hunger' in his kingdom lexicon to connote righteousness, sancti-fication, salvation and exaltation and so on. We also have the advantage of already knowing when we read these stories again, that Jesus will go on to make feeding in the church its central sacramental identity.

So is it possible when He says to Philip, predicated on the imminent arrival of many thousands who are ostensibly 'seeking the kingdom',

"and where shall we buy food for these people?"

that He means something on top of actual food? Is it possible that when the literal food (a miraculous bread) was created, therefore, it was created in this context in the service of an enacted prophecy?

Now, the sharper theologians among you are going to pull things up short and say that whilst we might accept that this miracle does cast Jesus in a Moses motif (as feeder of Israel), the Elisha reference won't fly. In the Elisha story the gentiles were fed. Elisha was called to the gentiles because of Israel's faith-lessness, something that Jesus underscores in His own teaching about Elisha. So, Jesus isn't really using this imagery too wisely by feeding five thousand Jews.

This is where Matthew's, usually ever so Jewish, gospel rises to the challenge. In Matthew, Jesus performs this same miracle twice; once for a Jewish audience and once for a gentile one. In both cases thousands were fed. One lot from five loaves and two fish, the other from seven and a few fish. They were fed in pretty close succession too. Also interesting is where, in the Jewish feeding, it's mainly the disciples who have compassion on the hungry folk, but in the gentile one they are silent. It's left to Jesus to point out that these folk have effectively been on a three-day fast to see Him and He doesn't want them to grow faint on the journey back. So, He makes His Jewish disciples wait at tables for them. A lesson they, sadly, won't remember when it comes to setting up the governance praxis of the early church.

Let me make two more hermeneutic points then. Smarter people than me have pointed out that these miraculous feedings can be seen in continuity with another feeding, one which is not miraculous as such, but is the last supper. The continuity is a common thread of language. The language that is used to describe Jesus' actions in giving thanks for and distributing this food on all of these occasions is slightly formal. Of the kind that denotes a symbolic meal; a meal like Passover. John points out for good measure that the feeding of the thousands was "very near" to Passover.

In an actual Passover meal Jesus again gives thanks, looks to heaven, breaks bread and distributes it to followers. This time with wine as well. This time it is just His intimate followers but the pattern, scholars tell us, is the same. Looking solely at Jesus' last supper with the disciples and the quite explicit references in it to Moses and Elijah, we have no trouble fitting it into an eschatological scene spanning the exodus and the revelation. Since we have no trouble in loading this small private meal with that sort of significance, why not the two large-scale fully spectacular public versions which preceded it as well?

Looking at Jesus' miraculous feeding of the five thousand of Israel, and the four thousand, it is possible to see these as an inclusive feeding of Jews *and Gentiles* in an enacted prophecy; an enactment which as we have said, all the while, echoes Elijah, Elisha and Moses, and pre-echoes the resurrected Jesus in the revelation. In fact, we could by rights call these 'the first suppers'.

Now, I know what you might be thinking, this hermeneutic has gone a bit elastic right? I am over-fitting the argument. I mean, if I wasn't over-fitting here there would still have to be more to it, right? We'd need some corroboration that Jesus *intended* the feeding of the five thousand to be charged with this significance; ideally, for a full house, it would be demonstrably charged with the significance of the old covenant – the Passover (the exodus narrative), and the new covenant Jesus was forging – the kingdom of God. Of course if I could squeeze the 'inclusion and exclusion paradox' of the kingdom parable of the great wedding feast itself, then that would make things pretty tight, sure enough.

In the version we have in John 6, the feeding of the five thousand was a miracle that took him 302 words to recount and qualify. He goes on to briefly describe the evening and morning after the feeding of the five thousand using a further 197 words. All the more surprising since Jesus walks on water in this time. Then he has Jesus re-visit the feeding of the five thousand, but John needs a further 917 words so that Jesus can explain the miracle in the context of His own kingdom. Here are those 917 words in full. Notice, before you read them, there are resonant features along the very lines I have been painting to look out for:

- A direct and explicit reference to Jesus bringing the exodus feeding narrative bang up to date, and then some.
- A firm re-statement of Jesus' figurative thirst and hunger motif.
- A recalcitrant people who do not all have faith.

- A transcending of food imagery with a radically spiritu-alized and personalized eschatology.
- A pre-reflection of the language of 'bread and wine to body and blood' that Jesus will use in the last supper.
- An explicit statement that Jesus himself invested this feeding with a spiritual significance as its dominant fact.

Furthermore, for my agenda, this sermon results in a "sword of division" outcome. Many disciples, jaded by these claims of Jesus, leave. This is the sermon I talked about earlier. The one designed to make them leave. I've left John's version in all its glory. I'm not up to the task of fully unpacking it without burning another whole chapter – which I don't think you want. I've also resisted the temptation to annotate. I'm hoping, after all my labors in introduction that this speaks for itself. Here it is:

> When they found him on the other side of the lake, they asked him, "Rabbi, when did you get here?"
>
> Jesus answered, "Very truly I tell you, you are looking for me, not because you saw the signs I performed but because you ate the loaves and had your fill. Do not work for food that spoils, but for food that endures to eternal life, which the Son of Man will give you. For on him God the Father has placed his seal of approval."
>
> Then they asked him, "What must we do to do the works God requires?"
>
> Jesus answered, "The work of God is this: to believe in the one he has sent."
>
> So they asked him, "What sign then will you give that we may see it and believe you? What will you do? Our ancestors ate the manna in the wilderness; as it is written: 'He gave them bread from heaven to eat.'"
>
> Jesus said to them, "Very truly I tell you, it is not Moses who has given you the bread from heaven, but it is my Father who gives you the true bread from heaven. For the bread of God is the bread that

comes down from heaven and gives life to the world."

"Sir," they said, "always give us this bread."

Then Jesus declared, "I am the bread of life. Whoever comes to me will never go hungry, and whoever believes in me will never be thirsty. But as I told you, you have seen me and still you do not believe. All those the Father gives me will come to me, and whoever comes to me I will never drive away. For I have come down from heaven not to do my will but to do the will of him who sent me. And this is the will of him who sent me, that I shall lose none of all those he has given me, but raise them up at the last day. For my Father's will is that everyone who looks to the Son and believes in him shall have eternal life, and I will raise them up at the last day."

At this the Jews there began to grumble about him because he said, "I am the bread that came down from heaven." They said, "Is this not Jesus, the son of Joseph, whose father and mother we know? How can he now say, 'I came down from heaven'?"

"Stop grumbling among yourselves," Jesus answered. "No one can come to me unless the Father who sent me draws them, and I will raise them up at the last day. It is written in the Prophets: 'They will all be taught by God.' Everyone who has heard the Father and learned from him comes to me. No one has seen the Father except the one who is from God; only he has seen the Father. Very truly I tell you, the one who believes has eternal life. I am the bread of life. Your ancestors ate the manna in the wilderness, yet they died. But here is the bread that comes down from heaven, which anyone may eat and not die. I am the living bread that came down from heaven. Whoever eats this bread will live forever. This bread is my flesh, which I will give for the life of the world."

Then the Jews began to argue sharply among themselves, "How can this man give us his flesh to eat?"

Jesus said to them, "Very truly I tell you, unless you eat the flesh of the Son of Man and drink his blood, you have no life in you. Whoever eats my flesh and drinks my blood has eternal life, and I will raise them up at the last day. For my flesh is real food and my blood is real drink. Whoever eats my flesh and drinks my blood remains in me, and I in them. Just as the living Father sent me and I live because of the Father, so the one who feeds on me will live because of me. This is the bread that came down from heaven. Your ancestors ate manna and died, but whoever feeds on this bread will live forever." He said this while teaching in the synagogue in Capernaum.

On hearing it, many of his disciples said, "This is a hard teaching. Who can accept it?"

Aware that his disciples were grumbling about this, Jesus said to them, "Does this offend you? Then what if you see the Son of Man ascend to where he was before! The Spirit gives life; the flesh counts for nothing. The words I have spoken to you—they are full of the Spirit and life. Yet there are some of you who do not believe." For Jesus had known from the beginning which of them did not believe and who would betray him. He went on to say, "This is why I told you that no one can come to me unless the Father has enabled them."

From this time many of his disciples turned back and no longer followed him.

"You do not want to leave too, do you?" Jesus asked the Twelve.

Do you remember what the twelve said? It's a great thing, the thing that they said.

So, we have three versions of the communion meal, not one. Three symbolic people groups are fed using them: the disciples; the nation of Israel; everyone else. Significantly, after the one where the Jews were fed, Jesus' new Israel – His twelve disciples – have another food problem on their hands. Why has that which remains from this feeding, where everyone had their fill, resulted in more than we had to start with? What can this multiplication mean?

Jesus was good with food. He increasingly had it both figuratively and physically represent Him in His dealings with people and His teaching about the kingdom. Actually, He spoke of an agenda way beyond this which was for people to "feed on him", an argument He had been slowly building to a crescendo the whole time.

The strange crescendo comes when the popularity of His miracle working and teaching is at its zenith. This sees many thousands turn up unannounced on at least two occasions. They come because they want something from Him. They want healing from diseases, comfort. They want to hear His teaching on the kingdom, counsel. They want an alternative to the establishment, revolution.

What do a lot of people want from the modern church? They want healing, sometimes actual healing, more often a metaphysical kind, a wholeness agenda. Nothing wrong with that. Also, built into every version of church I have ever seen, they want teaching, counsel. Nothing wrong with that either. The result of these expectations can be symbolically summarized in those two backbones of any successful church ministry, the pastoral care and the presence of "sound teaching" often only referring to doctrine. Wrap these elements up in a decent set of ritual praise and prayer bookends and you are, in lots of ways, a sorted church.

Now look at Jesus and ask yourself something. When He had established a sorted popular church movement just like that, why did He break through their expectation with the giddy spectacle of trying to arrange an intimate meal no one asked for? In increasingly spectacular and – from His personal safety point of view – risky ways Jesus gives them healing, miracles and teaching. Then, at the pinnacle of the "success" of that strategy, when thousands are literally chasing Him for more, He blows a hole right through it. He takes it to a new level in both practically and metaphorically demonstrating that He actually wants to center it on "a feeding"; a feeding which, when He explains its significance, will actually cause thousands to *stop* following Him.

What I want to say on the back of such a lengthy explanation is really rather simple and it is that, at its conception, Jesus founded the church on the principle that it would be centrally defined as a place of sustenance, not of counsel. I think there are three simple but profound implications for us arising from that.

So, here's a Gadfly moment then:

- Am I saying that the church centered on counsel, doctrine, ethics and homiletics is the wrong approach?
- Am I saying that Jesus gave the church a supernatural responsibility to have its people feed on Him?
- Am I saying that a communion meal as the sacramental centerpiece of the church cannot be a ritual, therefore, but has to release deep practical implications?

Yes, that is exactly what I am saying.

We need to change what we mean by preaching and teaching

Jesus says men and women don't live by bread alone, but by every word that proceeds from the mouth of the father. James says be few of you teachers, for they shall be judged more strictly. Peter says let anyone who speaks, speak as one speaking the very words of God Himself. This should scare us a little.

The calling of preaching for and in the church is prophetic. It is not simply to teach wisdom or pass on cultural values. It is to be a supernatural sustenance of the people. The energizer of the movement. The bible expects 'signs and wonders' to follow the preaching of this word. So, if we are serious about it, we can tell if it is being executed properly with a standard that is not intellectual or theatrical, but entirely practical. To what degree do church leaderships set out to observe if this principle is at work? Would it worry them if it was not? It should. The writer to the Hebrews says:

For the word of God is alive and active. Sharper than any double-edged sword, it penetrates even to dividing soul and spirit, joints and marrow; it judges the thoughts and attitudes of the heart. Nothing in all creation is hidden from God's sight. Everything is uncovered and laid bare before the eyes of him to whom we must give account.

If the bible equates Jesus with "the word of God come into the world" and the role of the church is to preach this 'word', then preaching in the modern church should be bending its very will on getting Jesus into the room. This is so that the people may, as He himself indicates, feed on Him. If you accept that then you don't need me to tell you why doctrines, and homiletics, worthwhile and entertaining as they may be, would be the wrong focus. Preaching is to exercise prophetic authority on behalf of Jesus and have an observable supernatural effect on the health of the body. Although I would add, in line with Jesus' appetite for a cool setting and a great line, there should be a little of the theater in it still.

Jesus doesn't want to counsel the church, He wants to feed it. As Rob Bell (love him or hate him) puts it, you can use modern preaching to generate the sprung platform from which the Holy Spirit does His work, or you can use it to build a wall which lets people know which side they are on. Jesus' own paradigm, when He was speaking to the man upon whom He would build the church, was that he needed to be on a mission to "feed it", not define it. So when it comes to preaching and teaching in the UK church today what have we (aided and abetted by empiricism, post-modernity and so on) done with that commission? What have we done with Jesus' mandate for the church to be driven by feeding?

Well, notice at least three metaphorical pathologies that show we have effectively stalled it:

1. Admonishment and correction, sure as flour is flour, have a place in the pulpit. But beware a baker who never stops beating the dough long enough to let it rise.
2. Systematic theology and sound doctrine, sure as eggs is eggs, have a place in the life of God's church. But be wary of the church that keeps putting stale bread on the table and then criticizes the people for their lack of appetite.
3. Philosophy and charismatic apologetics, sure as butter is butter, give vitality to God's message. But be wary of the church that calls you to make your own bread whilst only providing the sugar.

There's nothing wrong with preaching which brings counsel, it's wholly necessary. It's totally ironic that at the feeding of the five thousand Jesus had intended the disciples to be on a retreat. Kingdom work turned up though, lots of it, and feeding those people who were outside of the kingdom took the priority. Counsel is not the focus of the kingdom.

We need to change the balance of our efforts

If we deny the church an (unhealthy) focus on counsel, as expressed through too much pastoral care and not enough effective mission then counseling itself cannot be the definition of what church is for. So I might as well just say it and be done with it. The purpose of church is to advance God's kingdom, not to build God's hospital. There I've said it. Much as I don't like military metaphor (neither it seems did Jesus) any army you can think of has a medical core, but it would be a whole other thing to make the medics its corps. This logic means that the church, and those that lead it, need to balance their efforts accordingly. This means they will expend as much effort mobilizing the strong as they do taking care of the weak.

In accepting that approach it's an easy point to score to suggest that the classic "pastor or leader" controversy that troubles and divides most congregations will turn up. Actually, it's never as black and white as that, most people would recognize the need for both in different seasons. Most places might also recognize that few ministers are double-jointed in that way. So if you bend them the wrong way they have a habit of snapping.

Without resorting to clichés, it's possible to see that the churches that want to deploy their central leadership resource (and only paid staff member) on counsel, will only judge him or her "a good minister" – and the church "a loving church" – on the execution of that role. This creates a danger that the church will grow in numbers by attracting people who perpetually need counsel. Its leaders will then wear themselves out providing care and course-correction. If they are effective at all, they will only be effective at that.

I can hear the appalled protests from here, did not Jesus implore people to come to Him for rest? Yes He did, but He didn't use that word like we do. When Jesus supernaturally fed five thousand people it was as an act of mission, of heaven breaking through to earth. The church whose *re-interpretation* of that mission is weekly tearful ministry times, long pastoral care rotas, small and medium group life focused around "freedom" courses and one to one ministry aimed at "personal spiritual development" has tipped the balance too far in terms of counsel. If you think the church is meant to be the spiritual hospital of the world, you won't feed people as much as give them medicine.

This is something which I think we should do with all our power, which may surprise you. However, it shouldn't be our defining context. We should be doing that *within* a different defining context. It's the defining context, which every New Testament letter will shout from the rafters. The church is the dramatic proving ground for an advancing kingdom.

The kingdom of God is not a matter of words...

The advancing kingdom is something which Jesus testified that forceful women and men would be needed for. They needed to be sustained to forcefully advance it. He blazed a trail unto death in support of that point. A death which He said, in a worldwide way, released the "bread of heaven" unto that mission. A death He required us, in a worldwide way, to celebrate as our central sacrament, until He returns. A church centered on feeding. Feeding on Him. It's forceful stuff.

So, for me, herein lies the difference for the central definition of church, counsel matters (of course it does) but sustenance is critical. Jesus, in the final analysis, never "drove away" the people who came to Him expecting more free bread. They left because the bread, just like God's grace, wasn't totally "free" in the end. The bread, like grace, in the longer term, has to be accepted on the terms being set by its provider. That requires a significant reformation of the meaning of the concept of "free". With the consumption of Jesus' bread came a radical expectation of how the power it provided would be expended. To accept Jesus' full definition of the bread of heaven come into the world was not just to partake in a routine nourishment from what Christ had done for them. It was also to accept the risk of what He wanted to do with them.

Many people would walk long distances and go without food for days when they thought they were following their counselor who, over a free meal, would tell them how to get to heaven. Few kept it up when He claimed they must, as He had done, be an unrelenting people who stop at nothing to bring that heaven down. Many people will sign up and commit fully to a church which has a terrific pastorally caring heart and really stimulating doctrinally sound teaching. Deep down we all know there has to be more to it than that. The church can and should do these things well. However, they absolutely have to be a sideline in the service of Jesus' real agenda for His church. That same agenda to demonstrably and forcefully bring heaven down into this world.

Jesus' central metaphor and mechanism for bringing heaven down was for us to "consume Him as a meal" into ourselves in a way which is transformative and sustaining. Jesus, ever the agitator, says to those who wanted to eat His 'free' bread, understand:

The Spirit gives life; the flesh counts for nothing. The words I have spoken to you—they are full of the Spirit and life.

His church, without falling into the trap of becoming dogmatic, fizzy or hard-hearted, must become, likewise, unswerving. Counsel in the church is important, critical at times even, but sustenance is her calling. She is the bread of life now for herself and for the world. The church's greatest link to the person and identity of Jesus is and remains, at His instruction, a sacramental division of bread to all. We will always celebrate the inclusion of that, of course we will. However, just like the original disciples at the most spectacular inaugurating event of Jesus' kingdom, we too will find that God's provision of bread enough for all brings an unexpected imperative. That imperative, on the lips of Elisha and in the praxis of our savior, is the challenge of what to do with the bread that is left over.

Bread, mad as it seems, that has been dipped in Champagne.

Chapter 6

God Meets Us at Our Edge, Not at Our Center

Jesus of course tells, shows and offers us the thing we need to advance the kingdom of God. That thing is intimacy with God. Now people might heave a sigh and think that in stating this I am getting with the program at last. That the calling of the church is to bring God into the center of our lives through praise, prayer and manifest spirituality displayed in the church.

I haven't got with that program I'm afraid. There are days when I just sit and despair over the lack of an alternative expression of church to the one we have. After all, think about it, almost all of the points I am making in this book might take a healthy push back from any vibrant church. They might agree with some of what I am saying so much that they've already got the T-shirts printed. Here's the thing though, it's not about agreeing with an idea. It ought to be about how applying that idea takes you somewhere.

Somewhere different.

I find churches largely not on that sort of journey. If some of them are on a journey it is happening so slowly as to defy a human lifespan, and that just doesn't scan when it comes to a decent definition of dynamic. What's it like at your places? Here's a playful litmus test, imagine your comfort levels and those of other church members during these announcements:

1. We have decided to ban the use of the Lord's Prayer in open worship unless it is spoken in modern English.
2. We will be meeting fortnightly from now on. During the off weeks we want people to work out what best use they could make of the Lord's day individually and in groups.

3. The next three Sundays are going to be teaching Sundays, all adults are required to attend a one-hour bible study after which the church will meet in interactive groups around three short sermons.

4. Everyone is going to be given a life application journal and be required to collect evidence that they are putting their faith into action. The minister will meet with every member quarterly to review progress and suggest means of support and development.

If we did a credible time and motion study on what the average church actually does with its time rather than what it says it does, what would we discover? What would your church be spending the vast majority of its time and energy on? Would it really be best described as "innovative community dynamism"? Or would it be "deferent variation" around a weekly meeting? How much of the church's time and resource is actually focused on holding inward looking gatherings? Sub-question: how much are those gatherings actually focused on doing much the same things every week, month and year? It's a big question, what should the church do, should it endure or should it journey?

I think part of the motivational structure to the answer to that question is found in whether the church orthodoxy makes an appeal to a "right" to meet God "in the center". The center of personal devotion. The center of worshipful community praise. The center of ardent spiritual prayer. I would never doubt that this is a source of relationship with God for the individual Christian or for a whole church. What I would profoundly doubt is that anything so static will lead to the kind of intimacy with God that is actually on offer in the bible and, in particular, through Jesus therein. This is because, in my reading, both are defined by extreme dynamism at every point.

My concern with a primarily centralist agenda is that it is a force for conservativism. It is conferring value on keeping things roughly the same. There is nothing malicious about this. In some ways it's just a failure to ask if things could be different at all. Christians in the centralist paradigm can exchange the risky glory of a dynamic journey with God for an appearance of dynamism which is really about accepting different roles in a lifecycle. So, *our role* in church changes with time, but church itself doesn't really change or grow or take any real risks. Church can, potentially, judge its own dynamism in busy-ness, noise levels or just plain rhetoric about dynamism being mistaken for dynamism. When it does, the church is in danger, largely by omission, of accepting an endure agenda.

The dynamic alternative to enduring like this is not speaking more ardently about the need to be going on a journey. It is to go on it. The bible invites us to journey to the very edge of ourselves before God. If we were to do that collectively it would be to the very edge of what we mean by church. If we set off on such journeys we would find the God of risk. He is always waiting for us at the edge.

What I want to do then is make this case, not through my own polemic but, as I am constantly trying to do here, through a reading. This reading will exemplify the relationship between intimacy with God and the risk posed by the journey. We will look at four bible stories which, for me, speak plainly about this. I want to talk about people who became intimate with God, very intimate. I need to apologize that they are all male (again) but you'll have to trust me that I've chosen them on the basis of their significance to my point. I want to point out that the defining characteristics of their intimacy is not found in the increasing sense of 'the God of the center' but in a, sometimes brutally, painful sense of the God of the edge.

What I'll want to say is shouldn't an intimacy like that be very attractive to the church? My fear is that you will say 'no', of course. To pull this off, I need to beg your indulgence in quite a long section using quite a bit more exegesis than I have been doing so far. I hope leaning more heavily on the bible like this is all right. After all, you can't really make a point about the long, painful and powerful journey you have been on if you have only ever been seen looking at the postcards on the spinny thing outside the tea shop.

What a look at these journeys might show us is that we must not expect to meet God forcefully if our interest is in our own need to endure.

God meets us at the edge, Moses

Moses never had it easy, well, that's not true, he had it very easy indeed to begin with. His birth and early months were not without peril, true, but they were hardly formative. He grew up in a palace and presumably had the best of what that had to offer. Sure he might have had a speech defect, although a proper scholarly reading of that seems to suggest that he wasn't one for public speaking rather than had a bad stammer. Sure there might have been a little bit of talk about his ethnicity from time to time, but he seems to have turned into a handsome and strong enough guy all the same.

Certainly strong enough to kill a trained soldier in hand to hand combat in an outrageously illegitimate attempt to ingratiate himself onto his mother race. They not only found that bizarre behavior but they didn't even recognize him as one of their own. Why would they? When the implications of his misfired national zeal threaten his safety, Moses proves his mettle by legging it. He meets some girls, he does some brave stuff, he gets a job as a shepherd and the rural life seems to suit him because he settles into it quite nicely thank you for something like forty years. He gets married and has a kid (I'm always slightly amazed at how few people remember this). His father-in-law is a priest of some god or other but that doesn't trouble Moses overly it seems.

Moses, on the face of it, decided all in all that the best thing to do was endure. So he gave up on his zeal, perhaps for the loss and trouble it had caused him. With that he gave up on journey. He might even, upon reflection over the years, say that God had blessed this decision with good things: home, family, income, safety. What a spectacular underachiever he really became; when you consider that God had made him for journey.

As an old man, when all this compromise is so much back catalogue, a bush catches fire and everything changes. The nation he seemed passionate enough about to kill forty years previously, is in trouble. The God of that nation, no less, wants to enlist Moses' help to lead it to freedom. God wants to use Moses' knowledge and experience of the court of Pharaoh to build an advocacy platform. That platform will generate on a national scale the result that Moses couldn't even approach on a local scale at the point of his pathetically misguided sword forty years previously. God, ironically (after forty years in the wilderness!) wants to consummate Moses' own back story. How could Moses refuse?

He refuses.

God insists though, and that pattern is set for the rest of their relationship. God very much hadn't met Moses in the center of his situation as it was, God sent him an envoy to call him to an accounting for his destiny, one that would take place very much at the edge. Sometimes that was the ragged edge too. The ramifications of God's offer and Moses' acceptance were found in an uncomfortable calling to a dynamic stormy relationship between them. This can even be seen just in their conversations, never mind what they achieved, take a look:

So, post-burning bushery, Moses lays down the will of the Lord for Pharaoh. Result? Bad news. Even at this early stage Moses is able to go back to God and say:

O Lord, why have you brought trouble upon this people? Is this why you sent me? Ever since I went to Pharaoh to speak in your name, he has brought trouble upon this people, and you have not rescued your people at all.

Of course that was not the end. God, through Moses, piles on the miraculous and the downright weird and powerful stuff. So, in time, the superpowers are humbled and the Israelites, armed and weighed with plunder, do indeed leave Egypt, the land of their slavery. God does, verily, rescue them and, in the subsequent journey, rescues Moses from his own weakness. When Israel sees what the guy has achieved out of his faith, they put their undying trust in him.

Yeah, right. A few days of hardship later and Moses has to cry out to God and say:

"What am I to do with these people? They are almost ready to stone me."

For the want of water in the desert, they turn on him, as they will again and again. God knew they would and yet God constantly squeezes this man Moses between the rock and the hard place. What I want to point out though, in recounting the story of that journey to the edge, is that with all that hard stuff came great stuff too. If the rough was flinty rock, the smooth was silk. In accepting the painful challenge, Moses also opens the way to powerful blessing. God says to Moses:

I am going to come to you in a dense cloud, so that the people will hear me speaking with you and will always put their trust in you.

Which they did after a fashion – a pretty twisted fashion, it has to be said. But God was true to His word, is there a much cooler moment in the Old Testament than:

Mount Sinai was covered with smoke, because the Lord descended on it in fire. The smoke billowed up from it like smoke from a furnace, the whole mountain trembled violently, and the sound of the trumpet grew louder and louder. Then Moses spoke and the voice of God answered him.

Moses spoke (Adam speaks), God answered (and he is no longer banished). Little bit wow really. And God keeps laying on the honey:

> Come up to the Lord, you and Aaron, Nadab and Abihu, and seventy of the elders of Israel. You are to worship at a distance, but Moses alone is to approach the Lord; the others must not come near. And the people may not come up with him.

Taking things out of sequence slightly, but Moses had a mojo, it went like this:

> Whenever the ark set out, Moses said,
> "Rise up, O Lord!
> May your enemies be scattered;
> May your foes flee before you".
> Whenever it came to rest, he said,
> "Return, O Lord,
> To the countless thousands of Israel".

Unfortunately the edge that I want to discuss here is not in Moses' story of triumph but in what happens to his relationship with these people, himself and his God when the enemy *is* the countless thousands of Israel.

> Go down, because your people, whom you brought up out of Egypt, have become corrupt. They have been quick to turn away from what I commanded them and have made themselves an idol cast in the shape of a calf. They have bowed down to it and sacrificed to it and have said, `These are your gods, O Israel, who brought you up out of Egypt.' "I have seen these people," the Lord said to Moses, "and they are a stiff-necked people. Now leave me alone so that my anger may burn against them and that I may destroy them. Then I will make you into a great nation."

Favorite bit alert. God says to Moses, you see how all this has only taken a month and a half to fall to bits?

> *"Now, leave me alone so that my anger may burn against them and that I may destroy them. Then I will make you into a great nation."*

Was there ever a more distressingly beautiful offer in the bible?

But Moses doesn't leave Him alone.

Because Moses sees that this is both the test and the invitation that it is. Moses feels the pressure of the whole back story haunting him. God, ever the patient one, says to Moses, I can roll the timeline back. I promised Abram that I would make him, one man, into a great nation. You, Moses, one man, are still his offspring; I can do that as easily with you as I can with these thousands of calf worshipping ne'er do wells.

Moses feels the sheer weight of the promises of old, the promises that he knows, from the burning bush forward, that he has been forcefully selected to move forward. God says, let's rub it out and start again. I'll start it with you, just like I started it with Abram. Interestingly, Moses is not just invited into one pair of Abram's shoes, to be the nation fatherer, he is also invited to play the role of Abram on the plains of Sodom. To be Abram consulted by God on the coming destruction.

He is being offered a place in the genealogy of grace.

God has revealed to His servant beforehand that destruction is coming, why? Because, just as it was with Abram, He is interested in sharing the burden. Moses doesn't want God to push the story back that far. Moses doesn't want to have to go back to Abram, to have to be the new Abram, Moses wants to be Moses. Moses wants God to push the story forward. So he takes a risk and disobeys God right there to His face, he doesn't 'leave Him alone' at all. Oh no. He dares to seek to ease God's pain, just like Abram did, by reminding God who He is:

> *But Moses sought the favor of the Lord his God. "O Lord," he said,*
> *"why should your anger burn against your people, whom you*
> *brought out of Egypt with great power and a mighty hand? Why*
> *should the Egyptians say, `It was with evil intent that he brought*
> *them out, to kill them in the mountains and to wipe them off the face*
> *of the earth'? Turn from your fierce anger; relent and do not bring*
> *disaster on your people. Remember your servants Abraham, Isaac*
> *and Israel, to whom you swore by your own self: `I will make your*
> *descendants as numerous as the stars in the sky and I will give your*
> *descendants all this land I promised them, and it will be their inher-*
> *itance forever.'" Then the Lord relented and did not bring on his*
> *people the disaster he had threatened.*

Gorgeous restating of the plan. Don't make me into Abram, be
faithful to Abram through me. Moses is getting it and getting it
tight. He, who didn't even want the gig, is learning to wrestle
with his maker. Out of his already profound relationship with
God he can not only see how humanity saddens its God, he can
seek to INTERVENE. He understands that with a God like this
we are not doomed, that something can be done, and that he can
be the minister of that something. Something can be done. Wow.

What is it that can be done when the faithless people face
destructive judgment? Well, the servant of the Lord can throw
his life into the pot to save theirs:

> *So Moses went back to the Lord and said, "Oh, what a great sin*
> *these people have committed! They have made themselves gods of*
> *gold. But now, please forgive their sin—but if not, then blot me out*
> *of the book you have written." The Lord replied to Moses, "Whoever*
> *has sinned against me I will blot out of my book. Now go, lead the*
> *people to the place I spoke of and my angel will go before you."*

Moses doesn't get to be sufficient; he doesn't get to be Jesus. But
most of the nation survives the wrath of God and that, given the

sin in question, is a monstrous feat of grace-wielding from the stuttering one. So, the vehicle moves on, God says to Moses:

> *"Leave this place, you and the people you brought up out of Egypt, and go up to the land I promised on oath to Abraham, Isaac and Jacob, saying, `I will give it to your descendants.' I will send an angel before you and drive out the Canaanites, Amorites, Hittites, Perizzites, Hivites and Jebusites. Go up to the land flowing with milk and honey. But I will not go with you, because you are a stiff-necked people and I might destroy you on the way." When the people heard these distressing words, they began to mourn...*

Too right they did, what if another Red Sea moment was needed? Thankfully for them:

> *The Lord would speak to Moses face to face, as a man speaks with his friend.*

So, soon after, one of those conversations goes like this:

> *"You have been telling me, `Lead these people,' but you have not let me know whom you will send with me. You have said, `I know you by name and you have found favor with me.' If you are pleased with me, teach me your ways so I may know you and continue to find favor with you. Remember that this nation is your people." The Lord replied, "My Presence will go with you, and I will give you rest." Then Moses said to him, "If your Presence does not go with us, do not send us up from here. How will anyone know that you are pleased with me and with your people unless you go with us? What else will distinguish me and your people from all the other people on the face of the earth?"*
>
> *And the Lord said to Moses, "I will do the very thing you have asked, because I am pleased with you and I know you by name."*

Between the lines moment, Moses says if you are pleased with me and with the people then come with us. God says, I am pleased with you (and I feel intimacy for you), that's why I've changed my mind, am going to put up with a stiff-necked people bent on destruction and I'm going to hold back from destroying them because I am (well) pleased with one of them.

Wow squared.

And this is not lost on Moses. At this profession of intimacy God has pulled back the curtain. Moses understands he can make a decision, he realizes there is a further edge here, he begins to understand the scale of what is possible in this relationship between God and himself. Yes, it is very much in a context of Moses' passion (compassion even) for God's hapless sinning people, but this is an 'I am' moment standing on the shoulders of what has been revealed in the story so far and so Moses' next move is his greatest:

Then Moses said, "Now show me your glory."

There it is, destination soul. Moses gets what God is doing bringing the people of Israel into the promises of Abram, promises which are to bless the whole world. In the under-standing of that Moses also gets another thing; that deep, intimate relationship with God is not only desirable, but is possible. So, that is what he is given. Two more quotes then before we get to the real edge. When Miriam and Aaron challenged Moses' authority God says this to them:

"When a prophet of the Lord is among you, I reveal myself to him in visions, I speak to him in dreams. But this is not true of my servant Moses; he is faithful in all my house. With him I speak face to face, clearly and not in riddles; he sees the form of the Lord. Why then were you not afraid to speak against my servant Moses?"

When the whole nation challenged Moses' authority God becomes exceeding angry and Moses is offered a second chance to metamorphose into Abram. God offers again to make Moses, whose only child is not even a full Israelite, into the nation of the promise. God wants to destroy the nation Moses has protected thus far. Moses, who must be exasperated with them himself, makes another impassioned plea. This one is very different from the other times though.

This plea does not, this time, depend on what Abraham has done; it is not a plea to the back story of Abram, Isaac and Jacob. Moses makes a plea to his own journey of how God brought these people out under Moses' staff, and concludes with something he is getting very good at:

> "Now may the Lord's strength be displayed, just as you have declared: 'The Lord is slow to anger, abounding in love and forgiving sin and rebellion. Yet he does not leave the guilty unpunished; he punishes the children for the sin of the fathers to the third and fourth generation.' In accordance with your great love, forgive the sin of these people, just as you have pardoned them from the time they left Egypt until now." The Lord replied, "I have forgiven them, as you asked".

You have forgiven them up to now when I have asked. Now I need you to do that again. None of this passes without condition, I'm glossing over the bits where God says "Really? You know it will only be temporary?" As He does here again.

No matter. Moses' deep relationship with God and his consequent longing for God's purposes on earth are the only things that stand between this people and their destruction. Time and time again Moses learns that as God's servant, he can stand in the gap. So he keeps throwing himself in that gap. Jesus himself credits His own ministry as the ultimate expression of what Moses started here.

So the Red Sea crossing, the miracles the like of which had never been seen before were all lightweight compared to what Moses achieved in relating to God. His own journey is about relationship, intimacy and depth. But that won't be enough. You see, like Gideon, it was not enough for Moses to experience God inside of the 'Moses and God' project, spectacular as that has been. Moses was one of the people of Israel, Moses was part of a necessary plurality, and he had to experience God in community, as part of that plural. Just like Gideon and many others after him would, Moses learned that particular lesson not at the safe center where the comforting God comes to bless but at the challenging edge of his relating to God who had come to move him on. God didn't just push Moses to that new edge; He pushed him well past it.

The people, despite Moses' visionary conviction, power and commission, miss Egypt, it's all they've known and their memories of its reality were short. They are not content with being carried on the wings of God almighty and fed daily by Him with bread that fell from heaven. They sing a song of back to Egypt. Moses feels with this political ill wind blowing that he is (again) in peril for his life, because he will oppose the back to Egypt party.

One night he hears the singers wailing at the entrance to their tents, 'oh Egypt where we ate without cost' (cf. Jesus in the revelation, the true eating without cost song). God was exceedingly angry. Not good. The bible says Moses was troubled; also, not good. A bit of Moses' trouble was, however, that he was back in this position again. Why did God keep letting this happen? What happens next is that he loses it for a moment, with God. You can read the whole episode in Numbers eleven but here's a paraphrase. Hint, read this in an angry voice:

'Why have you brought this trouble on me, what did I do wrong that I get the job of looking after all these (ungrateful, unreasonable, miserable and potentially murderous) people?

Are they my children? Am I their father? Did they come from my womb? Am I their mother? Why did you tell me to carry such a bunch of babies in my arms, am I their nurse? *You* promised their forefathers you'd take them to a new land, but why do I have to carry them there? Where can I get food for all these babies, how can I feed them, they are crying for their dinner, can't you hear them? I can't do this! I can't carry all these infants by myself. They are too heavy. If it is going to be like this then just kill me yourself. If you like me at all, then do it yourself, don't let them do it.'

Moses' journey is to the ragged edge of the apparent futility of the journey itself.

So, first, God eases the organizational pressure a little. He proposes a system of local government. A spiritual anointing is given to new leaders (some against their will) who now have a mandate to help Moses govern. God says:

"They will help you carry the burden of the people so that you will not have to carry it alone".

So, God heard Moses' complaint then...

God says fair enough, these people are too heavy for you, I'm not going to strengthen you further to cope, there's a limit to what even you can take. I'm going to lighten the load and make the project depend on a community not a personality (something God would get right from the off with Joshua). Even though I don't trust the community, I only trust you.

Maybe Moses thinks, about time too. But God says Oh, and another thing. I've written you a speech for tomorrow. I want them to hear that I don't trust them. Here it is and this is what I want *you* to tell these people, Moses. *You* are right, they are very much on the edge of killing *you*, taking control and turning the wagons back to Egypt, so tell them this. And here's a hint Moses, read this in your angry voice:

Consecrate yourselves in preparation for tomorrow, when you will eat meat. The Lord heard you when you wailed, "If only we had meat to eat! We were better off in Egypt!" Now the Lord will give you meat, and you will eat it. You will not eat it for just one day, or two days, or five, ten or twenty days, but for a whole month – until it comes out of your nostrils and you loathe it – because you have rejected the Lord, who is among you, and have wailed before him, saying, "Why did we ever leave Egypt?"

Moses learns that God will accept Moses' view of his own limitations. When he finishes hearing the speech that God wants him to deliver, Moses learns that doubt begets doubt:

Here am I among six hundred thousand men on foot, and you say, 'I will give them meat to eat for a whole month!' Would they have enough if flocks and herds were slaughtered for them? Would they have enough if all the fish of the sea were caught for them?

God says, maybe less than calmly:

"Is the Lord's arm too short? You will now see whether or not what I say will come true for you."

God pushed Moses to the edge, in order to agitate his faith. God says stick your neck out son, it will be OK, make a speech tomorrow that there will be meat. Do it in such an inflammatory manner that, if there is no meat tomorrow, they will certainly lynch you. And tell them I am angry with them, tell em good. Put your head in that noose you've feared the whole time Moses, put it right in and pull it really tight son. It's time we dealt with this. My arm is not too short, yours is...

God pushed him and pushed him and pushed him to the point where he cries out in the sort of bitterness the prophets are famous for, Moses isn't the only prophet who ends up asking

God to 'off him' rather than face the consequences of what his leadership has or has not achieved. That failure, however, clearly includes the fact that Moses feels that the God he has convinced these people to follow all this time, has also failed. So God makes a gallows of both of these "failures" and asks Moses to stand on it. Moses, who by now has the instinct to do as God asks, won't sleep well tonight.

God's reply to Moses' complaint about futility (as it is with all the prophets who bring it) is get back in there. But then, because this angst is very real, because the personal danger is very real and because God's anger at faithlessness in Him is also very real, God provides the breakthrough to the next part of the journey. The faith that calls out to God for a vindication, not a blessing, is the thing that so often releases this.

Be careful to look at *what* God provides in this situation; bread from heaven, water from a rock, herbal remedies, quail in the desert, salvation from foes within and without, yes, all that. For Moses in particular though God provides him with the space in their relationship, to completely lose it.

Moses is allowed to rail and rage at God about all this, and to be neither destroyed nor replaced. He has been pulled tight into God only to find that this kind of close intimacy gives him more space.

God provides space.

Moses is learning he has not been called to be some puppet of the almighty with a magic stick and a stutter. God drives him to the edge, just like Gideon in the winepress – although this is the far tougher gig – so that Moses can pull himself up to the full height of the relationship that *God wants* with Moses.

God pushes him really hard, right to the edge because it's only at that edge that Moses is going to be able to meet Him, face to face, like Eve did, like Adam did. And when Moses sits down and thinks all this through, and thankfully writes it all down for us, we know as he knows, this has been the making of him. It's a hard making. It's a hard God at times.

This makes him understand that God's compassion for sinners has a fullness, a timing and a meaning. He understands how much more there is to God than the here and now, and that it is possible to see His glory and live. To do so had given him the confidence to face all that was ahead, one of the first citizens of glory walking on the way of grace.

God doesn't let him slip into the errors of Knox and Calvin and countless others who will need a closed-ended God. Moses, at the visceral level, will understand and experience that full intimacy with God is not only possible but it is positively desirable. Even though this will make him into a freak in the eyes of others, he wants to achieve this. So, God, seeing and respecting this, sets up the circumstance where Moses can actually embrace the fully paradoxical nature of knowing God. His reward for doing this is to understand one more thing about God which blows everything else out of the water. God has one more (all-surpassing) edge for Him.

That very physical edge is THE edge, in fact, of Moses' whole story. It's the edge of the Promised Land. The journey to find and claim this land has consumed the entire second half of Moses' whole life. God takes him to the very pinnacle of everything his life and struggles have all been about, God takes him to the edge of the Promised Land... and then doesn't let him in.

If that is not appalling enough, God does this only *after* having told Moses that the whole project will end in failure very soon. God says, when you die, these people and the hope you had for them, will die with you, and, as we both know, shortly after this conversation you are going to die. It won't take them long to go off the rails. They are not going in to this Promised Land to which you have borne them. Not only that but I'm not letting you in either.

Dude, that's harsh.

The origins of this conversation have been hanging over Moses for a long time now. Way back in the day, when Moses and

Aaron (and Miriam, the star of the show who was the first among them to have faith enough to chase a baby down a river and speak to Egyptian princesses whilst they were bathing), when the three of them were learning their art, an incident occurred.

Moses and Aaron are in deep trouble because the people, oddly enough since God did make them take a desert road, have run out of water. Moses goes to God for the solution. The solution, says God, and there is some way in which this is supposed to authenticate Moses' continued calling, is to walk up to a nearby rock with his (magic) staff in his hand, speak to the rock and water will issue forth. Moses doesn't do that. Moses is angry, Moses thinks God is angry, Moses gives the whole thing a bit more flair and theater. In doing so Moses loses focus, he makes it about Moses.

> *The Lord said to Moses, "Take the staff, and you and your brother Aaron gather the assembly together. Speak to that rock before their eyes and it will pour out its water. You will bring water out of the rock for the community so they and their livestock can drink." So Moses took the staff from the Lord's presence, just as he commanded him. He and Aaron gathered the assembly together in front of the rock and Moses said to them, "Listen, you rebels, must we bring you water out of this rock?" Then Moses raised his arm and struck the rock twice with his staff. Water gushed out, and the community and their livestock drank. But the Lord said to Moses and Aaron, "Because you did not trust in me enough to honor me as holy in the sight of the Israelites, you will not bring this community into the land I give them."*

The game for Moses was over before it had really begun. They didn't do what they were told. They were told to speak to the rock, not hit it with the magic stick. They were told to speak to the rock, but they couldn't resist speaking to the people first *"Listen, you rebels"*, nice. They were told to let the people know that God would provide the living water with grace, with a word. They took the glory *"must WE bring you water"*. They provided it with anger – Moses raised his arm and struck the rock twice with his staff.

They didn't do what they were told. God made the consequences clear. It seems an unusual punishment all the same, neither of you are getting into this promised land now, because you did not trust me enough in front of the people, when it mattered, you let me down.

Fast forward now as Moses walks towards his death, the manner of which, just like the prophecy at the watery rock, he has seen effected in Aaron's passing already. This water from the rock incident has been a thorn in his flesh. Moses knows, even after all of his approaching God for the people and getting God to be gracious to them, that when it comes to his own personal story he had already failed. I'll let him tell you in his own words:

> ...the Lord told Moses, *"Go up into the Abarim Range to Mount Nebo in Moab, across from Jericho, and view Canaan, the land I am giving the Israelites as their own possession. There on the mountain that you have climbed you will die and be gathered to your people, just as your brother Aaron died on Mount Hor and was gathered to his people. This is because both of you broke faith with me in the presence of the Israelites at the waters of Meribah Kadesh in the Desert of Zin and because you did not uphold my holiness among the Israelites. Therefore, you will see the land only from a distance; you will not enter the land I am giving to the people of Israel."*

If you find God unfair here, so do I. So, I am sure, does Moses who goes on record himself as pleading with God about this defining moment.

> *O Sovereign Lord, you have begun to show to your servant your greatness and your strong hand. For what god is there in heaven or*

on earth who can do the deeds and mighty works you do? Let me go
over and see the good land beyond the Jordan – that fine hill country
and Lebanon…

God, like a parent, says He doesn't want to talk about it anymore:

"That is enough," the Lord said. "Do not speak to me anymore about
this matter. Go up to the top of Pisgah and look west and north and
south and east. Look at the land with your own eyes, since you are
not going to cross this Jordan."

If you are slightly narked at God, so am I. If you think that all that
stuff about how God speaks with Moses face to face like a friend
is completely undone in this huffy, capricious even, act where
God remembers Moses' mistake, and lets that define their
relationship, you are in good company.

For centuries, it seems to me, preachers have wrestled with
exactly this sort of thing in the nature of God and have found, as
they have had to, in favor of a capricious God. This has led to
hundreds of years of sermons about: Even though Esau sought
his lost blessing with many tears, he was not heard; Even though
David begged God not to kill the child, his request was refused;
Even though Saul was God's chosen one, God was saddened that
He had made him king. Fill in the rest yourself, there's plenty
more where those came from.

Moses is perhaps the pinnacle example: "even though Moses
asked God to forgive him from the lifetime of honor and service
he had grown into after this one mistake, God *is not* ever willing
to forgive those who refuse to honor Him as holy". There's a hard
edge to this God. So, to cope, we just have to concoct in the Moses
story (and the many, many others) a riddle-maker God. In that we
acquiesce to a notion of a God who ultimately is going to make
us experience rejection. Maybe it really is the last bastion of our
self-appraising, self-destructive souls, to seek to be rejected by

God. After all look at the evidence:

> *Since then, no prophet has risen in Israel like Moses, whom the Lord knew face to face, who did all those miraculous signs and wonders the Lord sent him to do in Egypt – to Pharaoh and to all his officials and to his whole land. For no one has ever shown the mighty power or performed the awesome deeds that Moses did in the sight of all Israel.*

If even HE can't get into the Promised Land, who can, right? That's our only conclusion from this story. Well, that depends on your hermeneutic.

When I used to stop and think that God would not even forgive Moses himself – after everything he had suffered and done to get forgiveness for the people time and time again – for one act of anger; when I realized that God then told Moses (on his death bed!) that the whole project had, in fact, failed. It used to make me angry. Because, I don't want a riddle maker God, I don't want the Calvinists to win the day. In my upset about this, for a very long time, I missed them.

Those two words.

Two words. Following what is, after all, a huge chunk of bible to wrestle with – where God does an unusual amount of talking. The non riddle making God is offering Moses a final edge for his journey and He is offering it in just two words.

Moses is taken to the mountain top and shown (maybe even supernaturally shown) all of the Promised Land for which he has toiled relentlessly and then, spectacularly, God pulls back another curtain. Moses is thus invited into an intimacy that calls him, amazingly, once again to but *broaden* his gaze. God asks Moses to let go of himself. Moses is given something that feels like a sword through the heart of him and told to accept it. He is told you are not going to cross "this Jordan".

Two words, "this Jordan".

"Why will you not cross this Jordan, Moses?" says God.

'It is because I sinned against you a long time ago and did not honor you as holy', says Moses.

'No', says God, 'It is because you have earned a better crossing and I am taking you into that'.

To see Moses' death at this point as a defeat is surely to miss the point of Christianity. It is to give in to every stuffed shirt that ever stood in a pulpit and held up a God who perpetually tells us that we are never good enough. That God will always need some heavenly paradoxical card trick to make it all right, but only in the end.

Moses is honored by God all the way through his journey and then, especially, at its end. Moses is honored by God through death, as the consummation of what was, to date, the most spectacular level of intimacy achieved with God since Eve and Adam. The reward for that intimacy is to cross *another Jordan*. To cross into even more intimacy.

There is another promised land. Moses has moved the story on and got it ready. He was never going to complete it because, however grand this part of the story becomes, it is only a hiatus. This, for all its turbulence and power, is a mere shadow of what God has in mind. So Moses dies unrequited of his part of the "wandering and trying to find a home" story, for sure, but that's because God takes him to the true home of his story and "this Jordan" is not the way there.

Moses doesn't die as one of the last. He goes home as one of the first.

I've always been angry with God for not letting Moses into the Promised Land, but it suddenly strikes me in writing this, there's no need for that anger, because God did let His faithful friend into the (ultimate) Promised Land.

God met Moses at the edge, not the center.

God meets us at the edge, Elijah

James and John, the sons of thunder, go with Jesus on a mission to a village. The village rejects Jesus' message. James and John, thunder in mind, say shall we call down fire from heaven? Jesus might be annoyed with the question. Why do they say this? Well, because Jesus is the new Moses and Moses more often than not when he is being rejected has God barbeque the offenders. Also, in their minds and the minds of many onlookers, Jesus is Elijah (reborn) and Elijah was a fire-bringer. Unlike Moses, Elijah, it appears, could actually summon the fire; he was the fire-starter. Twisted, right?

So, if you are Elijah first time round, how cool is this. Your entire nation has run off with fertility gods and orgies, typical. The king of that nation has invited the pagans into his court, which anyway is supposed to be God's court. He's even married one of their whoring princesses. She is hell-bent on stamping out the local religion, pushing this Yahweh character into obscurity, this she does with sex it seems, lots of it. She puts her missionaries in every town and they whip up a nice little frenzy, do a little dance, make a little love, get down tonight...

If you are Elijah you are on a one-man mission from God, you might, somewhat foolishly, believe you are the only man who can do this, but that charges you with a level of zeal that we've not seen since Samson. You set up a battle royale with them there fertility prophets and you face the people with a choice. It's a choice when they get off their beds of rebellion that they remember deep in their psyche. They've heard it before. Choose God.

If you are Elijah you are an ox of a man because by power of personality alone you defy kings and authorities and you call whole cities to account. You can bring the circus to town, and bring it you do. You have the confidence to challenge hundreds of the prophets of Baal to come and fight little old you. He says let's define this space, let's see who is God. Let's put the whole show to one almighty test. You want to sacrifice to father nature? Fine, go ahead. But let's do a double header. You set up your sacrifice, I'll set up mine. Not so fast with the matches, big guy, this is god we are talking about, right? Your god is mighty and made everything right, your god owns you, right. So, get him to light the fire for ya. Too tricky? Tell you what, if your god can't light a little bonfire and my God can, you are so toasted.

Admittedly that's a précis of one of the all time great confrontations in the bible, but you are very familiar with the story. God turns out to be God. Elijah brings a fire so decisive that it even burns up the rocks. Why? Interesting tangential question, glad you asked.

My theory is that God did not want this place to turn into yet another high place, and for people to prostitute themselves to Elijah's pile, so to speak. Just like Gideon's ephod, there is corruption in powerful icons.

Also, it's a testament to how angry God is, not that he melts rocks you understand with an unusual fiery anger, but that He melts these rocks. Israel has at various points in the journey set up piles of stones as a testimony. It started with Abraham, Jacob kept it up, Joshua did it, at various times and for various reasons these were set up as testimony to what God had done. These rocks were not going to be like that. God didn't want these rocks at all. There was another rock coming. One that would fill the whole earth. Cue a whole chapter on Jesus and Daniel that you can thank me for not inserting here.

The thing to see is that Elijah, as the servants of Yahweh go, is a world heavyweight, he is at the top of his game, there is nothing he can't do as they drag away the startled corpses of five hundred prophets. The people are, because of him, praising God once more albeit temporarily. So when Princess Jezebel breathes her own murderous fire that's hardly going to dent the mettle of such a guy right?

But it does dent. Elijah tumbles into an enormous paranoid

depression. On the back of this great victory he just can't take it anymore. He has been living on his nerves all this time and they are, quite frankly, shredded. He needs to talk to God. No really, he needs to talk TO God, not with God, that would have been easy. So Elijah takes himself to an edge, quite literally. He does this to meet God, quite literally. He embraces his mental breakdown and sets off to confront God within it:

> He came to a broom bush, sat down under it and prayed that he might die. "I have had enough, LORD," he said. "Take my life; I am no better than my ancestors." Then he lay down under the bush and fell asleep.
>
> All at once an angel touched him and said, "Get up and eat." He looked around, and there by his head was some bread baked over hot coals, and a jar of water. He ate and drank and then lay down again.
>
> The angel of the LORD came back a second time and touched him and said, "Get up and eat, for the journey is too much for you."

Elijah's edge is to go into the desert and ask God to kill him. Proper depressed then. A bit like Moses had been. You have to see God's sense of humor prevail here. The drama queen prophet prays to die and then falls asleep and what's the first thing you have him see when he wakes up? An angel. There has to be a momentary flash of panic there.

Anyway, instead of embracing his death wish he finds the angel is cooking breakfast. She/he/it says you can't make this journey, it's too much for you, have a muffin, in fact, have two. She strengthens him on God's behalf and leaves saying the journey is too much for him.

"Too right it is" thinks Elijah, "that's why I'm out here trying to euthanize myself... wait a minute, what journey? Who said anything about a journey? I never said I was going on a journey!"

In my version the angel, just out of earshot, says 'yeah right, that's why you come on all portentous and make your way *into*

the very wilderness God originally brought your people *out of.*
And when you get there, you sit under a bush, what were you
expecting? That it would burst into flames? What journey indeed,
you know where you need to go, loony boy...'

God wants to talk TO Elijah too, it seems.

It becomes a pilgrimage. The fact that it will cost him to talk to
God probably suits Elijah's theology at this point. At the heart of
Elijah's 'God story' sits another depressive like himself, Moses. At
the heart of Moses' 'God story' is a place. It is called Horeb. Horeb
is the place where the silence caused by Eden was finally broken,
where God, once more, was willing to risk friendship with the
sons and daughters of Eve. Risk friendship with one in particular.
Risk using this friendship to pour out the water that would wash
away the stain of humanity forever. Even though using that man
as the vessel, would break him.

Horeb was always extremely significant to Moses, God sent
him out on that mission from there and promised to meet him
back there when it was done, a promise that He kept.

Moses went back to Horeb one other time too, a very profound
time. You know the story, rock of ages cleft for me and all that.
Horeb, the place of silence breaking. Horeb, the place of law
revealing. Horeb, the place of glory seeking. Where it all started.
The place where God's resolve was set. Horeb, where Moses was
at an edge where God not only met him, but God let Moses see
Him, see His glory. See it and not die.

Elijah's own pain needs some of that right now. So he knows
in the very marrow of him, where he needs to go. The journey, of
which the muffin angel spoke, is to Horeb. It is a brainstem
decision. Incidentally, it'll cost him forty days and nights in the
desert to get there, hmm, interesting.

He makes it. His brainstem has found the very place where
God meets his prophets. In person. He goes into a cave and sits
down on the edge.

The angel of the LORD came back a second time and touched him and said, "Get up and eat, for the journey is too much for you." So he got up and ate and drank. Strengthened by that food, he traveled forty days and forty nights until he reached Horeb, the mountain of God. There he went into a cave and spent the night.

And the word of the LORD came to him: "What are you doing here, Elijah?"

He replied, "I have been very zealous for the LORD God Almighty. The Israelites have rejected your covenant, torn down your altars, and put your prophets to death with the sword. I am the only one left, and now they are trying to kill me too."

The LORD said, "Go out and stand on the mountain in the presence of the LORD, for the LORD is about to pass by."

Then a great and powerful wind tore the mountains apart and shattered the rocks before the LORD, but the LORD was not in the wind. After the wind there was an earthquake, but the LORD was not in the earthquake. After the earthquake came a fire, but the LORD was not in the fire. And after the fire came a gentle whisper. When Elijah heard it, he pulled his cloak over his face and went out and stood at the mouth of the cave.

Then a voice said to him, "What are you doing here, Elijah?"

He replied, "I have been very zealous for the LORD God Almighty. The Israelites have rejected your covenant, torn down your altars, and put your prophets to death with the sword. I am the only one left, and now they are trying to kill me too."

The LORD said to him, "Go back the way you came, and go to the Desert of Damascus. When you get there, anoint Hazael king over Aram. Also, anoint Jehu, son of Nimshi, king over Israel, and anoint Elisha, son of Shaphat, from Abel Meholah to succeed you as prophet. Jehu will put to death any who escape the sword of Hazael, and Elisha will put to death any who escape the sword of Jehu. Yet I reserve seven thousand in Israel—all whose knees have not bowed down to Baal and whose mouths have not kissed him."

At this edge what Elijah gets (and no way can we conclude that he was expecting this) is an insight into the depth of his own pre-existing relationship with God. His judgment is that he needs this deeper encounter so he takes a self-imposed wilderness journey that reaches the far edge of mental health. He wanders in the desert. He even gets the spiritual green light of angelic re-enforcement for what he is feeling and doing. For God's prophet he goes on an ironic journey, an anti-exodus pilgrimage. He goes back to the start of the story he has been progressing up until now. He gets to the 'sacred place' and finds a comfortable cave to sit in. He is, of course, expectant, very expectant.

But then a funny thing happens. He hears from God in his usual manner. He has undergone this momentous journey for something that usually happens to him in his own kitchen. He, the prophet, just gets "the word of the Lord". Well, that's what he has been getting all along. So God doesn't show up in any way, not yet, God just tunes Elijah to the usual station.

He must have been a bit let down. God not only speaks to him via the utterly conventional wireless channel He has been using all along, but uses it to ask an entirely counter-intuitive question when we consider the manner in which God has mediated the journey to bring him to this point. He asks him, 'what brings you here?'

Elijah opens the emotional floodgates anyway and gets the whole thing off his chest. There seems, coded in that, a bit of a snipe at God as to why Elijah's own work, even when it is as truly amazing as the great mount Carmel circus, doesn't dent the soul of the very people it is supposed to be about. Elijah says to God, don't you know we are losing? The covenant might as well not have happened, there's nowhere to worship you anymore, you've got no mighty priests anymore in any case, you've only got me left and they are going to off me fairly soon and then where will we be? We are losing, well, you are losing... Elijah is utterly committed to a God who can melt rocks when called upon to do so, but he wants to know where that gets him when that God's people are hell-bent on erasing their God and it seems to be working.

Now we have it. Elijah's big question, the same as Moses' big question: why are you a failure, God?

THEN God says, OK I'll be there in a minute. The wireless tunes out. God wants some face time. Then we get manifestation. God brings His own circus. You've heard enough sermons on this by now, suffice to say God causes all the manifestations of Himself that Elijah might be familiar with to occur and, to Elijah's increasing confusion perhaps, God is absolutely not manifest in any of His previous calling cards. Till we get this still small voice. Till we get this, dare we say it, weak God. Elijah recognizes immediately that this is his cue. How excited do we let him be in this story, I think very, but he is in for a shock.

After all these shenanigans and a bit of false start conversation Elijah is now where he wanted to be, he is now standing in the presence of the Lord of Hosts, the Almighty Creator God. Elijah expectant of indescribable revelation. Then he gets to hear THE SAME QUESTION that God asked on the wireless earlier.

Different channel, yes, but SAME QUESTION.

What are you doing here Elijah?

Nothing has changed because of this encounter. God is going very much out of His way to make it appallingly plain to Elijah that his relationship with God was *already* fit for purpose. It didn't need a pilgrimage into the darkness of the desert of his soul, it didn't need to go to another level, it was sufficient for the will of God to be ably expressed.

God makes His presence pass by and His presence is, at first, defined by an absence, just to build the tension and help Elijah face the irony of his presumption. His presence then turns out to be a voice. That's the same thing Elijah has been having all along.

Elijah has been IN God's presence all along. The dummy. God, the great leveler, takes him to an ironic edge, to show him the startling worth of what he already had.

Then they get to business. Elijah gets some jobs to do and at the end of these he gets to hand in his resignation because God tells him to anoint his successor. Which can only mean one thing, right? Well, actually, it doesn't mean that exactly, God has an innovation up His sleeve there. Before that one, however, the biggest revelation God can bring to Elijah at this edge has been threefold:

One, go back the way you came, this is not the place, you need to be where you were doing the things you were already doing. The things I wanted you to do.

Two, you are nearly there; I know it's been hard, but you are nearly there. Well done. The battle is going to turn my way, and I want you to be instrumental in prophesying and delivering the people into just that. We are not losing son, just keep your focus on the long game.

Three, and stop being so completely up yourself will you, it's mighty irritating, you are not the only one left you prima donna, there's seven thousand of you for goodness sake. I don't have to tell you everything.

There is one other thing God does soon after though. Just like Moses after a fashion, God tells Elijah that it is time to come home. Just like Moses with Joshua, after a fashion, a young servant character is introduced, Elisha. He gets the anointing and the training (a speed version of the Joshua story). Then, in a range of supernatural events worthy of a much longer treatment, Elijah gets taken home in a limo.

Just like Moses, God ends his life, but, confusingly, not with death at all, but by taking him somewhere and leaving his garments behind with a pregnant sense of a commission which is continuous with the power that God exercised through the man who once wore them. Which also hints about the man who will wear exactly that uniform again. He would be called John (but Jesus called him Elijah all the same).

Elijah goes all the way to a very personal edge. He meets God there only to discover that he already had deep intimacy, but in the maelstrom of his own view of himself and his commission he hadn't recognized it. On account of this intimacy, it was not too much trouble for God to meet him at that edge. God fashioned this encounter into an overture which consummated that intimacy. That consummation was for God to recognize, just as He had done with Moses, that for all the power his mighty servant had been able to display, it was his frailty that had been spent, so God invites him home.

God meets us at the edge, Samson

Nowhere in the bible does a character get worse treatment by us than Samson, there's just no dealing with him. In his own life this was spectacularly true. In a prototypical way we do to Samson what we run the risk of ending up doing to Jesus. It's just so much more obvious with Samson. We reject the meaning of his life in favor of the myth of his life. Because the myth is just too damned attractive a story and, as the old journalism adage is said to go, why let the facts get in the way of a perfectly good story?

We refuse to have the whole of Samson's story because the whole of Samson just raises too many more questions about God than it provides anything approaching satisfactory answers. Actually it would be smarter to ignore him, but we do recognize though, painfully, that we can't totally let go of such a story as this. The trouble is, to hold onto only the part of his story we really want to use, we end up neutering the whole and misrepresenting the deeper facts. This is to our cost both theologically and in terms of our humanity. This is a risk we also run with Jesus' story of course.

The real story of Samson has to be the masterclass in how we have a God who meets us at the edge. Take a précis of the facts, as the bible is unabashed in giving us:

> *Again the Israelites did evil in the eyes of the LORD, so the LORD delivered them into the hands of the Philistines for forty years.*

Samson was provided because of sin in God's world.

> *A certain man of Zorah, named Manoah, from the clan of the Danites, had a wife who was childless, unable to give birth. The angel of the LORD appeared to her and said, "You are barren and childless, but you are going to become pregnant and give birth to a son. Now see to it that you drink no wine or other fermented drink and that you do not eat anything unclean. You will become pregnant and have a son whose head is never to be touched by a razor because the boy is to be a Nazirite, dedicated to God from the womb. He will take the lead in delivering Israel from the hands of the Philistines."*

An angel predicts his birth and in it he is, unequivocally, the property of God. In the Old Testament the tradition of the Nazirite – the dedicated one – was usually a choice, Samson gets no such choice.

> *So Manoah asked him, "When your words are fulfilled, what is to be the rule that governs the boy's life and work?"*

Samson's father wants to know what his part is to be in the upbringing of such a special child. He doesn't have one, although his wife does, and there's a reason for that. Manoah would have been on solid ground to conclude that this visitation would bring forth a great leader and savior of the people. He would have been wrong though. God didn't need a great leader, He just needed a savior.

The woman gave birth to a boy and named him Samson. He grew and the LORD blessed him, and the Spirit of the LORD began to stir him while he was in Mahaneh Dan, between Zorah and Eshtaol.

The reason was that human discipline was not necessary; the boy was predestined to be a conduit, a lightning rod, nothing less. He wasn't being set up to become famous for his self-control. So, much to his parents' horror, Samson (the Nazirite set apart by God) chooses a Philistine to be his wife.

"She's the right one for me."

What neither Samson nor his parents knew was that Samson had no real choice in this.

This was from the LORD, who was seeking an occasion to confront the Philistines; for at that time they were ruling over Israel.

Off on the marriage project Samson encounters a young lion intent on killing him.

The Spirit of the LORD came powerfully upon him so that he tore the lion apart with his bare hands as he might have torn a young goat.

Insert honey-based sub-story immortalized on Tate and Lyle's Syrup tins to this very day. Samson has potentially uncontrollable fits of supernatural strength. He holds a wedding feast (interesting) and proves that he is a betting man. Setting his wedding companions an unsolvable riddle, he goads them into a bet where he will be the winner. They give in to this foolishness and it all turns ugly when, in order to win, they pay the bride a visit and threaten to kill her whole family. Nice.

The future Mrs. Samson proves to be emotional, perhaps

understandably. The smug companions solve the riddle and Samson sees, perhaps not unreasonably, that a woman can be used against him. This is not a lesson he will prove willing to learn.

> *Then the Spirit of the LORD came powerfully upon him. He went down to Ashkelon, struck down thirty of their men, stripped them of everything and gave their clothes to those who had explained the riddle. Burning with anger, he returned to his father's home.*

Samson has a problem with anger. God knew this.

Things turn ugly. Samson seems to be thinking shortly after these events that everything might be fine again. How could he think everything might be fine!? Was he well in the head? Good question. He went to see his wife whom, it has escaped his attention, he is not technically married to, but he has consummation in mind. He discovers she has been passed to another. He is offered an alternative wife, but...

> *Samson said to them, "This time I have a right to get even with the Philistines; I will really harm them." So he went out and caught three hundred foxes and tied them tail to tail in pairs. He then fastened a torch to every pair of tails, lit the torches and let the foxes loose in the standing grain of the Philistines. He burned up the shocks and standing grain, together with the vineyards and olive groves.*

Shock and awe.

The Philistines burned Samson's not quite father-in-law to death in a revenge killing, so...

> *Samson said to them, "Since you've acted like this, I swear that I won't stop until I get my revenge on you." He attacked them viciously and slaughtered many of them.*

This means war, quite literally and the Philistines go up to Judah, spreading out for battle. The people of Judah are given the choice, war or Samson. Then three thousand men from Judah pay Samson a visit to ask him:

"What have you done to us?"

He answered:

"I merely did to them what they did to me."

Not sure Samson knows what "merely" actually means here. Pretty sure that Judah knows what he is capable of. When it was guerrilla style, they were probably on his side, but open war, that's not going to fly. They get his consent to hand him over. They say, we won't kill you, we will only tie you up and hand you over to them. Which is the same as killing him but hey ho.

As he approached Lehi, the Philistines came towards him shouting. The Spirit of the LORD came powerfully upon him. The ropes on his arms became like charred flax, and the bindings dropped from his hands. Finding a fresh jawbone of a donkey, he grabbed it and struck down a thousand men.

It was too late; it was a rumble, were the advancing Philistines really going to stop once they had killed only Samson, er, no.

There's no doubt if you were in Judah that day that you realized you had something rather impressive on your hands in Samson, a bit like a nuclear deterrent, even if he's not much chop in the poetry department. Then Samson, identifying himself as God's servant, for the first time in our hearing, and needing a miracle because, super-human or otherwise he is only human, cries out to God.

Because he was very thirsty, he cried out to the LORD, "You have given your servant this great victory. Must I now die of thirst and fall into the hands of the uncircumcised?" Then God opened up the hollow place in Lehi, and water came out of it. When Samson drank, his strength returned and he revived.

God brings him water from the rock, wow. Samson is Israel. The people choose him as a judge, showing they are not much of one themselves when it comes to assessing character. Samson led Israel for twenty years in the days of the Philistines. In those twenty years he proves three things, one; he has a thing for the ladies, two; he knows how to unlock his own strength without the spirit of the Lord directing it and three; he actually loves the God who made him.

Some time later, he fell in love with a woman in the Valley of Sorek whose name was Delilah. The rulers of the Philistines went to her and said, "See if you can lure him into showing you the secret of his great strength and how we can overpower him so we may tie him up and subdue him. Each one of us will give you eleven hundred shekels of silver."

Samson fell in love with her, but she, it appears, loved money more than her bodybuilder boyfriend who, it was fair to say, was a better looker than a thinker. Samson's great weakness was that he couldn't stand being nagged by a woman that he loved. He trivialized his calling, to lead Israel, and his strength from God which even he, the idiot, had attributed to the symbol of his Nazirite status over the actual power in its calling. He lets everybody down. He lets his hair down. It's not important that his strength left him. It's important that, for the first time since his conception, God left him.

One has to ask though, whether God was not behind the weaknesses of Samson more than He was the strengths. We, who know the end of the story, can still see how God will put this turn of events to a great use. However, throughout this story it is Samson's fundamental mental instability that is God's real weapon and this is both a noteworthy and an unconventional thing. It's what makes Samson unpalatable beyond the two-dimensional character on the Sunday school wall. It's that one has to ask, did God make room for a seriously mentally ill man to be numbered among the saviors of His people? One is tempted to conclude, yes He did. One has to ask, did God know what kind of grizzly non-future such a savior would face? One is tempted to conclude, yes He did.

Then the Philistines seized him, gouged out his eyes and took him down to Gaza. Binding him with bronze shackles, they set him to grinding grain in the prison. But the hair on his head began to grow again after it had been shaved.

Now, the rulers of the Philistines assembled to offer a great sacrifice to Dagon their god and to celebrate, saying, "Our god has delivered Samson, our enemy, into our hands."

When the people saw him, they praised their god, saying,

"Our god has delivered our enemy
*   into our hands,*
the one who laid waste our land
and multiplied our slain."

While they were in high spirits, they shouted, "Bring out Samson to entertain us." So they called Samson out of the prison, and he performed for them.

When they stood him among the pillars, Samson said to the servant who held his hand, "Put me where I can feel the pillars that support the temple, so that I may lean against them." Now the temple was crowded with men and women; all the rulers of the Philistines were there, and on the roof were about three thousand men and women watching Samson perform.

Samson the slave, whose strength no longer saves but makes bread for the enemy, Samson the performing monkey, jeered by the oppressors of the people he used to lead to victory, Samson the blind joke, subdued ...reaches to the edge of himself.

Out pours the most heart-wrenching prayer, bar one, recorded in the whole bible. It sums up the roaring incomprehension of a man ravaged by anger, torn to bits by bad judgment and poor mental health, raging at his circumstance and committing the whole stupid catastrophe into the hands of the one he still dares to call sovereign, sovereign of this freak show! Yes, even of this:

> *Then Samson prayed to the LORD, "Sovereign LORD, remember me. Please, God, strengthen me just once more, and let me with one blow get revenge on the Philistines for my two eyes." Then Samson reached towards the two central pillars on which the temple stood. Bracing himself against them, his right hand on the one and his left hand on the other, Samson said, "Let me die with the Philistines!" Then he pushed with all his might, and down came the temple on the rulers and all the people in it. Thus he killed many more when he died than while he lived.*
>
> *Then his brothers and his father's whole family went down to get him. They brought him back and buried him between Zorah and Eshtaol in the tomb of Manoah, his father. He had led Israel for twenty years.*

It ended where it began, and you have to ask two things of that end.

Was it ironic that Samson died cruciform praying about his abandonment and, in giving his death as an offering, completed God's purpose for his life, stated at his birth, by overcoming His enemies?

Was it acceptable that God brought him into this world with no other apparent choice but to follow that path?

God met Samson at that very edge and Samson seems to have

relinquished everything for that one indwelling moment.

So, Samson pushes us to our edge of our comprehension of God, which is why we can't quite easily tell such a story. It is about how much it really costs to belong to God. In part it unseats us from the captaincy of our own souls, something that just doesn't sit right with us modern educated folk. In part we see it points, forlornly, to the (similarly) pre-destined fate of another man who will be tortured, mocked and die to bring God's victory, to a new Samson.

God meets us all at the edge, Gethsemane

It's a tough shout in Christianity as to which is the more powerful statement of who Jesus is. Setting aside the fact that the answer is really an empty tomb; which says more about Him, the cross or Gethsemane? Jesus bled on the cross and died from both physical and metaphysical wounds. Jesus bled in Gethsemane because of the sheer stress of what He was going through and what He was about to. They are a pair, Gethsemane and the cross; one is the anticipation of the other.

Jesus had met His father at many edges. There had been several attempts on His life. He had to have intimacy with Satan, through direct conversation (when He was delirious) and through washing Satan's feet, albeit posing as the feet of another. Jesus had also been physically exhausted on a number of occasions and one can only begin to imagine how great His frustration really was at having to bring the message He brought sitting in a boat and shouting to a bunch of very easily distracted and harassed sheep. Some of whom would be baying "crucify" all too soon.

Jesus knew exasperation, that in a few short months His whole message, the entire project to save the human race from witting annihilation, hung on the bunch of half-witted teenagers he'd assembled from the spare parts of Palestinian society. You can write your own lists, there are a lot of edges in Jesus. The cross or Gethsemane, which is the rawest? It's hard to tell them apart. They are polar opposites on the scale of Jesus' intimacy with His father.

In Gethsemane He draws yet on the full authority of His sonship to come into the absolute presence of God. In that communion He brings the fullness of literally absolutely everything to bear on that relationship. Also, more parochially, He brings the fullness of the empathy his last thirty-two years had caused Him to experience. He spreads these out on the ground like Hezekiah's letter and then He bleeds over them. He brought what He must face to a father He knew, because of its very nature, would not face it with Him. A father who, in order for its effect to be absolute, would desert Him.

He weeps, He bleeds, He defines Himself in God's presence with more than what a thousand Psalms could hope to convey. He holds up His fundamental inseparability from God – Deep calling to Deep. Then He turns to face a fact. The fact is this: in the end, none of this relationship will avail Him. The cup He drinks willfully severs it. At this point, He can barely go on.

He even, foolish as it was, went to check on His disciples. Why? Maybe to give them some insight into what He would need from them at that time? Maybe to seek some solace in the tiniest fraction of what would be left to Him, in love-relating terms, when God, His father, abandons Him? Or is it just to prepare His companions for the collateral pain they are all about to endure as His journey closes in an apparent catastrophe that they won't comprehend or cope with? To train His pall-bearers Himself. We are given insight (with Him) to see that reaching for these relationships was folly. He found them sleeping, they weren't the least bit ready; they would be no use to Him at all, come the hour. So he goes back to prayer, seemingly alone but actually in communion for a fraction of a moment more.

Jesus faces in those prayers what will come. Separation from God. The cross is its expression; Gethsemane with every drop of blood is, paradoxically, its most bitter antithesis. Every moment of intimate prayer to a loving God, every second of connection shared, every iota of support received, actually drives the knife in deeper. It merely accentuates what will be taken away. This is what will be lost, this is the cost, this is what will be taken this, this, this. No wonder He feels close to death in it.

Jesus becomes the anti-story to our story. Jesus willingly surrenders his inseparability from God as the solution to our separation. To return a possibility for us that once again, as a race no less, we could reach for God in the way that He now does. In this act He is going to become fully human. We have to assume that the full mantle of humanity will leave Him stripped not just of this relationship, this level of communion, but of any certainty about God at all. That He might fully be us so as to fully die in our place. His last few breaths are spent making the searing pain of this, on top of the tortured agony in His physical being, abundantly clear to all.

God meets Jesus at THE edge, everything else is as naught.

If I don't feel to have done that last section justice, forgive me. How could I, without another entire book?

It needs a much longer and far cleverer treatment, than I could ever hope to give it.

In search of an intimate death

The three key stories I chose to begin this section have three things very much in common. One, they pre-echo Jesus Christ and His achievement, as we have just discussed it. Moses and Elijah turn up at the transfiguration for a reason. They were emblematic and prophetic lives which pointed the way to the life of the kingdom of God coming forcefully here to earth. Samson, although he only gets an Oscars' type name-check in Hebrews 11 is, for me, a definitive, flawed fore-type of Jesus in the manner of his praying to the God who had deserted him and bringing down the enemies of that God with his own death. In Samson's case the enemies were people, in Jesus', they were sin and death and Satan. I feel my more visceral point is well made there, although few theologians would tarry long over it.

The reason I feel this point to be well made is because of the two other things these stories also have in common. They have two amazing similarities. Those are intimacy and death. Intimacy: crushing, powerful, tear-wrenching, confused, appalled, elated, unexpected, consummated intimacy with God is possible. That's why these stories endure. And death, they all end in death.

They all, except for the confusing reversal in Jesus' case, end in the supplicant meeting their maker at their closest most intimate point. The close of their intimacy story in Him is meeting Him in their deaths. For Moses, Elijah, Samson and Jesus, intimacy with God reaches its pinnacle in facing and accepting death.

Moses: The sheer power of personality and the burning of righteousness is something which God was pleased with, something that drew God into creating a unique relationship that had not been seen since Eve. A God who wants to speak as a friend, face to face. God consummates their relationship with a spectacular gift of perspective in the context of an imminent death.

Elijah: The sheer power of personality and the unquenchable fire of confident spirituality; something in which God felt reciprocal confidence. God knew the whole of that man and clearly delighted in the heady cocktail of his mighty spirituality and fragile self-knowledge so that, at every turn, Elijah was given what he needed, not what he wanted. To keep his spirituality vital. God consummated their relationship with an intimate unpredictability. Even to the point of giving him an unpredictably novel kind of death.

Samson: The sheer power of personality and the unstoppable nature of the flesh. Not in the Paulean sense but in the sense in which God can course through your veins. Samson was a man after his time; he was a flashback to Eden, the quintessence of what "all flesh" could not achieve. Paradoxically, in the hands of his maker, he was the celebration of what it could. We'll debate for centuries whether he was an instrument or a puppet. He saw himself as a celebratory instrument and gave himself up to be, in the most intimate surrender, a conduit. God consummated their intimate relationship in the absolute crescendo of a glorious death.

Jesus: The sheer power of personality through transcendence. More to say there, but there's a whole section coming.

All of them, except Jesus, died looking into a land that was not yet there, which is partly what Hebrews 11 is trying to say. For each of Moses, Elijah and Samson, their intimacy with God reaches its pinnacle in death. Their deaths have been given to us to point to something. Jesus' death is the pinnacle of that something. Jesus' death is anticipated in and concludes their stories. It is His death which shows us that, when it comes to relationship with us, God does not want to meet us in some here and now, some temporary manifest center of our making. The God of Moses, Elijah, Samson, Jesus, Ruth and Mary had always been pointing in the same direction.

Home.

The corollary of that, which an amazing number of churches (in the history of the Christian movement and even today) and individual Christian servants have gladly learned, is the acceptance that death is only another edge. It is not to be feared. Something we learn both on the lips and in the behavior of Jesus. Home, for us, is death, which, core to Christian hope, is not the end of intimacy, in fact it is the reverse. Jesus has walked through the valley of the shadow of death so that we shall fear no evil. When He did, He then spread a table to set a feast for us. A wedding feast.

In death we consummate this intimacy, that's our home – as

bygone hymn writers were only too keen to celebrate. If this intimacy works at the level of a person, how much more could it do so at the level of the church?

So, here's a Gadfly moment then.

- Am I saying that intimacy with God is a reward not a right, and is found most deeply when the church accepts that it is to journey into risky dynamism rather than endure in faith and calling?
- Am I saying that the church needs to meet God not in the center of thankful supplication for blessings received but in the edge of a maelstrom of confrontation with Him about what has not been achieved?
- Am I saying that the church, just as Moses, Elijah and Samson did, must give up her right to be the best judge of her own character and accept that painful challenge is God's way to powerful blessing?
- Am I saying that God mediates that journey of the church for a purpose which only pulls back a further curtain to transcend both that journey and its destination?

Yes, that is exactly what I am saying.

To find and be found in intimacy with God is something that we need in spades to be God's people in our societies and on this earth. So we need to journey into risk. God meets them, Moses, Elijah, Samson, Ruth, Abigail, Esther, Rahab, Deborah, Tamar, Priscilla and almost all other significant biblical people, at the edge not the center. God, singularly, meets His own son at the quintessence of the edge which so defines the human condition – that of doubt in God Himself. This He does, according to Jesus Himself, to show the church "the way".

Jesus seems to be saying through His actions and to his disciples, the way to find God is in a journey of risk-taking not in home-making. So what have we made of that? The challenge to the church seems pretty plain to me. It's a proportionality question. *Either in* profound worship acts or in deep social action, and certainly in the myriad of microscopic and society-wide explosions of grace actions where they can in fact be conjoined (and at their best), are we anticipating meeting God at the edge by, well, going there?

Certainly in the traditional western church there feels to be, and maybe ultimately this is unfair but let me say it anyway, there feels to be a desire to stand still and have God come to us. If He will do that then what's on offer is that we will cosset Him at the center of something quite anodyne, actually. Why do we want Him at the center of our churches like this? I think it is because we have a craving that He would be something fixed. This perhaps justifies the paranoia of our need for the endurance of the church and its ordinances in the face of our own fears, let alone any other commentators', for their relevance.

If we pour our energies into setting up a church, which is, as I have said already, a hugely taxing thing to do given all its complexity and compromise. If we set that up and then we don't sense intimacy with Him *in it* what can we do? We can fake it of course, always a possibility. We can compromise on less, the favored option in the mainstream church. We can needlessly bruise and stretch our faith, as if we are somehow to blame for His absence. We can adopt monastic levels of stillness, better fasting and praying or louder worship to seek to occupy the void.

We can be the "must try harder" people.

But let me ask it again, what happens to us, however hard we try, if people just do not see Him in the place we have made for Him, in praise of Him, to honor and recognize Him? Do we ask them to believe He is there, anyway, when the cleaner conclusion, tough as it might be, is that He doesn't want these things and is actually to be found somewhere else? What I think happens when we accept this possibility is that we take a leaf out of the books of Moses, Elijah, Samson and most of all Jesus. We journey. We journey in our God. In so doing we bring Him a question which itself is actually not seeking a blessing, it is looking for a confrontation. Why are we failing God? Why are you failing? Then we sit down at the edge of this risky honesty and wait to see if He will show up.

Every single one of the people in the bible who did this was radically challenged and changed by God who rewarded their tenacity with intimacy and with revelation. Stop and think about the appeal of just a handful of significant bible stories that were not covered in this section but could have been. Let's take a quick walk down a gallery of people whom, perhaps based exactly on our particular circumstances, we could seek to emulate. Let's read the church in their meeting with God which takes place, of course, at the edge:

We could need to see ourselves, when we worry over the effectiveness of our witness, as Jacob; Jacob who challenges God that the great multiplication of Israel has not happened. That in all likelihood division in his own family is about to be its undoing. Jacob who left the Promised Land alone to wander in exile and who, by the river of his own doubt, comes back into it alone. He prays to hold God to account for what is not happening.

God shows up, but not as the God who was expected, the one who might reveal some other great thing to him and cause him to build another altar and carry on buoyed in his faith. None of that. God shows up as a wrestler, an intimate, a bone bender, a sand in the eye, sweat in the grip on the neck, a wounder. And Jacob goes away totally changed both in name and in commission to go and be what God wanted from him.

When we worry about our impact on the bastions of this corrupt world, we could need to see ourselves as Joshua. Joshua who finds that when God shows up to the party, God is not on his side, because his side or the other side is not what God is about. God is not petty or parochial and the mission that fills Joshua's windscreen, and powers his fears, is not definitive of God's identity or purpose at all.

God does not show up (the armies of the Lord have not turned up) to aid and abet Joshua's life dream for the people of Israel and bridge the painful gap between his leadership ability and Moses'. Not at all, they have turned up to allow Joshua's little gig to be a part of what God is doing. Joshua wants to ask if God is at the center of what he is building and God says, don't be daft laddie, you have a role at the edge of what I am doing, now look lively because things are going to get seismic around here. He goes away changed in his commission for leadership with a wider view of God.

We who worry about the relevance or impact of the church on its young people could need to see ourselves as Gideon. Gideon calls God to account for the futility of the end game that has been led by the previous generation, and what a waste of time it means to seek the God of the past to have anything to do with the young people of the future.

God does not show up to comfort him. God shows up to goad him into action. God calls him right out of himself, out of his comfort zone and forces him to put his actions where his mouth is and throw aside his security blanket. He is caused to find God through the force of the sort of self-defining moment that only young people seem willing to risk. To define himself running with supreme confidence into impossible battles.

We who, by history or otherwise, are a church clouded by violence or complicity with it, by sectarianism, or silence in the face of it, or any other range of sins, could need to see ourselves as David; David who learns that God can, and will, kill his firstborn son as a punishment for his sexual greed, oh, and the fact that he is a murderer.

We could need to be confronted, as David was, that God is deeply angry at our failures and will not prosper us in them or protect us from their consequences just because we are penitent.

We could meet a God who, when their consequences come to bear, will expect to be worshipped all the same. How many churches do "truth and reconciliation" with their own pasts in this sort of a way and take the punishment that God metes out and then get up, bathe, eat and praise him?

We who have given in to a sense of helplessness as a church in decline could need to see ourselves as Ehud. As the one who confronts God by going on a suicide mission to at least look into the eyes of God's enemies and oppose them with a clever sleight of hand.

The God who shows up there revels in Ehud's audacity and leaves him alive to bring more of it to bear on the situation. The God who shows up there rewards the scandalous level of risk his servant was willing to take and is very pleased with it.

We who work in the broken places could need to see ourselves as Ruth, who remains so true to her faith and her word that she is utterly unflinching in the face of the bad judgment of her mother-in-law whose bitterness has completely infected all her thoughts and decisions. Would we persevere in the love of God's one and only church in other communities thus infected?

The God who shows up there is channeled through Boaz as he gently refuses her sacrificial offer of sex and instead covers her up in an act of prophetic grace and chooses a more risky path for both of them.

We, especially in the modern well-to-do church could need to see ourselves as Esther; Esther, someone who is in need of an awakening from a Disney princess daydream to the reality of the failures of justice in this world.

The God who shows up there wants her to sacrifice her young life to prevent genocide and He is unflinching that it was for a time such as this that she was given such a privileged experience, and now she is expected to make that privilege count.

We, especially perhaps in the church in the Middle East or Africa could need to see ourselves as Abigail. Abigail who has been living in relative stability sees that destruction is coming. She takes it upon herself to stand in its way personally and sets off to be a peacemaker in the middle of the threat by tackling it head on.

The God who shows up there allows her to put herself completely at risk from everyone around her and from the threatening stranger. She goes on a mission to throw herself in front of the young ego-charged, protectioneering David and through that which God has made her, prevents him from butchering her town and pushing himself off the rails completely.

The church in Thailand, or even Amsterdam, could need to see itself as Rizpah, a concubine. One who was complicit with the illegitimate kingdom, one who had sullied herself, who then rises above that status and sets up a profound protest movement. Who, at great embarrassment and discomfort, spent an entire season outdoors in all weathers protecting seven decomposing bodies (two of whom were her sons) as a protest offering to God for justice against the violence that kings and rulers bring about.

The God who showed up there was a God who did not answer a single prayer of the elite in Israel until her case was settled in the repentance of the powerful. The legacy of a concubine is retained in His canon as one of virtue.

We who are perhaps located in or near the inner city, UK could need to see ourselves as Mary; Mary who bears the shame of a teenage pregnancy out of wedlock and who protects within that a deep concern for the sovereignty of God. She does not feel the need to cry out for justice for herself. She, who sees what society becomes when you are on the fringes, cries out to the God of the edge.

The God who shows up in that situation gives her a testimony that the rich are being sent away empty because God, it turns out, has a heart for militant, pregnant teenagers.

All in all, we, the church, could read ourselves into being

around these the riskiest of stories of people who go to the edge and meet a sovereign God and achieve great things. Let's face it, that is what we long to do. We could do worse than let their stories suffuse our reading of ourselves.

I think you are probably getting it. For reasons best known to Him, God meets, hears and completes people at the very edges of who they are and what they can do in sometimes extreme circumstance. Often this is where the faith concerned is as ragged as it is ever going to get. Often this is where they are putting their own dubious back story or damaged lives on the line for repentance, to prevent sin or call for personal or social justice.

When the people in these stories took on the challenge of the edge – in preference to the peace of the center – God powerfully blessed them. It's not that they were dealt with lightly by God in this. When they give Him this sort of space, they come away limping, they are pushed to the ragged edge of their humanity and their faith in Him. The power of that blessing is that He gave them not what they wanted, but what they needed.

If God's church is seeking to experience and indeed to be a thin place where God's will for the world and what we do actually meet, then she might do worse than to start by reading these – and other – stories of our God in more than a homiletic manner. She might actually read their original intensity *into* her own situation. For that to be effective she will have to give up on an agenda that expects God to validate her character at the peaceful center. She will have to journey to the edge these stories point to. It is this journey that is the intimacy that will change the church.

God clearly, if you follow my agenda, treasures dynamism, risk and fear at the progression of the cutting edges of His kingdom. God is a God of tension, even if that kills you – sometimes especially if that kills you. He may want you to enjoy Psalm 23 moments, resting by quiet waters, but these have no meaning if they are not the reward of intimacy which comes to you when you walk through the valley of the shadow of death to achieve them.

That's why the church cannot focus on becoming a center of anything. This is why the church has to risk all. It needs both to be willing to go to, and to be willing to be 'the edge' for this world. It needs to do this in the unsafe and uncertain knowledge that it will encounter a forceful God there. This comes with a promise that if the church does this, it will become His ultimate sacrificial community, His vanguard of the new world. The gates of hell will not prevail against the onslaught she will bring on this world.

The very experience of this sort of journeying is an acquiescence to God to mediate the terms of the journey. What we will find is not a riddle maker God, but a master navigator who mediates the journey of the church for a purpose which pulls back a further curtain. A curtain that will reveal what we sometimes call our "all in all", that God will show us how He transcends both the journey and its destination. In so doing they will both be put into the service of His design.

This is a design which enables the members of His church to transform into new humans, humans who reside in a constant ache for home. This ache is the means by which every one of us distances ourselves from this passing world. This is defined not by the way we judge or reject it. This is defined by the way we walk around within it, courting the intimacy of our God. This is defined by the way in which our resultant, manifest, risk-laden love of this world is a high testimony to just how lovingly we seek our home in Jesus. That is why we will live in and journey to the edge as a costly and thoroughgoing expectation of the transcendence of an intimate death.

Big words, I know, I can't really back them up with anything I've done.

Thing is, Champagne is always immanent, it is always opened when something very real is happening, something defining, it is always opened for a reason. It marks the place.

Champagne at a wedding always shows greater things are coming, that is its purpose.

Summing Up Chapters 4 to 6

This seems like another good place just to stop and take stock. Let's take a short hard look at what I've tried to say since last time we did:

In chapter four: We talked about getting the hermeneutic wrong and turning our reading of God, the bible and Jesus into something omni-inclusive and unwilling to cause offense. We highlighted quite how much of our hermeneutic needs to be about making a right judgment. There is no inclusion into Christianity without conditions. The weight of those conditions is one's life and/or death – as a spiritual metaphor and even literally. This radicalism calls us to, as Jesus did, exclude any who will not pay that cost or who wish to haggle over it. The ultimate challenge of Jesus is that we are not the ones who choose Him, He chooses us.

In chapter five: We concluded there was a hermeneutic of church in Jesus' passion that it was to be a place of, and a people dedicated to, the sustenance of others. That feeding was to be with the food that they needed, not necessarily the food that they would want. This led us to call into question a church which decides to define itself as attractive via a singularly pastoral ethos. Essentially that was to say a love without risk or condition was not at all like Jesus' love. The church needs to judge itself not on the basis of its ritual integrity or even the societal influence of its mission but on whether it feeds people with Jesus himself.

In chapter six: We sought after, and found, a hermeneutic of relationship with God which showed a God who was keen to meet us at the very edge of our being rather than at the center – somewhere that might have, on first inspection, seemed the more obvious place for the church to focus its efforts. We called for greater personal and corporate risk-taking in allowing God to push us to the edge of what we are comfortable knowing about ourselves. There we would find a new country of the soul where we find God to be both more threatening and more intimate. We realized that there is a calling for the church in this too. A calling to read its identity not in the aesthetic endurance of our honorable institutions but in longing for intimacy with a dangerous God and the risky journey which takes us into it.

Where to now? Well, we need to press into my objective to unveil more of a hermeneutic for church through a hermeneutic of Jesus. We need to do this more and more fully through the bible used in the ways we have already seen and, of course, being read *through* the Jesus we find therein. To fully accomplish this we will now have to introduce larger subjects without the aid of our Gadfly moments to sum them up. What we can do is attempt an almighty Gadfly moment as the closing chapter.

We will begin this section with another "reading of Jesus". This one will explore some views of His coming kingdom principally by examining what He actually said to His disciples and detractors about it. This, we will see, is about conferring a kingdom on us and how, in consequence, this could become resident in us. This will prove a complex and sometimes puzzling storyline arcing through His call to sacrificial love.

In chapters seven and eight: Maintaining that momentum we will begin to detail how the church might rediscover a fuller, riskier hermeneutic of Jesus. One where God calls to its/our deeper being and not to the institutionalized one we have pushed to the fore. We will be seeking to challenge a picture of the bible as a static authority source. Instead we will have to allow our reading of Jesus to inject a dynamism into its interpretation and to perturb its traditional authoritative meanings. This will come as a challenge not to read Jesus in the bible but to read the bible *through* Jesus.

In chapters nine and ten: When all this is done we will seek to wrap things up by describing what a church pursuing such a kingdom today – by reading itself into being through such a Jesus to do so – might look like. What we will see is that particular church practices intimacy and risk on a staggering (world changing?) scale. That conclusion will close the circle of a hermeneutic of church through a hermeneutic of Jesus.

Hope that is going to be interesting...

A Reading of Jesus 2:
Great Ideas of the Half-told Kingdom

I have maintained at various points along our way that we should be bold enough just to read the scriptures as intelligently as possible respecting the fact that God wants to communicate with us through that reading. I am going to try to stick with that now even though we are getting into more academically contentious and complex texts. If you really do need a theologian in your pocket to read the bible, then we are all sunk anyway...

In His direct exposition on the kingdom, rather than His cryptic story-telling, Jesus said some things that turned every listener's world upside down. This seems to be part of the reason Jesus had already created such a powerful platform of ideas with His stories. That way people would be able to reflect more fully on the 'great ideas' of the kingdom He would then introduce. Great ideas of the church in fact.

So it is Jesus' kingdom expositions that start to radically unleash the hermeneutic I've spent the whole book building so far. Once you go on to couple them with the crucifixion they are utterly amazing. In them you see Jesus calling His church of the half-told kingdom blinking into her radical existence. Here are some of the key ones in brief:

"Blessed are you, Simon son of Jonah, for this was not revealed to you by men, but by my Father in heaven. And I tell you that you are Peter, and on this rock I will build my church, and the gates of Hades will not overcome it. I will give you the key of the kingdom of heaven;"

"But I am among you as one who serves. You are those who have stood by me in my trials. And I confer on you a kingdom, just as my father conferred it on me, so that you may eat and drink at my table

in my kingdom and sit on thrones, judging the twelve tribes of Israel."

"The kingdom of God does not come with your careful observation, nor will people say, 'Here it is', because the kingdom of God is within you."

For Jesus' definition of the kingdom three facts (at least) become plain: the church has the key to it; it is conferred on His followers; it somehow is confirmed "within you".

In some (because it is only some) of His kingdom parables, Jesus' kingdom is a half-told transformative story pivoting on the presence of an exterior grace source in the world. The tares can't transform, the workers can't make employment, the tree can't suddenly fruit. It all has to happen by the agency of a powerful loving figure who is "other" to what the existing system is failing to bring.

Jesus hints and says repeatedly that God is effecting that agency through Him. He is the generous "way" that the kingdom of grace has begun to come into the world. This is why the parables of the kingdom have to remain as stubbornly half-told as I have described them. We are supposed to ask 'when do we get to hear the second half? Who holds the key to it? How and when will the endings arrive?'

I would argue, once we couple His kingdom parables to His prophetic proclamations, that Jesus, in two distinct and completely unpredictable ways, declares a set of endings which redefine the kingdom of God with staggering force. One of those ways is the church and His assertion that God's kingdom has been conferred onto her.

A Conferred Kingdom

The 'kingdom of God' in Jesus' time had a non-allegorical meaning. There was a reality called the kingdom and it directed the first-century Jewish expectation of their unfolding history. What they were expecting was obvious. Some of the disciples (and some of the non-disciples) in the Jesus story had been obsessing around the idea that Jesus was going to somehow be able to restore the (military) kingdom of Israel *now*. He, on the other hand, had avoided association with that agenda or with anything more than a hint at the subversion of Rome. At one point He went into a short exile to prevent a group from pressing this agenda onto His movement. Jesus needed to tell them, show them in fact, that His kingdom was not what they were expecting.

So, it is not a surprise that Jesus critiqued this military expectation. Sometimes this was openly – *"for all who draw the sword will die by the sword"* is a fairly good example. At other times it was it in His more cryptic sayings. The *"reed swayed by the wind"* speech about John the Baptist is overt criticism both of the self-seeking complicity of the Herodian dynasty and the folly of the way of revolution. Jesus, precisely because He taught parables to thousands that began *"the kingdom of God is like"*, appeared to be setting out an alternative kingdom stall.

Jesus' kingdom stall left His religious detractors sorely put out. After all, this particular marketplace was already a pretty crowded one (in which He said they were like children sitting and moaning at each other). Like the scriptural overlap between the military story of Kings and the sacramental story of Chronicles, this marketplace had priest-like figures and soldier-like figures all jostling for people's attention. David and Solomon had kinda blurred the edges of 'the king' and 'the priest' thing in any case. So, when one of David's relatives comes to the market and sets up a bold new stall in the corner which attracts and excites many customers, there might be tears before bedtime.

When that relative of David is happy to be hailed with *"hosanna to the son of David"*, they want to know pretty sharpish what kind of wares He is selling. This is why they are constantly bleating *"if you are the Messiah then tell us"*, that sort of thing. Jesus has to skillfully side-step their hermeneutic bickering. So He wouldn't take sides on who had authority in their version of the kingdom, or on which of their sects had the right theology of resurrection, or which would be given full charge of the inheritance. He wouldn't be drawn on any of those expectations. When they did get some sort of answer out of Him it was always a critique of their claims and of themselves. In these Jesus asserted, using His oblique puzzling statements, that it was they who did not know the scriptures and it was they who lacked the power and authority of God behind what they were doing. He also pointed out on a number of occasions that, on the plain face of it, they should be concluding the opposite about Him; that He had come as the finger of God.

So, when it becomes far too popular, they try to throw His stall out of the marketplace. First they set the old religious trap 234b for Him: 'convict of blasphemy and stone to death'. Here, He confused them by quoting Psalm 82 claiming that it says we are all 'gods' (sons of the most high). A psalm that goes on to predict, of course, that those who fail in mercy will die like "mere men" all inheritance forfeit. When that ploy fails they set the old military trap: *"is it right to pay taxes to Caesar or not?"* hoping for a hastily mounted confession of sedition. Here, He confused them by saying that it was not He who needed to ask which side He was on but they who had failed to ask themselves the question of their true kingdom identity. He knew who His father was.

So, from these simple examples and much other evidence, we can see that Jesus was seen as a critical player in the priestly and in the military forms of the existing "kingdom narratives" of the day. It comes as no surprise that there was an expectation that He would seek to be seen to be fulfilling one of them.

The shocking truth about what Jesus was *really* planning with the *actual* kingdom of God still reverberates around the globe today. No wonder He initially explained it in confusing parables.

Jesus' kingdom needed to stay an incomplete puzzle because there were some things about it He was yet to disclose. Jesus hadn't come to set up His stall to sell a new version of their kingdom. He'd come to take over the market. He'd come to authoritatively set up an innovative and alternative kingdom. He'd also come to give that whole kingdom away. Whilst everyone was expecting the kingdom, no one, except Jesus, was expecting the church.

Jesus' church wouldn't be called to roll up all their hope into a decisive military and messianic action, what they were to achieve was going to need to be way more powerful than that. He was going to innovate 'a church kingdom' so powerful that Rome was not the issue, the gates of Hades were the issue. These, it seems, would be unable to stand against the onslaught. How do I know this? Because Jesus says it and then He does it. Jesus is at one point overwhelmed that Peter has unlocked part of this mystery very early on, so He bursts out:

Blessed are you, Simon son of Jonah, for this was not revealed to you by men, but by my Father in heaven. And I tell you that you are Peter, and on this rock I will build my church, and the gates of Hades will not overcome it. I will give you the key of the kingdom of heaven;

Here is Jesus already saying to Peter two profoundly interesting things. One, I'm founding a church on you. Two, that church will be given the key to the kingdom of heaven. Wow. Peter comes down with a crash ten minutes later, but you have to give him his moment in the son.

Jesus, later on in His dealings with 'the twelve', shocked all onlookers and subsequent hearers when, in what He believed to be a quintessential act of kingdom, He knelt and washed the disciples' feet for them. We've covered that at length but let me remind you what He said:

Do you understand what I have done for you? ...You call me 'Teacher' and 'Lord', and rightly so, for that is what I am. Now that I, your Lord and Teacher have washed your feet, you also should wash one another's feet. I have set you an example that you should do as I have done for you. I tell you the truth, no servant is greater than his master.

You are not to be greater than your master, and your master is one who washes your feet. Jesus uses that provocative challenge to give them a commission to love one another as He loves them. After that particular Passover meal things turn, of course, in a very dark direction for everyone as the enemy mobilizes. Jesus comforts them by forewarning how all of this is going to end, and by reminding them that He is the way to the father and that the Holy Spirit will enable them to remain in Him even if He is no longer physically there. He then revisits that same shocking Passover speech only to intensify it.

My command is this: Love each other as I have loved you. Greater love has no one than this, that he lay down his life for his friends. You are my friends if you do what I command. I no longer call you servants because a servant does not know his master's business. Instead I have called you friends.

A friend is considered better by Jesus than a follower, especially if the friend is one who, out of that friendship, serves. Nearing the very end He takes time to say to them:

The kings of the Gentiles lord it over them; and those who exercise authority over them call themselves Benefactors. But you are not to be like that. Instead, the greatest among you should be like the youngest, and the one who rules like the one who serves. For who is greater, the one who is at the table or the one who serves? Is it not the one who is at the table? But I am among you as one who serves.

You are those who have stood by me in my trials. And I confer on
you a kingdom, just as my father conferred it on me, so that you may
eat and drink at my table in my kingdom and sit on thrones, judging
the twelve tribes of Israel.

Nearly the last thing that the living man Jesus of Nazareth had to
say was this: The kingdom is being handed over to the servants.
Their only qualification to receive it is that they transform
themselves into 'servant-friends' in the model Jesus Himself
exemplified. We need to screech to a halt right there, because that
was *not what anyone* in this story thought was going to happen.
That is a monster innovation. That, even now, is as scary as a
scary thing. Jesus says He is *giving them* the kingdom? God isn't
keeping it? Jesus isn't taking it back to heaven (or wherever) for
safekeeping? He's leaving it – here. Is He mad?!

No He is: *taking the very nature of a servant...*

Jesus exited the world scene in an ultimate act of
hybridization where He insists that it is as His roles of king,
servant *and* friend combine in their foot washing complexity they
confer His kingdom *onto them* with the authority of the father. It's
as simple as that and practically the last thing He says on the
subject. We have to stop and take a long look at this. Jesus, like
Jonathan before David, confers his rightful ownership of the
kingdom on the one He loves. He dresses us in His clothes. He
gives us His inheritance instead of judgment and death. After all
of His stories and actions aimed at shaping a truer understanding
of what the blessed thing is meant to be, after bringing it
personally to earth, Jesus says this isn't my kingdom anymore,
I'm conferring it onto you, just as God conferred it on me.

This true kingdom is not to be a choice between jihad and
religious authority. It is not even a small, semi-naked intimacy
between God and the individual – a single foot-washing by a
personal savior. Jesus inaugurates a kingdom of authentic, costly,
vulnerable friendship by asking the human race to forego such

things as 'lords and masters'. This is a community mandate of intimacy with God offered to the whole of the world. The church is to come into being as the living testimonial that a 'servant-friend people' *can* put an end to strife.

Clearly I've given it my best shot, but I haven't got words for how shocking that should be. The kingdom has been given to the servants who are, in that act, conferred the status of friends. Friends with God then. Marvel at that fusion of necessary intimacy, necessary plurality and necessary personal critique of the authority of what the scriptures were actually saying on a vast, vast scale. Jesus washed their feet to say, I give up the way of Lordship and favor love instead. Now you go and do the same for the whole world. Start a worldwide movement that will want intimate, costly friendship to be *the sacramental life* that points the way to God.

As for all the other people who came to Him chasing all the other kingdoms (and those that still do today) Jesus turns them away empty. His disciples were not promised the kingdom as a military victory in their political life, they weren't to segregate from the world and wait for an afterlife; they weren't even given good news about that to share in this life. It was conferred on them, not as a faith proposition for themselves, but as the new world order.

Everyone was expecting the kingdom; no one was expecting the church.

Before the full shock of that can even land, Jesus brings another innovation. The kingdom expressed through the church will be, as God had always intended, *a resident kingdom:* So we find:

> *"This is the covenant I will make with the house of Israel*
> *after that time," declares the Lord.*
> *"I will put my law in their minds*
> *and write it on their hearts.*
> *I will be their God,*

and they will be my people.
no longer will a man teach his neighbor,
or a man his brother, saying, 'know the Lord'
because they will all know me,
from the least of them to the greatest,"
declares the
Lord.

It is probably because of the fact that Jesus conferred a revised kingdom of God onto His remodeled Israel (who were to be sacrificial servant friends) was already so shocking that no one was the least prepared for this second innovation. Jesus just keeps piling on the shocks to their worldview. He doesn't want to confer a kingdom *onto* His disciples, He wants to confer it *into* them.

Just like God never really wanted to give a law to His people to guide their hearts and minds from an external standpoint, a distant God, He wanted it to be a law which was in their hearts and in their minds, so they would know Him, a near God. The kingdom Jesus proclaimed, therefore, had to take up residence in His disciples, in His Church. In part that was how He was going to be with them to the end of the age and that was how a band of recalcitrant teenagers were going to change this world irrevocably. When Jesus announced an innovative kingdom with a servant friendship ethos He wasn't finished, He was just getting started:

> *Once, having been asked by the Pharisees when the kingdom of God would come, Jesus replied, "The kingdom of God does not come with your careful observation, nor will people say, 'Here it is', because the kingdom of God is within you."*

In 2013 (when this book was finished) there remains some controversy over what Jesus actually meant when He said *"because the kingdom of God is within you"*. Some scholars hold that Jesus wouldn't say such an innovative, immanent thing about the kingdom on the back of all His eschatological and mysterious "not yet" language. They, to my mind, are bringing a predetermined hermeneutic to the text. In any case, they carry on; He certainly wouldn't say this to the Pharisees. So they overwrite this occurrence of *"within"* by using a more neutralized *"among"*. Jesus was in fact talking about Himself as the kingdom of God incarnate and not some other referent.

Some other scholars say this is a load of old dingo's kidneys because every other use of the same phrase that they can research *does* mean *"within"* so they are keeping it simple and sticking with that. Jesus, counter-textually almost, meant what He said. I'm on their side. This is exactly the sort of bruising innovation I think God would bring to change a failing storyline with finality. Jesus brought wisdom as a teacher, for Him to say the kingdom of God is within you doesn't instantly mean it is in everyone, or in the Pharisees to whom He is speaking for that matter, it's a statement of truth, not a statement of fact.

Jesus, in any case, doesn't seem to me to be saying this *directly* to the Pharisees as a compliment. He is saying that:

"The kingdom of God does not come with your careful observation."

They are *not the ones*, utilizing the current "looking" behavior of their generation, who are going to see the kingdom come. That looking behavior was, in part, the search for a military messiah to overthrow the oppressor and bring Israel out of Egypt once more. They sought, preached and taught this classic 'vindication narrative' that was shot through all the Old Testament prophetic scriptures on which, in a time of occupation, they had pinned their hopes. Jesus of course had already said that a diligent study of these scriptures should have revealed Him to them.

Keeping with His theme of "observation", directly after that we find Jesus making another kingdom proclamation:

> Then he said to his disciples, "The time is coming when you will long
> to see one of the days of the Son of Man, but you will not see it."

Why will they long for this, whatever it is, and why won't it
come? Arguably, He says this for at least two reasons: First, Jesus
is going to be brutally and slowly murdered in front of their eyes
without them understanding that this is how He intended to
bring the kingdom down and hand it over. So, the other storyline
that such events clearly *do not* point to: amazing military victory
over the oppressor and self-determination for Israel, would have
been way easier to watch.

Second, the continued pursuit of that amazing military victory
over the oppressor and self-determination for Israel is going to
jade that oppressor off so much very shortly that Rome is going
to redefine oppression for them with finality. Israel, in this time,
will never get back up and sing that song again.

It is at that (historical) point – when the temple is burning to
the ground, a ground which is opening up to receive the dripping
blood of every young man in Jerusalem aloft along the road on
crosses – they are all going to long to see the victory of the days
of the Son of Man as they understood the scriptures to have been
promising it. It's not going to come. Jesus says:

> *"but you will not see it"*.

Jesus, having compressed a thousand years of history and
prophecy into a single statement, isn't finished there. He
continues the theme. It's a short sentence in place of a long
exposition but notice that Jesus wasn't the first Messianic figure
in this period, He was in a long queue, and He wouldn't be the
last. So Jesus says:

> The time is coming when you will long to see one of the days of the
> Son of Man, but you will not see it. Men will tell you, 'There he is!'

or 'Here he is!' do not go running after them.

If you *are* looking for the Son of Man, says Jesus, then stop. Do not run after the next *"one"* who pitches up with a candidacy. They should not follow the next Messiah in line. The reason He gives is this:

For the Son of Man in his day will be like the lightning, which flashes and lights up the sky from one end to the other. But first he must suffer many things and be rejected by this generation.

Unpack that then. One, do not follow the next (revolutionary) Son of Man figure, or the one after that. Two, the (real) Son of Man is going to have something called *"his day"* and that is going to be on a fairly big scale and broadly visible to, well everyone, without ambiguity. Three, before that day, however, the (real) Son of Man must suffer many things and be rejected by *"this generation"*.

So, he is around right now.

He will not be marked out to you by bringing *you* the victory you long for, but paradoxically by suffering and rejection at *your* hands.

This is very odd and hard to grasp.

Jesus then proceeds to put His version of the *"day"* (of the Son of Man), into a context His listeners will know very well:

Just as it was in the days of Noah, so also it will be in the days of the Son of Man. People were eating, drinking, marrying and being given in marriage up to the day Noah entered the ark. Then the flood came and destroyed them all.

It was the same in the days of Lot. People were eating and drinking, buying and selling, planning and building. But the day Lot left Sodom, fire and sulphur rained down from heaven and destroyed them all.

He cites two of the biggest "days" in the Hebrew scriptures. The days wherein people, before Abraham and after Abraham, have experienced judgment and destruction from God. The great flood and the destruction of Sodom and Gomorrah. These days (like the coming day of the Son of Man) are decisive judgments on the world and have two things in common. One, the judged ones were oblivious until it was too late. Two, the judgment *"destroyed them all"*.

This is heavy stuff.

Of course we know, and so do Jesus' listeners, that in both these stories, one on a world level and one on the level of the proto-family of Israel, there was a salvation sub-text – very few, but some, were saved. So, Jesus now reminds them of a couple of things lifted from His own teaching. In particular He highlights again:

"the one who tries to keep his life will lose it, the one who loses it will find it."

This, of course, is a reference directly to a qualification He gave for being one of His disciples. The plot thickens. So, who is going to lose His life, Jesus?

They ask Him where this drama will occur. Still keeping the kingdom very much a puzzle at this point He says to them:

"where there's a dead body, there the vultures will gather".

Another translation I am aware of is not vultures but eagles. It works with both. Israel has failed to recognize the day of her visitation and she has rejected the mother hen's wings. The eagle, the symbol of Rome, is going to come instead. The oppressor whom they might believe the kingdom should overthrow is going to come and kill and destroy with finality and as the instrument of judgment of God. Israel is as good as a dead body when that decision is forged. Heavy prophetic stuff. Jesus predicts the complete end to their present, failing kingdom storyline. This He does to make way for the God of innovation.

So what, I hear you ask, has all this got to do with the kingdom of God being *"within us"*? Well, I don't think I've ventured to stick my hermeneutic neck out quite as far as this before, so here it is, laugh or cry:

One other pointed detail in this complex "son of man cometh" speech, with all its many (and immanent) references to judgment and destruction of Israel and the world, is that Jesus adds this odd little twist that doesn't quite fit a first-century storyline. That judgment appears to have both a temporal manifestation – Rome is going to come and wipe the place off the map, and an eschatological one – the Son of Man is going to come like lightning in the sky (after his tribulation).

One of these seems to stand for an earthly realization and one a heavenly. Jesus is referencing 'a thin place'. Possibly, once we understand the resurrection, He is referencing *the* thin place. Jesus mashes the earthly and heavenly storylines together. Earth and heaven are combined without any apparent apology. He then conjoins them with a storyline that is as old as storylines – the flood, the first judgment on all flesh come down. For good measure He juxtaposes these to the last close call that Israel's family had on the old burning sulphur front. This is about that axe at the foot of the tree, isn't it Jesus?

He then resolves that entire mash up by saying this:

I tell you, on that night two people will be in one bed; one will be taken and the other left. Two women will be grinding grain together; one will be taken and the other left.

First up *"on that night"* refers to Jesus' own shorthand in His teaching of God's judgment/the kingdom/the Son of Man coming *"like a thief in the night"*. Second, it strikes me, bizarrely, that this references a time zone difference, some sleep, some work, they are in different time zones; this is a world-level event. Third, way more important by far and finally getting to my point: Jesus' kingdom narrative here actually forms itself around the innovation He has already pointed out to the Pharisees. That the kingdom of God cannot be seen if you think of it as (totally) external. It can be seen *"within you"*.

So when God comes to the bed with two people in it to do "the taking", there is going to be something different about 'the one who is taken' and 'the one who is left'. Right? Jesus' hung imperative is that 'the one who is taken' will be the "kingdom within" one. It is in understanding this, Jesus says to the Pharisees and to His disciples that you will all recognize who the Son of Man is *today*.

It's me, says Jesus.

I'm not just conferring the kingdom onto you, as if that innovation isn't bruising enough, it is to be a resident kingdom, which will be *within you* only if I am.

> *I pray also for those who will believe in me through their message, that all of them may be one, Father, just as you are in me and I am in you. I have given them the glory that you gave me, that they may be one as we are one.*

For my hermeneutic, Jesus is saying the deciding factor for the one who is taken when the Son of Man/Final Kingdom comes is not a sociological, historical, religious or even a physical storyline. It is that the 'one who is taken' personally owns the story of the Son of Man who 'suffered many things and was rejected'. This, we are all agreed in this telling, is clearly Jesus himself. 'The one who is left' even as they listen to Him now, is the one who does not accept Jesus.

As we look on, all this time later, we are of course more privileged to know the extent of the suffering and rejection the Son of

Man must undergo to achieve this kingdom. So we can now affirm what Jesus was only alluding to when He spoke these words then. The 'one who is taken' personally owns the death of Jesus.

This is how you will, according to Jesus, inherit His kingdom.

So we see within Jesus' highly complex, and partially occluded, narrative of the coming judgment and destruction, the 'kingdom within' acts as a temporal down-payment to avert that judgment and destruction even if you lose your life for Him. This eternal kingdom within is arbitrated by Him. It is arbitrated on the evidence that the weed has transformed into wheat; it is the last person standing at the marketplace running into the fields before dusk; it is the tree, a year later, bearing much fruit. When we combine His stories and His proclamations, the kingdom within acts as a sort of long-term deposit given to the one who believes in Him. Or, as I'm sure it says elsewhere:

Now it is God who makes both us and you stand firm in Christ. He anointed us, set his seal of ownership on us, and put his spirit in our hearts as a deposit, guaranteeing what is to come.

Or, as we have already studied earlier in the book:

I tell you the truth, no one can enter the kingdom of God unless he is born of water and the spirit, flesh gives birth to flesh, but the Spirit gives birth to spirit.

These then are the two high value items on my stall. The two big bang theories of Jesus' parables and proclamation of kingdom. They won't win me any theology prize, because they are pretty obvious and simple really:

One, the kingdom of God is the church. Jesus *conferred it upon* intimately accountable servants as a mandate to an externalized servant-love for the world in this present age.

Two, the power of the kingdom of God is deposited *to be resident within* the people of that church by Jesus Himself.

And Death and Hell have nothing left to say.

In all this, Jesus invites us to experience Him as the king of the great half-told story. The story of the consummation of Jesus and the kingdom of God. This is a story played out on the spatio-temporal stage of a world God is not finished with. Thus the story has two sides.

For the one side we use the shorthand of the "now kingdom", this refers to the church's communion with God and the offer of Jesus for (all of) us to be enduring "as one" with each other just as He and the Father are. That communion powers our love for each other and our love for the world. These are Jesus' standard for the evidence His conferred kingdom has come "now".

For the other side we use the shorthand of the "not yet" kingdom, this refers to the consummation or inheritance of the church which practices this now kingdom. The presence of the Holy Spirit of Jesus within the believer - and rolled up into the necessary plurality of the sacrificial servant love of the church - is the evidential deposit He leaves us.

Communion and consummation, the now and the not yet kingdom; the conferred and the resident kingdom. A heavenly Mobius strip. They are both the kingdom of God. The church of Christ is, in fact, only completed if it represents God through both. When we do this, collectively and individually, according to Jesus, we will then become the ultimate thin place ourselves. The kingdom will come on earth as it is in heaven.

Where will the church get the inspiration to flesh out what it means for her role in the world today? By reading Jesus, that's where. After all, He promises to be with us now <u>and</u> until the (not yet) kingdom comes.

So, we should keep Him close.

Real close.

Chapter 7

Rediscovering Joy in Reading Jesus
(Part 1)

The church has been handed the key to a kingdom. One that is conferred onto us and which has to be resident within us. This kingdom has a 'now' part which we therefore have to celebrate. It has a 'not yet' part which we have a mission from Jesus to speed the arrival of. This is its job description given by Jesus to His disciples, and we are they.

It is imperative therefore that this celebrating and speeding have to be done whilst keeping Jesus, the 'author and perfector' of the kingdom, as close as possible. One way given to us to achieve this is that we can read about Him. The spiritualized nature of this reading confers a textual life onto the necessary plurality of the church. Such a life will only be evident when the church constantly rediscovers, for the exact times and places where it finds itself and for its mission, the joy of the hermeneutic of Jesus. That joy needs to be manifest in our spiritual relationship with the bible, overt teaching from it and existential expression of it. We will concern ourselves with that over the four chapters to come.

This will be the slow-burning ending to my argument, and I really hope I've saved the best till last. I hope too, by this late hour, that you know what I mean if I use this word 'hermeneutic'. I don't mean some dusty academic concept to describe how we read ancient texts. I mean it as a living concept to describe the way the bible, and, now that we get more fully to it, Jesus therein, reaches out and grabs a hold of your soul. If we apply a hermeneutic of Jesus that allows us to "read ourselves" in this text, to appropriate textual life, we will be changed. We will also understand a very different calling for the church from the one she might have at the moment.

When I talk about Jesus reaching out from the text to grab hold of our souls I am not, of course, making that classic modern Christian error of collapsing my worldview into a lazy Platonic sense of 'soul body dualism'. I am tapping into the, far superior to my mind, philosophical position of How to Train Your Dragon:

> **Gobber:** *"If you ever want to get out there to fight dragons you need to stop all of ...this."*
> **Hiccup:** *"But you just pointed to all of me".*

For those who know and love that film you understand where I am going. When I say God grabs my "soul" I mean a God who is, in and through this scripture in general, and Jesus therein in particular, pointing to "all of me". This is a complex gesture. In fact it has, to parody that Darwinian thorn, an irreducible complexity. That's why books about Christianity with simple in the title are doomed from the off. It's not simple.

That irreducible complexity is how the church can appeal to me. For a start, I'm a complex guy. For a second, I am fearfully and wonderfully made by my creator as a being who responds to poetry, who is taken to strange places by music, who feels "other" a lot of the time, who is aware that within me there is a spirit and a truth which is not of my own making, now appealing, now convicting, now groaning, and able to encounter (occasionally) an inexpressible and glorious joy that comes from without. This spirit is also able to be reaching to play a part in that necessary plurality that makes the church innovative and edgy. Combining with other like spirits therein we rejoice in the depth of *our* maker and how, with a little bit of dragon training, He makes it possible for us to join spirits with Him.

I once heard an aside in a sermon (not even the sermon itself) which changed my view of God. Is this not what sermons are supposed to be for? It was in a school hall (funky church) and the preacher was commenting on the "how long, how high, how wide..." etc. is the love of God. He didn't even know he was being profound; it was a filler to the next point.

He said something like this: we all get long, high, wide because we use them all the time. He said that deep was not something we use commonly in a way in which it could confer any understanding of God. He said to get that sense you have to imagine that, in an instant, the hall in which we stood was filled with water and we remained where we were. That, he said, would give us a hint of deep. Especially if we then thought, this is how God fills the world.

I had a profound shift in my thoughts about God that day. Why? Well, because this was a very good way of putting it, my intellect celebrated with his metaphor. Moreover, I, a great lover of the Jonah story, particularly love Jonah's view of God:

You hurled me into the deep,
into the very heart of the seas,
and the currents swirled about me;
all your waves and breakers
swept over me.

Because I, like the psalmist does, think that is a highly re-usable idea in the evocation of God:

Deep calls to deep
in the roar of your waterfalls;
all your waves and breakers
have swept over me.

Because God's compassion, our lost-ness, the truth, conviction of faith, sorrow for sin, the unrequited pursuit of joy, the list goes on, are all, in the bible, things that are described as 'deep'. It's a big word. Because the work of the person of the Holy Spirit is about the deep things of God.

It's also because, as a case in point, although I can't ever fully explain it to you, the sea always reminds me of God:

Special Flotsam

If I surrender to the waves
Not raging
Their pearled tissues dividing
In grey green fascination
Pledging

If I were subsumed
Absorbed of all
In cleansing gone
Aloft

And tumbled rhythmic in the night

This loosened brows, this tangled hair
Uniform of purpose, hue, line
Not mine.
If heaved with mighty sinews
If awesome breakers
Stroke my face in molecules of promise
Of twirling jointed rhythms
Of the lighted life
This present vehicle decries

If I surrender to the waves
Not raging
To absolute support succumb
Spared as I am
This particle dwelling here

Relieved of tempest heart that twists and lies
And fails
Relied supplicant upon that force
Bent still this wicked, wicked frame

A special flotsam
Ever held.

Relived as I am I am
Still succour fables maritime
A special flotsam I
Ever held
For serenity divine.

Good thing I live in Birmingham then...

My point is this. When I read the bible, and in that living text find that God points to all of me, that's not something I can fully understand myself, it is not something that even stays constant, it is only something I can *be*. For the church too, to use the bible, and Jesus referenced therein, should not be a discipline which is "of the earth", however comfortable we would be if it were. It is not something we can fully understand, it is a spiritual thing. Of which Jesus says:

The wind blows where it pleases.

What makes our bible authentic for living is that when it fails modern systematic standards of coherence, and I don't just mean in terms of its factual accuracy or consistency, it is not diminished. Intellects are coherent. Spirits are not.

When it comes to Jesus then, much as we are often told we do, we don't need to acquire an elaborate intellectual scaffolding that might be holding up His story. He is self-sustaining because, in the reading of the bible, He is encountered as spirit. This is a spirit which is communing with me, a reader, who also has spirit. Together these brood, not over facts, but over truth.

I can burn all of my seventy-five years on this and still not get to the end of such an encounter. The bible and I, in a constant interact where both – through Jesus – change constantly. Where that becomes a truly joyful thing is when you multiply the effect it can have by a church-wide expression of it to celebrate and speed the kingdom.

Well, it would be.

You see, I think the church maybe needs to rediscover its hermeneutic of Jesus for its mission and teaching; it needs to unleash the consequences of such a level of reading. This is because we, the church, must through our "reading" of Jesus combined with a reading of "ourselves" – both of which, let me say it again, are spiritual not rational disciplines – seek to become more real.

This short chapter starts us on the final leg of a hermeneutic journey into four propositions then:

1. The bible is not the ultimate authority, Jesus is, even if, paradoxically we have the bible to thank for being able to understand that.
2. Jesus meets more fully those whom He completes in the most costly way.
3. Jesus invites us to experience Him as the king of the half-told kingdom.
4. Jesus said he had come to make a new kind of wine, this proves to be a (champagne) blend of intimacy and of risk...

The bible is not the ultimate authority, Jesus is

What am I going to say on this subject when rows of shelves in the theology library patently cannot agree upon the starting point of it? Well, all through this book I've tried to wrestle with saying something new to you, out of respect really. So I'm going to stick to that pattern here and just give you the thoughts of a Gadfly, not a theologian.

The Pharisees, Chief Priests and 'Rulers of the people' in the gospels are, by and large although not always, the baddies in our narrative. Jesus says this to them:

You diligently study the scriptures supposing that by these you possess eternal life, these scriptures testify to me and yet you won't come to me to have life.

They found that unsettling.

Jesus goes on to make many other statements claiming that their whole religious underpinning to life was actually being fulfilled in His ministry. The authority to do so, He claims, is given by the fact that the scriptures themselves actually predicted this. Jesus sees His own life as an enactment that fulfills large tranches of prophecy concerning God's entire project for the nation of Israel and the world. He says to them, before me there was only a pregnancy and, now I am here, there is birth and new life.

They found that profoundly unsettling.

In one of His sermons Jesus takes up the motif: *"you have heard it said... but I say to you"*, and He goes way beyond the Rabbinical exegesis commonly denoted by this idiom because He attempts to fully *re-interpret* the whole law of God (albeit make it tighter, not something we always notice). When you hear this from within the pre-existing cultural expectations of the time you only have one question on your mind. His detractors came to obsess over it. 'Who is this guy?'

Frequently in the gospels Jesus takes a rest from His public debates with "the establishment" and just strikes out to meet individuals. To them He makes the same sort of authoritative claims, only they are more personal and more interesting. In fact it is the encounters with "more real" people that are some of the most interesting places where Jesus challenges the institutions. So when Jesus meets the Samaritan woman at the well this is one such encounter.

When we read this story in churches we tend to focus on His discussion with the woman about her 'sin'. We think her a sinner because Jesus points out she has had five husbands and is living with a man who is not her husband. We do this scarcely stopping to entertain the idea that she might be the victim of domestic abuse, or serially discarded due to infertility. Anyway, I'm doing it now, focusing on that part of the conversation. What is much more intriguing for our purposes is why Jesus wants to engage with her at all. I mean why point to her? Was it accidental, a chance meeting? Yeah right.

Jesus has been sent. Her God wants to be a much bigger part to her story. The mechanism for this engagement will be every bit as clever as any debate Jesus might have with the Pharisees' established 'church'. It is also much more natural which is why we perhaps don't notice. This is an encounter where He wants, just as He does with the Pharisees and the religious Jews, to subvert an idea of the established authority of the scriptures and of how they should speak. Here's how He does that.

To this woman from this culture facing this encounter with who it is this man *appears* to be, scriptural authority works in two ways. These are her ethnic identity and her worship practice (actual or nominal, we are not sure which it is). So it is not accidental that she says to Jesus 'do you know whose well it is you are sitting beside and asking me, a Samaritan, to draw you, a Jew (who hasn't had the foresight to bring a bucket), water from?' This is our father Jacob's well. Read 'our father Jacob' as 'my ancestor, my identity'.

In this statement she is therefore opening an appeal to the authority of the (history) scripture. She uses it to claim a racial and political heritage that still very much matters at this time.

This claim acts in two ways, it is first a point of differentiation from Jesus (and His racial heritage) and connotes with it all the bad blood that has passed between the two sets (she may not have heard Him preach the parable of the good Samaritan). Second, it is a point of association with God and His calling of Israel to be His people. This well here – that I am allowed to draw water from – was the well of the one and only Israel (remembering that his name started out as Jacob). The authority of the scriptures support my identity.

Further into her exchange with Jesus she explores the authority of scripture a second time, but this time she wants to appeal *against it*. She challenges Jesus that you Jews say we have to worship God in Jerusalem and it is not permissible to do that here on this mountain (famed of course in the Jews' back story as a symbol of apostasy). That worship claim, in the mind of the Jews, is rooted in the authority they draw from the (worship) scripture to identify the temple system, the priesthood and their political corollaries in the perpetuation of a geophysical God around Jerusalem. Huge areas of the Hebrew bible are dedicated to establishing little else, so they would seem to be on solid form here. The woman's interpretation of this is that it is nothing more than a form of military, political and social control. Naturally she, and every other Samaritan with her, wants to challenge and reject that particular (scriptural) authority on worship practice, which she doesn't like, whilst simultaneously upholding the authority of the one on identity, which she does. Luckily Jesus wants to challenge the authority of scripture too. Moreover it is no accident He has now come in person to her precious well to tell her as much.

Stop and marvel at this God. Transport the story if you will to Scotland, and see God meeting a young nationalist at the foot of the Wallace Monument. Transport the story to Palestine and, oh, wait a minute, that's where it did happen. The God of the gaps doesn't do "accidental encounters". This woman, her well, her life, her back story of identity and scriptural authority have come up before Him.

So He sends Jesus to meet her need, the need to draw a different water. Actually this is the water of the *necessary* internal critique of the whole scriptural system of authority and to everyone's shock, not least hers, He is successful. Here's one radical shard He now plants deep into her mind:

Believe me, woman...

What this woman wants to believe, and we are not entirely convinced of her commitment to it as anything more than a sectarian polemic in real terms, is a God locked into culture, geography and history and boxed in by tradition. This gives her a scripture, diminished by the political agenda of tribalism and a God perhaps not worth worshipping on those terms...

Jesus' challenge?

Believe me, woman, a time is coming when you will worship the Father neither on this mountain nor in Jerusalem... Yet a time is coming and has now come when the true worshippers will worship the father in spirit and in truth, for they are the kind of worshippers the Father seeks. God is spirit, and his worshippers must worship in spirit and in truth.

Believe me, not what is written that you have held onto thus far. You have been reading (more likely hearing) those things (those scriptural authorities) as being about fixing you to a "when" and fixating you on a "where". They were actually supposed to point you to a "way" – I am that way. Believe me this is not to a 'when or where' this way leads to the one *in whom* you are to be.

Jesus, we know, has a profound impact on her expectations of God in this appeal – one that was not divorced from her actual way of life though, and may have brought some judgment on it.

True to form though, God does not just want to connect with her as an individual. This woman, like Gideon, Moses, Samson and all the others is called to the necessary plurality of the nation she claims fealty to. God wants this influence He has had on her to be expressed in the plural and this woman, whose name we never hear, does not disappoint Him.

Jesus connected significantly with her – through a challenge to *her reading* of the authority of the scriptures. He replaced that with a call to recognize the Holy Spirit's desire for the restored worshipping nation through His own mission. His reading is so powerful and compelling that she immediately becomes an instrument in bringing this revelation to her whole town. They then drop everything and spend several days with Him on account of her conversion which culminates in a mini revival. All from a conversation about the authority of the scriptures and how the one who is initiating that conversation has transcended that authority.

When the disciples find Jesus at the tail end of this encounter they say to Him, do you want something to eat. He says He has food they know not of. In a minute, when the people of the town get here, He is going to share a meal of it with them.

A bit like a sacrament.

As every preacher that ever stood on a platform knows, there are of course implications from these sorts of encounters which are more than spiritual. Jesus, so the scripture informs us, believed in a 'realized eschatology'. He taught us to pray *"your kingdom come"* not as an act of piety but as a vow to be a part of it happening with your living, even with your dying, with your being. So, as well as communing with individuals, like this woman, Jesus goes back again to the established church of the times to tell them too.

When they are challenged by Him, they get defensive and quote the authority of scriptures as a barrier to Jesus the whole time. The law says this, Moses says that and you need to get on board or things are going to get ugly. Jesus quotes the scriptures right back at them the whole time about lacking mercy, being snakes, preferring sacrifice, ignoring the vulnerable, being complicit in blood thirst. He says trust me, things already are ugly.

He does this paradoxically to uphold the original intent of the authority of the scriptures that say these things. He wants to prove to them that they don't understand that intent at all. This is not just argument, He is serving them notice. He is systematically stripping them of their right to claim any imputed authority from these scriptures. These scriptures, says Jesus, do not confer authority on you independently of your fulfillment of them. In short, says Jesus, they point to all of you. So in engaging with the Pharisees and their chums on the authority of scripture he publicly challenges them to give Him an account:

> Woe to you, teachers of the law and Pharisees, you hypocrites! You give a tenth of your spices – mint, dill and cumin. But you have neglected the more important matters of the law – justice, mercy and faithfulness. You should have practiced the latter without neglecting the former.

Now here's a thing. The Pharisees and co. were keeping the law inasmuch as it was easy to understand. When the matter at hand was practical it was easy. What does God want? God wants a tenth of my stuff? Cool, I'll get the direct debit mandate signed right away. I'm all sorted, where's my prayer shawl?

Jesus says to them, you give ten percent of your value to God, and that's no bad thing, but you have somehow mistaken that to mean that He is, therefore, satisfied that you have kept His law. That god is too small. Your god is a mere quantity surveyor and you regularly teach this about Him because you, the ruling classes, find quantity easy to come by. So where's the bother in making it an orthodoxy? You make the rules, make flashy offerings of your large ten percent and then go and consume widows and orphans with nary a thought. As your god is a quantity surveyor you bend the intent of the scriptures because you think they give you the authority to claim this about Him.

I've come to serve notice on you, says Jesus, God is a quality surveyor. That's why His (perfect) law is not wholly practical, it is also esoteric. So tell me, you who measure in and by the authority of the scriptures, how have you accounted to Him for the things in it that cannot be measured? Justice, can you measure this week's amount of justice? Mercy, can you measure the percentage of mercy you've dispensed this year? Faithfulness, do you even know what that is? And the answer, clear to anyone, is that Jesus is sure they don't have a clue, not even ten percent of one.

The meaning of authority

Modern Christians need to hear these same challenges. That's what I want to say. We have sometimes fallen into the same trap as the woman at her well had in that we to tend to want to see our scriptures a bit like she did. We talk up the "authority" of it, the parts that we like and which suit our agenda of who is in and who is out. Like this woman we also have those authoritative parts we are not so keen on. So, when we do use the bible as an authoritative reference point we fail to recognize that only the tiniest proportion of it can even *be* used in such a way and in any case, as we ourselves have ably demonstrated over the entire history of Christianity, which part is constantly in dispute. That dispute is endemic; it's not just in the scholars' corridors, it's in the living room of every house group too. Yet cling we do to our ideas of "authoritative".

Actually, this is a diminution of the authority of the scriptures. It is actually a hermeneutic of communication. It creates a problem-focused theology within which we can, like this woman does, keep on communicating with one another about what we do and don't believe. We sort of say 'God has communicated His requirements so let us believe in them and practice them'. Then we argue for millennia about what He meant by them.

The hermeneutic that Jesus (in my humble opinion) wants to offer comes along in the middle of all that and says, you want to believe something? Is that it? Believe something about the how's and why's and where's of worshipping God. Then *believe me* when I tell you it's not about believing, it's about *being*. For Jesus, God is not offering communication, He is offering communion. These scriptures don't summarize His requirements they are one of the key ways that He offers Himself to humanity. And I have now come to sit by your individual wells, says Jesus, not to communicate that, but to consummate it.

A bit like a wedding.

We need to let Jesus' warnings of the Pharisees ring in our ears too. They don't understand the plain fact that the totality of scripture is screaming about justice, mercy and faithfulness and that these are not, never can be, of the earth. So, do we understand that?

Fine, we might have moved the game on a bit. I'm resisting all the old clichés like the crusades, and women wearing hats in church as much as I can. Fine, we do recognize justice and mercy and love and it's brilliant that this shows we are not the Pharisees. Are those recognized enough though? Have they become the very *being* of the church, or could *singing, thinking and speaking* about these things and easy giving to charities focused on them have become our ten percent? Are these the new mint, cumin and dill?

That was harsh; I didn't mean it to sound like that. I'm trying to say something more complex. Trying and failing. Come on Mr Arthur, pull yourself together.

Think about it like this, the most important things the bible speaks of, sings about, alludes to, weeps over, fantasizes about are in that class of objects linked to our metaphysical spiritual being, not (just) to our rational believing mind. Every church in the land, every day, wrestles with these things. So we do go to the bible as our guide, sure, but it's not rules we need, it is the inspiration to be able to:

"worship the father in spirit and in truth".

For as Paul says (and I know Jesus would have approved):

"...in Him we live and move and have our being".

Jesus demonstrated to the woman at the well, to the Pharisees and to all who had ears to hear Him that the scriptures call out about things that you *cannot measure yourself against* to please God. It calls out about things that have to become part of you; part of your being in God, not your believing in Him. The scripture points to all of you.

The implication, heretical as it sounds, is to accept that it is actually an (ancient and modern) error through systematic theology, orthodoxy, doctrinal statements or otherwise, to insist than these metaphysical things are now somehow fixed (measurable) in the twenty first century. What we have instead is a mandate to draw on the authority of Jesus (who amplifies the authority of scripture) to a holy discontent with a church that wants us to just believe the right things about God.

We are called to a desire to imbibe these things into our individual and plural lives as part of our being in God. To let these texts bring us to life precisely because we have read them through Jesus who is our very life. This is why Jesus says to Nicodemus:

"Flesh gives birth to flesh, but the Spirit gives birth to spirit. You should not be surprised at my saying 'you must be born again'. The wind blows wherever it pleases. You hear its sound, but you cannot tell where it comes from or where it is going. So it is with everyone born of the Spirit."

"How can this be?" Nicodemus asked.

Jesus wanted to say to him when you are born again of the Spirit you do not lumber around like the (cursed) natural borns of this world, you become like the wind, you appear to answer to no one, you blow where you please. You can't be measured, you can't be benchmarked; you can't be called to account. You become free to be what God made, and you were born to be in this wind-like state. And we all know to whom the wind directly, and only, answers.

Hands up if you don't long for that to be a description of the beauty of your church? Now, I know that you might be thinking 'pass the chamomile tea' at this point, isn't this all so much liberal hair-splitting? Playing with choice words out of context? It's not though. Let me make my point like this:

To offer so flat a prognosis of the purpose of the bible as to say that it has some kind of "final authority" only discernible in a systematically extracted governance – even if the way that is done is proper clever – is like trying to suggest that knowing the atomic structure of oxygen is the same as breathing. Everyone realizes that knowledge of the atomic structure of oxygen isn't breathing, breathing is when oxygen combines with our cells to keep us alive.

Oxygen, breathing, living. Word, spirit, life.

We should not read the scripture to one another competing for some authority to instruct each other to become different persons along some descriptive model or other. We should read it with each other because, in a way we cannot fully understand except to experience it, it is a living text, the reading of which imparts "other" unto us. Unto us a son is given. A son who says, unto you a Spirit is given. I am called to combine the effect of that idea in myself with the necessary plurality which God has called us to in the church. We need to realize we are called to breathe this text in. Like oxygen.

Oxygen would be of no use to you at all if it only inflated your lungs. To do its work, oxygen has to join with your cells. We have to make these texts, in all kinds of varied ways, a part of our being. To do this we must accept that Jesus never said to His disciples and to the church, therefore, all authority in heaven and on earth has been given to a document which will be compiled over the next hundred and fifty years or so. He said it

"has been given to me".

The bible is not the final authority, Jesus is.

We read about that Jesus who does not tell us to follow a code or even necessarily copy a behavior pattern. We follow one who says that unless you drink me, eat me, you can have no part of me and my authority. So if Jesus doesn't act as the bridge between God and our reading then the church is in a whole lot of trouble.

God, only in part through the bible, is pointing to all of you. Jesus, the quintessence of that particular gesture, remains its final authority.

So, here's a mini Gadfly moment to help rediscover the joy of hermeneutic of Jesus for the teaching of the church.

- Am I saying that we – who are born again into Him – have, as a birthright, individual and corporate freedom to read our bible "through Him".

Yes, that is exactly what I am saying.

You know that, I've been saying it from the front cover onwards. So let's press deeper in.

Chapter 8

Rediscovering the Joy in Reading Jesus (Part 2)

Let's become a little more practical now. If all authority in heaven and on earth has been given to Jesus, what does He do with it? Well, the majority of the gospel's air time is given to a Jesus who, in a range of ways, used it to conjoin His spirit with the spirit of others; He used it to complete people.

Jesus meets more fully those whom He completes in a more costly way

What we see, time and time again in our reading of Him, is that Jesus meets most fully with those He completes in a more costly way. The sharp eyed among you will notice that none of my examples of the "God meets at the edge" chapter came from the New Testament. Well spotted. I was keeping my powder dry to point something out. To point out that Jesus (who being in very nature, God?) also meets people most forcefully at the edge not at the center. To look at a few of those, I need to use a decent level of exegesis. I hope that will be all right. I'll try to do it in an engaging way. Even if this book turns out to be sermonologue it would be good if the sermon was at least interesting. To keep things at the right sort of length I'll stick to just four examples: a man, a girl, a woman and a boy. That seems straightforward enough.

A man

Who to choose? Almost every encounter between Jesus and individuals is shot through with tension. We've touched briefly on Peter, Thomas, Nicodemus, Judas, the rich young ruler, all big hitters, all worth much more attention than I have given them. I think, for a real sense of being met at the edge though, few could compete with Jeff. That's not his real name. We are never given his real name. When we join the story it seems to have been a long time since he heard it either. We find Jeff in Mark 5 and in Luke 8. Matthew, for purposes best known to himself, seems to have entered a parallel universe where Jeff appears as twins.

To get the full narrative tension of this encounter you have to back it up a little. In all three synoptic gospels there is agreement on when this encounter happens, and that, to me, is significant in itself. Not for exegetical reasons, but for the hope of a really good story:

Matthew: Jesus heals a leper, says a Centurion exemplifies great faith, heals many people, particularly it seems those who are supposed to be cooking dinner and those with demons. He refuses to take on a teacher of the law as His disciple – apparently the bonus scheme wouldn't have been to his liking – and He tells a young mourner that becoming His disciple is more pressing than his father's funeral.

Jesus wants to get shot of the crowd which he has been pulling, so he tells Peter and John to bring the tour bus round the back (well, boat) and they all head off. That boat is then beset by a furious squall whilst Jesus catches some zeds. The disciples, for the most part well-trained fishermen, are pooing themselves. So they wake Jesus up and He proceeds to rebuke the storm like a naughty puppy. The storm being the puppy here, not Jesus, that would be weird.

The boat puts ashore at the Gadarenes/Gergesenes/Gerasenes (the gospel writers each having forgotten to bring a notepad that day). Jeff and his twin brother, er, Jeff, pop up right nasty, only to find Jesus is more than a match for them.

The demons causing all this palaver have a quick chat with Jesus and, at their own request, are summarily dismissed into a herd of pigs. Pigs don't like demons it seems, so they all top themselves in a mass drowning. The whole town turns out to pray for the invention of the deep freezer right then. Failing that, they settle for asking Jesus, who is way too costly a Jew to have around if these are the consequences for their porcine economic structures, to leave. Some of them might have had pick axe handles. Jesus, having only just arrived, leaves.

Mark: Same gig more or less, although Jesus is in a teaching not a healing ministry prior to the raging-storm-trouser-filling moment. Jeff is on his own this time and we get a bit more information. He lives in the tombs, he has been growing stronger and chains can't bind him now. He spends the evenings wailing and self-harming. He's not in a good way and getting worse.

Jeff spots Jesus, runs up and falls to his knees. Much the same story as Matthew here with the coda that, when newly delivered, Jeff tries to come with Jesus in the boat. Jesus sends him home to tell the people what has happened. This Jeff does. Well done him. Mark says, as an aside, that Jeff appeared to have been possessed by a "legion" of demons, eep.

Luke: Fullest version of the story yet, that's what you get when the most excellent Theophilus needs a briefing, more details, better research. Agreeing with Mark, Luke says Jesus wasn't healing folk prior to this incident, He was teaching, oh, and refusing to accept the authority of his earthly family over Him. Thus, He instigated this odd thing that makes people in churches who aren't related call one another brother and sister, but oddly given Jesus' exact words, not mother.

Jeff's story is a bit like Samson in a way, it's a belter, so we belt it out, but we are not sure what to do with the complexity of it. One thing is for certain, Jesus takes Jeff to the edge that day, but not in a way too superficial a telling of the story might suggest. Jeff, who is amazing on his own, is also a game-changer for Jesus who uses him to step things up. Jesus, ever the fan of collateral impact, takes just about everybody else in the story to their edge that day as well.

First off, there's the edge for the gaggle of "disciples" that have come for the latest magic tricks and maybe some free bread and definitely some "interesting times" to live in (don't these people have jobs?), Jesus takes them to the edge of rejection. He gives them what they need, healing, miracles, controversial teaching and then, as He does from time to time, sets up a boat race; Jesus and the disciples in boat number one, the also-rans quickly chartering local craft. A tertiary function of the furious squall is to deter the lightweights. Because if you are heading for the next revival meeting and a storm as fierce as that kicks off, you lose your taste for evangelistic meetings. So the storm functions to separate.

There's an edge for the Twelve in the boat themselves, the storm has a secondary purpose, it sifts. There's not space here to talk about sailors in a storm who fear for their lives and find God's prophet calmly sleeping in the face of imminent watery death. I so wish one of the gospel writers had documented (for my convenience actually) an argument between Peter and Nathanial, say:

Peter (struggling at the helm of the battered ship): "Gnnnnrrrrgggggaaaahhhh".
Nathanial (stumbling up lashed by winds and sheet rain): "Pete Mate, I'm brickin it, is there anything I can do to help"
Peter: Hnnnnrrrrgggggghhhhhhaeeeeeehhhhhhh.
Nathanial: "Pete mate, are we gonna die? I'm too young to die, tell me what to do!"
Peter: Kinda busy here, big guy, if you want to make yourself useful then, instead of bugging me ya numpty, why don't you go and wake up Jonah over there, even a carpenter is going to be more use than you.

Jonah, wake up.

What's all this fuss, says Jesus, enough of it. The disciples are fairly hip to Jesus' miraculous powers over people by now, but they weren't ready for this. Ready for this in a place where they should have been the strong ones to rescue Jesus and prove their worth. They throw themselves on Him, and He rescues them. So, right there in what should have been their front room, Jesus rearranges their furniture yet again. Who is this, that even our winds and waves obey Him?

He's the image of the invisible God, numpty.

The boat sails calmly on and Jesus, with a wry smile perhaps, feels the wind is changing and time is short.

> **Peter:** "Alright captain Jesus, where to?"
>
> **Jesus:** "That way a bit".
>
> **Peter:** "Hard a port Nathanial my lad, put your back into it, no room for soft-handed lady boys on this ship. Ehm, Jesus, when you say that way, you don't mean…"
>
> **Jesus:** "We'll make port at Gerasenes".
>
> **Peter:** Right you are captain, I don't know who's going to need our services there though, if you said we shouldn't go through Samaria I've got no earthly idea what we are doing going to a place twice as unclean.
>
> **Jesus:** Did you say something Peter?
>
> **Peter:** Nothing of any interest, Jesus, coming up on Gerasenes, shall I choose a good spot to land?
>
> **Jesus:** No, let me choose. Set it down over there.
>
> **Peter:** Sure thing, Abraham Isaac and Jacob, does this day get any worse?
>
> **Jesus:** Sorry Peter, I missed that.
>
> **Peter:** I was just thinking Jesus, shall we head a little bit further upstream from the massive herd of pigs.
>
> **Jesus:** Head for the pigs.
>
> **Peter:** Right you are, where else would a good Jew choose to land?

So while the disciples speedily strap Tesco bags over their sandals and put pegs on their noses, Jesus leaps ashore, and sniffs the breeze.

Peter: Where to Lord?
Jesus: Let's head over there.
Peter: (bursting into short-lived laugh) No, seriously, Jesus.
Jesus: No seriously, let's go.
Peter: Of course, the Tombs, where else would a good Jew head just before the Sabbath, gotta love those fresh gentile bones...
Jesus: Peter, your mumbling is really starting to bum me off.
Peter: Right you are Lord. OK lads, head for the graveyard.
Lads: You what?
Peter: No mumbling now, follow Jesus.

For a first-century Jew there is only one thing that could make this scenario any more unclean.

Peter: Oh, look Jesus, a naked gentile madman and he's heading straight for us.
Jesus: Good.
Peter: Of course, good.

For the disciples to be out in the land of the gentiles, to have pigs on the hill, and on the wind, pig excrement underfoot, be in the vicinity of a gentile ossuary and to be about to be accosted by an uncircumcised naked man covered in cuts and blood and clearly out of his mind – it would be hard to imagine how Jesus could have contrived of a more skin-crawlingly unclean set up.

Maybe some lepers will come and watch, thinks Peter. Jesus pushed them right to the edge. But why? Jeff, that's why. The edge incarnate.

For a long time this man had not worn clothes or lived in a house, but he had lived in the tombs. When he saw Jesus, he cried out and fell at his feet, shouting at the top of his voice, "What do you want with me, Jesus, Son of the Most High God? I beg you, don't torture me!" For Jesus had commanded the evil spirit to come out of the man. Many times it had seized him, and though he was chained hand and foot and kept under guard, he had broken his chains and had been driven by the demon into solitary places.

If the disciples are having a bad day, Jeff is having a bad year. We don't get Jeff's back story. How does it come to pass that he is here and in this state? Is Jeff *to blame* for any of this, or is he the victim? Jesus is unusually silent on that front. The local people couldn't chain Jeff up. They didn't need to, the picture of raving, solitary, naked, self-harming, supernaturally strong, incredibly dangerous insanity is chains enough. Nonetheless, Jeff kneels before Jesus.

What do the locals call Jeff? Hard to imagine. What do teenagers call Jeff when they are daring one another to go near the tombs at night.

What do the local elders call Jeff when they are wondering whether the answer to a long problem might not be a short sword? What do the local community psychiatric nurses call Jeff? What would we call Jeff?

Jesus asked him, "What is your name?"

"Legion," he replied, because many demons had gone into him. And they begged him repeatedly not to order them to go to the Abyss.

I'm pretty sure, when a host of demons occupying a super strong madman answer in harmony "legion", that even the stoutest-hearted fellow on the field is going to take a little step backwards. This is where the gospel writers, if they were ever inclined to put words in Jesus' mouth to draw out the overall meaning of what

He was doing more clearly for their audiences (perish the thought) missed a big chance that might have read a bit like this:

> "Legion," he replied, because many demons had gone into him.
> 'I wasn't talking to you', said Jesus softly, 'now you son, what is your name?'
> 'It's, it's, it was, I mean I think it is ...it's Jeff, actually'.

There's an edge for Legion who is consigned to the pigs (bad news if you are a pig). Legion is pushed to the very edge of whatever and whoever he has been twisted to become. Presumably all that 'don't send us to the pit' is a bit "request denied". It's Legion's turn to feel what it is like to be made up of multiple raging-mad animalistic personalities careering in self-destruction. Unlike Jeff, they can't take it, and they go off the edge.

There's an edge for the people of the village who now have an edgy choice. Come out and cheer "The wicked witch is dead!" Or, as they choose to do, come out and count the cost of a God who removes the unclean from among them. It's a pretty big cost. That stays top of mind. They are speedily taken to an extreme edge.

Here is this prophet guy from across the water. He has come unbidden to see us. He has solved our biggest problem. He has given us a bigger one and He is just sitting there talking to, "is that Jeff?!" They look at Jesus and Jeff as a prospect. They look at Jesus and the pigs as a prospect. They do the math. Too much of an edge, and they beg Him to leave.

If you are the disciples you must be filled with two parts relief and one part regret at this development. After all, you are not completely stupid; you see the potential in this. So, a tiny bit reluctant maybe, you shrug and, Tesco bags still slipping in the filth, you untie the boat.

If you are the restored Jeff, nothing is clearer in your mind that day than this. Whoever this guy is, I want to go with Him. Oddly, Jesus the disciple collector, says no. He says (using Mark's cleaner script):

> *"Go home to your family and tell them how much the Lord has done for you, and how he has had mercy on you".*

This he does. In fact, the disciples swap e-mail addresses with him and later discover that Jeff didn't restrict this activity to his own family. He set up an evangelistic mission and toured all over the ten (gentile) cities of the area playing to packed galleries. His book, "Legions of Angels" was on the top ten list for three years or, as the bible puts it:

> *And all the people were amazed.*

None of them more than Jeff I'm sure. It won't have escaped his attention that, a few years later, as he laid on his bed replaying those words in his head *"how much the Lord has done for you, and how he has had mercy on you"*, that people had started calling Jesus "The Lord".

Last of all, Satan was taken to his edge that day. He completely overplayed his hand with that furious squall. That didn't work at all.

Jesus never did anything casually, why would He? His time on earth was short; He had a mission from His father that was frankly staggering given the constraints. But He also had authority from His father and that was more staggering still. He had a resonance within which the scriptures came alive in Him. That has to be important for His church too.

As I hinted when I came over all preternatural and blamed the storm Jesus had to calm on the devil, these stories serve to create a demarcation in the acceleration of Jesus to the cross. He knows the time is short. He begins to become a bit more public and a bit more poignant as He goes. Something that can be slightly lost for us.

When we look at Jeff, as I have suggested we do, he stands out as a prophecy surrounding uncleanness and being a gentile and what Jesus does with them. What these two, quite ultimate, barriers should do is keep a Jewish savior at arm's length. What happens instead is that we find there are no limits God won't go to in order to reach those He wants. Moreover, we find that legions of demons cannot stand in His way.

Jeff stood for the devil's increasing hope that uncleanness, possession and mental instability are barriers enough to keep his selected ones on the wrong side of the saving grace of God. He is proved spectacularly wrong. Which is a big problem for him, since what does that say about all the other gentiles who aren't nearly as bound up as Jeff was? If Jesus can liberate Jeff, who can't he liberate?

(I'm indebted to Stephen Aylin, my brother-in-law, in this inspired re-imagining of the story for a group of young people, he probably doesn't even remember he did it, but I do. The Jeff bit was my idea though).

A girl

There's a girl, she's twelve years old, she's a daughter. Nothing odd there. She meets Jesus and it is hard to imagine meeting Him at more of an edge than she does. It seems to be Jeff's fault, which is a tricky logic to back up, but let me try.

So Jesus leaving the dead legion of pigs bobbing in the lake comes back to Israel. A large crowd gathers (again). People are still hearing and distributing the story in that oral tradition buzz. I'm sure those who did have jobs and went to do them from time to time would return to the pack with the question. 'So what's he done now then?' Animated re-telling would ensue. That is, after all, our understanding of how the gospels were formed and eventually committed to text.

"So then that Gerasenes devil man came and fell on his knees right in front of him!"

"No way!"

"Yes way..."

So it's apposite and odd at the same time that at the very next moment when the buzz over this story is circulating – 'Jesus went to Gesarenes, but why would he go there, it's full of pigs and gentiles?' – that Someone *else* should come and also fall at Jesus' feet. Stunning in fact when it turns out to be the last man expected at the party. Jairus, the leader of the local synagogue. Surely this is too much?

> *Then one of the synagogue rulers, named Jairus, came there. Seeing Jesus, he fell at his feet and pleaded earnestly with him, "my little daughter is dying. Please come and put your hands on her so that she will be healed and live."*

The bible says, Jesus looked Jairus up and down and said:

'Shoe's on the other foot now though eh? You come here in your synagogue robes, you people who never stop opposing me, and then you need something, suddenly my miracles are not cheap tricks or the works of the devil, are they now? So I'm credible now am I...'

I'm kind of presuming you know this story well enough and you know Jesus did not do that, the bible simply says *"so Jesus went with him"*. The son of God went with the (mis)representative of God in this community. The Son of God chooses to serve the representative of God in this community. Jesus, not even giving his usual huffy retort 'unless you people see miracles, you will never believe', just went. Well, He accelerated.

On the way He picks up a huge crowd. A huge buzz. It will be, as it has been, hard to talk, hard to walk, hard to think. The chatter among the crowd must be huge. "Is that Jairus, what's HE doing here?!" – "and then all the pigs ran into the lake and were drowned, they did!" Jesus, unlike the disciples, doesn't lose focus in a crowd. He can hear Bartimaeus' feeble shouting over the top of one. He can hear whispered thoughts that He is considered a blasphemer. So this crowd's momentum also stutters because Jesus suddenly stops. The disciples get their notebooks out, proclamation incoming...

But Jesus doesn't proclaim. Instead He asks this bizarre question:

"Who touched my clothes?"

Jesus doesn't lose focus in a crowd, not for a minute. The disciples, as usual, take a whole bunch of time to come momentarily into focus.

"Eh, Jesus, everybody within a twenty yard radius has touched you in the last few moments, it's mobbed out here, I'm touching you now, what with all the pushing. How can you ask, 'Who touched my clothes?'"

Jesus had a lot of patience. I mean He could have said: "Peter, what kind of dummy do you take me for? I'm here too, I can feel that people are pushing us around, if I stop and ask a question like 'who touched my clothes' in the middle of this then I must have a reason, right, or do you think me some kind of simpleton?"

Maybe He just said that with His eyes.

Jesus never lost focus on the person in the crowd, never for a minute.

But Jesus kept looking around to see who had done it. Then the woman, knowing what had happened to her, came and fell at his feet and, trembling with fear, told him the whole truth. He said to her, "Daughter, your faith has healed you. Go in peace and be freed from your suffering."

Another person falling at Jesus' feet. That's three in a row, is it national falling on your knees day? First a demon crazed gentile, then a desperate synagogue ruler and now this trembling woman. What is going on here with all this kneeling?

What is going on is that Jesus is subjecting the world to His authority in preparing to die for it. He is accelerating towards the cross. Jeff stands for the fact that nothing a person, including a non-Jew, could do to screw themselves up utterly and to drive themselves completely to the farthest recesses of 'far from God' will be sufficient to escape Him in the long run. The Jonah factor applied to everyone.

Jairus, we are not yet sure what he stands for, because he is not standing, he is walking in hope.

This woman stands for Israel and the particular state into which she has fallen: Unclean.

Now, I'm going to do a weird thing here, don't get fazed by it. God seems to give people diseases for His glory. The diseases are genuine, the diseases are awful. So when Peter says to Jesus, *"who sinned, this man or his father, that he is blind?"* he is reciting the old accepted wisdom that God visits the results of sin on people through the generations, despite all that Ezekiel 18 has to say, but let's leave that. Jesus might know that we, reading that conversation some time later might very well be shocked by Peter's theology. So Jesus, ever the electric one, puts in a jolt of His own. No one sinned, this man has been blind (for forty years!) so that I might heal him and reveal the glory of God in his life.

Wow.

God let the man be blind for forty years (like the number of years Israel spent in the wilderness then?) just to show off Jesus' power at the appropriate moment. No time to go into that now though.

My point is this. Here is a woman subject to incurable bleeding. We don't catch her name, so let's call her Mary; there seem to be plenty of those hanging around this part of Palestine.

She, on many, many fronts, feels like another one of these. It feels that God has afflicted her. Why would He do that? Well, she, like the man born blind, can act as a prophetic sign. A sign to Jairus, to the crowd, to us and to herself. Here's how that works. Thanks to Rob Bell's unpacking of this story we can see that the cleansing of this woman is a miracle explained in ten steps:

This woman had faith in touching Jesus' clothes, this odd little fact is placed deep within the story. We, anachronistically, preach about her great faith, she only had to touch the edge of His garment blah, blah, great faith, that's nonsense. Since when, in your reading of the bible, did God add a fine-tuned detail like that which you were not supposed to ponder?

Jesus specifically (in Mark's version) asks 'who touched my clothes', not who touched me. That's a challenge to the woman, of course, to *be known* by God in her inner life, and in the healing she receives. God says, 'I'm onto you...' That's also a challenge to the crowd to ponder a moment, why this level of specificity?

'Hark the Herald Angels Sing' makes no sense at all unless you sing it at this point. One line in particular, "risen with healing in his wings". Jesus does not come back as a seraphim (angels don't have wings by the way) in that hymn, that would be Gnostic nutcase time. This is a (mis)quotation from Malachi.

Jesus, the Rabbi, wore a prayer shawl. Of the kind Moses was instructed to sew prayer tassels onto, a remembrance action, one on each corner.

Malachi says, when the sun of righteousness rises (read Messiah comes) he will rise with healing in his wings. It's 'wings' because that's how we translate it. Actually, for our purposes, without going into all the Hebrew schmebrew, it's risen with healing in the corners of his garment.

The woman says to herself (and not necessarily in a meek way, we add that to the story, it's not in the text at first), if this guy is the Messiah, then my incurable disease can be healed if I just touch the corner of his garment.

Jesus stops the whole show and says "who touched the corner of my garment?" The woman 'fesses up'. In so doing she is conferring on Jesus the status of Messiah, she is owning her faith in God's Messiah.

God's Messiah says "Daughter" (shorthand for the huge blessing 'daughter of Israel' and the last thing she's ever likely to have been called in over a decade) your faith (in the Messiah, for I am he) has healed you, now receive the Shalom of God. This she does.

This woman most likely was suffering from polymenorrhea, a debilitating disease which not only meant that she bled constantly but that she was, as a Jewess, permanently unclean, excluded and not able to touch anything, particularly anything holy, without contaminating it.

In one of only two of Jesus' 'passive miracles' (the centurion's servant being the other) there's a heap of controversy when He publicly declares that the, in this case shoplifting, protagonist has faith. The most unclean Jewish person in the village is declared to have faith.

So, accelerating all the way back to Jairus' daughter then; this woman is declared faithful and deserving of peace (shalom wholeness) and confirming of faith in the Messiah and a 'daughter of Israel' and no longer the most unclean person in the village. She receives this declaration standing in front of the most clean person in the village, Jairus. This will not be lost on him. This whole side-episode will have caused many fireworks to go off in his head, highly trained as he will be on 'corners of the Messiah's garment' and their significance.

Jairus, himself, has fallen on his knees before Jesus that day precisely because he is looking for a healing for someone who, potentially in his book, might *better deserve* the title of 'daughter of Israel'. She is certainly a daughter. Jesus' tangent with this other daughter of Abraham, however thought provoking, has only slowed things up.

This has slowed them up cunningly, if you are Jesus, because Jairus too, unbeknownst to himself, is also to be an enacted prophecy. Jesus is packing them in. Accelerating you see. Drawing men and women to himself more intensely, more laden with meaning as he heads towards His ultimate "drawing".

We have to, and I would suggest it is interesting and a duty to so do, think ourselves into this story. What did go on in Jairus' house that day? I mean come on, this guy is the leader of the synagogue. The party position on Jesus in that movement is not great – some of them have already tried to fling Him off a cliff for blasphemy. So what did happen? Well, let's tarry a moment on two readings.

Reading one: Resistance: Jairus is at home, he is attended by friends and relatives as the condition of his daughter has worsened. Prayers will ring through the house as people recite them and try to lift her to God.

Whispered counsel will reach Jairus' ears, wise words from wise friends. He may well be fasting at this point, praying more regularly and with more force than he ever has. He may well have to think his way through his Sabbath address this week, where he is going to read from? What is he going to confirm about Israel's great God?

Dispatches reach him, to confirm that it is not going well, breathing is shallow; unconsciousness deepens. A wise friend places a hand on his forearm meaningfully to convey strength in God's will, but the place is like a mausoleum, whatever they are saying with their lips, their eyes are convinced she is going to die. Suddenly a young man bursts in all wrong-sized shoes and hair unkempt. He's begun speaking before he has read the room.

"He's back, Jesus is back, there's a huge crowd gathering on the outskirts of town, what shall we do?!"

Looks silence the youth.

"What shall we do?" repeats Jairus, to no one in particular, "what shall we do?" and he stands up full of resolve.

"Jairus, leave him", says a voice from the corner, "someone else can go, nobody is expecting you to bother..."

"Bother", whispers Jairus, "everyone is expecting me to bother him, everyone wants me to stand up to his face and defend our place and our nation against him and his miracle working, don't think you can heal here on the Sabbath Jesus, we don't want any of that nonsense, don't think you can heal in our Synagogue Jesus it has no need of you, don't think you can challenge us with your healings to test us like you have done elsewhere, we are not impressed with your healing, we don't want that here!"

"Well said Jairus, but another time not today, not with your daughter the way she is, rest and pray, God will out. We all understand what you are going through." And Jairus just looks through him.

"We all understand why he can't go around healing here."

The door opens a crack, his wife catches his gaze. That's when he feels it. The drawing.

In hindsight he should have just left there and then, but he didn't, he wasted another hour arguing with them, letting them beat him down, but they did not succeed. "Enough of this, my mind is made up, I'll bother him to come to my home, here, if it's true our people don't need his miracle working then so be it, but I need it, if you say there will be consequences, so be it, let them come! Will it be of no consequence to me at all if I bother him to come here and she is made well? What price your disapproval, you speak as if you had no daughters yourselves..."

He leaves distraught. He finds Jesus, he humbles himself, Jesus accepts and does not humiliate. The healing of this woman interrupts, long enough for the faces to come through the crowd, a chill attends them. They are angry faces, as angry as they were when he swept past them out of the door. Faces that have settled on the sword.

"Your daughter is dead", they said. "Why bother the teacher anymore?"

Straight through the heart. Jairus' inner wall collapses. A door opens a crack; he catches the gaze of Jesus.

Ignoring what they said, Jesus told the synagogue ruler, "Don't be afraid; just believe."

Heady stuff, but let's allow another of the (many possible) readings before we progress:

Reading two: Acquiescence: Jairus is at home, he is attended by friends and relatives as the condition of his daughter has worsened. Prayers will ring through the house as people recite them and try to lift her to God. Whispered counsel will reach Jairus' ears, wise words from wise friends. He may well be fasting at this point, praying more regularly and with more force than he ever has. He may well have to think his way through his Sabbath address this week, where he is going to read from? What is he going to confirm about Israel's great God?

Dispatches reach him, to confirm that it is not going well, breathing is shallow; unconsciousness deepens. A wise friend places a hand on his forearm meaningfully to convey strength in God's will, but the place is like a mausoleum, whatever they are saying with their lips, their eyes are convinced she is going to die. Suddenly a young man bursts in all wrong-sized shoes and hair unkempt. He's begun speaking before he has read the room.

"He's back, Jesus is back, there's a huge crowd gathering on the outskirts of town", he looks to the others, "What shall we do?!"

All looks turn to Jairus.

"What shall we do?" repeats Jairus, to no one in particular, "what shall we do?" and he stands up full of resolve.

"Jairus, it's worth a try", says a voice from the corner, "he might be a trouble maker but we have investigated several of these healings ourselves, he really does heal, at a time like this what are you to care for appearances..."

"Appearances", whispers Jairus, "is that what you think we do here, is that what we are worth? Can our place and our nation be swept aside because it was only an appearance? Here he comes breaking our law with his miracles and they are all that matter, is that it? Moses did miracles, but he also upheld a law, this rabble who know nothing of the law chase him on land, on sea running after him like sheep! Are we not good enough shepherds for them? Is the Law of Moses an appearance? He heals on the Sabbath, is the Sabbath an appearance? He disrespects the synagogue, is the synagogue an appearance? He challenges our authority, is our authority an appearance? Shall we hand it to him and the key to the kingdom with it?! Is my service to God a mere appearance that you expect me to go to him?"

Deep in his house, a door slams. That's when he feels it. The drawing.

In hindsight he should have just stayed where he was, but he didn't, he'd wasted another hour arguing with them, and then he'd let them beat him down. "Fine, my mind is made up, I'll bother this itinerant to come to my home, here, I'll humble myself to be in need of his miracles, there will be consequences, but fine, let them come, it'll be of more consequence to me if I don't bother him to come here and she dies. What price is the appearance of my own disapproval, you speak as those who have daughters yourselves..."

He leaves distraught. He finds Jesus, he humbles himself, Jesus accepts and does not humiliate. The healing of this woman interrupts, long enough for the faces to come through the crowd, a chill attends them. They are complex faces, more conflicted now than when he swept past them out of the door. Faces that have seen the sword.

"Your daughter is dead", they said. "Why bother the teacher anymore?"

Straight through the heart, victory to the enemy with hardly a battle. Jairus' inner wall collapses. A door slams shut – in the gaze of Jesus.

Ignoring what they said, Jesus told the synagogue ruler, "Don't be afraid; just believe."

Well here's an edge and no mistake. Almost everything that the controversy of Jesus is about hangs on this little moment of inter-action with Israel's identity displayed in Moses' spiritual bloodline right here. This is so, irrespective of which story it is that is actually being played out because, annoyingly, we don't know which it is.

Jairus, who in Mark's gospel, is four times referred to as "the synagogue leader" as if the writer cannot understand what is unfolding. We are not told once, like a conventional narrative, we are told four times. Mark only stops calling him that to call him the girl's father. Jairus, synagogue ruler and father, has gambled and appears to have lost. At that particular moment, it must have felt like he had lost it all, been tricked out of it even. It's heady stuff. Jesus, having brought him to this edge, fixes him to the spot. "Don't be afraid". Afraid of what? It's an interesting question. When your daughter is dead you can't be afraid of that anymore can you? What was Jairus afraid of, what did Jesus see? Well, we don't know, but Jesus' sense of Jairus at this point is that he is afraid. Jesus meets that immediate anxiety categorically, revealing that, whoever Jesus turns out to be, He can see well enough into Jairus' soul.

Jesus, having fixed him to this spot, moves him on. "Just believe." Believe what? These are coded words, perhaps even private words. There would appear to be nothing for Jairus to believe that would come to aught. If this is Jesus suggesting that all will be well in some future place when Jairus' daughter is buried and the consequences of his momentary, but futile, faith in this Jesus falls on him from a great height. If Jesus is trying to suggest that Jairus somehow has to have faith in that this is God's will, the Lord gives and the Lord takes away. Or worse, if Jesus is imploring Jairus to have faith in Him that will outlive this still birth.

Well, that's nuts.

Then we get to it, the real edge. Jesus of Nazareth heals demon possession (big time) and, having stopped along the way to restore an "unclean" Daughter of Israel (Israel is mostly female in the bible, did you notice?), He sets his face resolutely for that house. The house where we have been told that a "little daughter" (of Israel) lies dead.

What few details we have, they are curious. Jesus in the whirlwind that is whipping around him with surviving a furious squall unscathed, the casting out of legions of demons, the cleansing of this un-cleansable woman, arranges that the next installment – in what is turning into a summer blockbuster run – is to be kept under wraps.

Whatever happens and how it is arranged, He manages to take Jairus, the men from the house and only three of his disciples with Him. Quite how the huge crowd pressing in on Him is dissuaded from jumping on the bandwagon is a lost fact. Whatever Jesus is going to do, it is going to be, by His own standards, and the standards of the momentum of His present mission, intimate. Personal.

Jairus, presumably numbed by all this, shows the way. Is Jesus really planning to try and be a guest at this funeral? Does Jesus really think that an audience with the synagogue ruler is still on the cards? Whatever is going through Jairus' brain, he leads Jesus to his house. A distraught house. A house of mourning. Professional wailers, as befits a man of Jairus' standing, are already drawing their full wages.

When they came to the home of the synagogue ruler, Jesus saw a commotion, with people crying and wailing loudly. He went in and said to them, "Why all this commotion and wailing? The child is not dead but asleep". But they laughed at him.

Laughed at Him or not, somehow in this bizarre little roller-coaster, the circumstance arises that a dead child, a mother, a father – the family that stands for God's synagogue – are left in the room. This is the first time Jairus has laid eyes on the finality of the situation. This is the first time he AND his wife have been drawn together over the trauma of the loss of flesh of their flesh, bone of their bones.

Is it really dawning upon Jairus at all that he has deliberately invited Jesus, Jesus for goodness sake, into his home at the peak of this? How has his wife responded to this wholly inappropriate invasion of their family at a time like this by a band of rock stars?

Jesus, Peter, James and John – the core of the family that stands for God's future church – are, mad as it seems, standing there too. In the bedroom of a dead twelve year old, Justin Bieber reaching out to them from the walls (in case future generations read this book Justin Bieber was/is a pop star much favored by girls of a certain age).

Peter, James and John have seen some crazy things as they have followed this Jesus. Things that they could not have expected at the outset by the Sea of Galilee. Even (or is it particularly?) in the last two days the game has moved on considerably. But what now? They are, all of them, in the presence of the finality of death. Jairus and his wife, maybe just staring into the middle ground. Peter, James and John possibly none too sure of their ground here. Jesus, on intense ground. Girl dead, heading for the ground.

So we come to her. For all we strain into this miracle, we are compromised by what we know is about to happen. So, take a moment to personalize this, all you parents in the room. This little daughter is dead. The power of Jesus' gospel has not yet been revealed, imagine you don't know that He defeats death. Imagine your little daughter lies there dead and Jesus has told you not to be afraid but to believe, believe what precisely?

Mark comments, somewhat poignantly I feel, that it is Jesus who led them into the room. Not Jairus. Whatever business Jairus had with Jesus on the whole "don't be afraid, just believe" front, it wasn't in that room.

> *After he put them all out, he took the child's father and mother and the disciples who were with him, and went in where the child was. He took her by the hand and said to her, "Talitha koum!" (which means, "Little girl, I say to you, get up!"). Immediately the girl stood up and walked around (she was twelve years old). At this they were completely astonished. He gave strict orders not to let anyone know about this, and told them to give her something to eat.*

You know, after all this time, we can't help ourselves, we read this in a blasé manner. This should be BOOM! And we have become all of course about it.

The greatest defining characteristic of this miracle is the power of Jesus' personality to overcome everything that screams from the pages against it. The most startling fact about it remains its seeming ordinariness to Him and His advancing kingdom agenda. Does He grandstand for a moment, pray to heaven, 'father you have heard me now vindicate your servant'? No. Does He say to those collected 'now you shall see the power of the father coming in His kingdom'? No. So does He do *anything* demonstrable that is aligned with His kingdom agenda? Yes, yes He does.

That part hinges on who it is that is lying there. That's the question at the heart of this miracle. Just like Jeff, just like Mary hot upon the heels of whose stories Jesus finds himself accelerating through this room, 'who is this' is the key question in the frame of these events.

If you are this little girl, are you passive in this story? If we are talking about Jesus meeting people at the edge then we get to this finally. This little girl, the name of whom Jesus does not even enquire for it seems, has gone the farthest away from anyone's reach it is possible to go and still be warmer than the surrounding air. She has died convincingly enough (for there is even still some conjecture that she was only in a coma).

What was, let's call her Susie, what was Susie's post-mortem experience? What was her journey, who accompanied her, whom did she meet, what was she doing? She was passing, whatever that can mean, she was doing it. Every part of the Christian belief structure cries out that, whatever it was, she will have been conscious of doing it. We stand or fall on that frail fact.

She was on her way to the very edge of all possible existence as a human being.

And then she hears a command, in Aramaic, the language of the familiar. It is straight forward, it says get up. She obeys, and what does she see? Here is this strange man in her room, he is holding her hand. Here are these other strange men behind him, they look a little freaked. Here are mother and father leaning, straining, rushing forward their faces aghast. And what of this man holding her hand? Well, it's a mystical question isn't it? But He is real, she can feel His touch, and when she hears His voice, she recognizes it as the one who called her out of death and into life.

BOOM.

And Jesus out of a motivation which we can only speculate is to do with the conversations that were held in Jairus' house before Jairus found the strength to seek Him; out of compassion for a little girl whom He does not want to turn into a freak show for the whole town, and nearby tourists as well; out of the intensity of the purpose of this bizarre sequence of events which seems to have been to offer Jairus and his house, the household of the synagogue, an intimacy with God finding its pinnacle around facing and accepting death; out of all this, Jesus sets them an almighty challenge and He makes sure they know He is serious. *Tell no one.* This is not for the crowd. This is not for me and my purposes (not yet). This is how God meets you.

BOOM squared.

As if to accentuate that, Jesus says, *"give her something to eat".* Let's get back to normal...

...and if you are making something to eat.

What do we make of the exorcised man, the cleansed woman, the resurrected child? Well, of Jeff we have said enough. However, for the woman and for the child there is one more thing to mention, one more accelerator. A fine detail we should not ignore in the sweep of the spectacle of the stage that Jesus is setting, testified by all three synoptic gospels, before He faces the cross. Mark, ever the mustard seed guy, says that the woman had been subject to bleeding for twelve years. He also notes that the child who was dead had been twelve years old.

Micro boom.

Jesus saves. This we know. But how He saves. Jeff is released against the odds and against the grain of everything Israel is straining for, as far as Israel is concerned Jeff could have gone to hell, not on my watch, says Jesus. Jeff stands for those who are not Israel, and yet are redeemable in Jesus' mission.

The woman and the child have the number twelve in common in their stories and this, to me, is no mistake or pathological attention to detail. This is just as meaning-laden as Jesus' decision to have twelve close disciples.

The cleansed woman stands for the state into which Israel has plunged, unclean. How unclean? Twelve years' worth. One year for each of the twelve tribes, completely unclean.

Jairus' daughter stands, not just in the life of Jairus and his wife, but in the symbolic praxis of Jesus, for the hope of Israel, her future, a future that is apparently dead. How dead? Twelve years' worth. One year of death for each of the twelve tribes. Completely dead.

Jesus stands in the midst of their fates as the great reverser of Israel's fates. Heaven bringer. Kingdom announcer. Healer, even of her death. It cannot escape our attention. The particular circumstances of the very real people and the very real physicality to which they are subject aside, these people, at the touch of Jesus, stand for all Israel's fate. These people have been placed there by the sovereignty of God to anthropomorphize His kingdom. They are, in and of His will and ownership of their lives and circumstance, tough as that is to bear, pre-destined as kingdom announcers. Their stories, through Jesus, enact the arrival of the kingdom of God.

How apposite that they should be so, as witnessed by the ruler of the synagogue no less, who is supposed to have that as his job description.

Mark says, did I mention that Jairus was the ruler of the synagogue? You'd expect that from John's gospel, he's the screenplay writer. Mark, straining at the kingdom leash the whole time, stops in these stories to ponder for himself not a kingdom proclaimed from a hilltop to thousands with imagery, but one demonstrated in an inner room to a significant few with intimacy. A few who had been humble enough – despite the great cost to their lifestyle and value system – to ask to see the king.

After all this has passed, Jesus says, let's eat together (let's pause for a normal touchstone of intimacy wherein undoubtedly we can discuss these and other things) if that is all right with you.

He eats (and talks) and then accelerates away.

A woman (and a boy)

We leave Jairus, his wife and their daughter to their sandwiches and travel to Nain. There we will find that a mother and son are waiting. What's about to happen is much bigger than raising someone from the dead after a few minutes. Eeek! Bigger! Jesus, I'm not sure my nerves can take much more of this.

Technically, we have to go back to Nain. If I'd been writing the gospel I'd have placed this story after the three we have considered so far, but, for Luke, the only gospel writer who tells this tale (see, better research), it comes before. Those helpful NIV translators seem to agree with me because, in the version I have, they put a little header note on this story linking it to the story of Jairus' daughter in particular. They seem to see them as a pair. Me too.

...because Eve and Adam were a pair. Just thought I'd throw that in there as a loss leader.

The particular question on my mind at this point in our proceedings has to be why didn't Sergio Leone and Hugo Montenegro decide to tackle bible narrative? They would have been made for this particular story; this day in Nain. In case that's a geeky reference, the former is a film director, famous for the Spaghetti Western genre, and the latter created their iconic scores – like the theme tune to *The Good the Bad and the Ugly*. That tune should be compulsory to play in churches whenever this story is told.

You know the drill by now, I want to look at this story and talk about who the key character was, is now and will be. This is, as promised, another one of those "Jesus meets us at the edge stories". I'm not sure what you are making of my broader theology at this point, since this is not a theology book, but this is another story where we are dealing with "a thin place". The kingdom which is not of this world, the great arena, is hovering "in the air" so to speak of this world. We become more aware of that due to Jesus' disrupting presence.

As Paul puts it, our battle is not against flesh and blood but against the rulers of this age, its principalities and powers. That's longhand for Satan and all his little wizards essentially. Accepting that these events have a spiritual dimension is critical for how we should be reading Jesus here. What we are seeing, what Jesus does through the bigger lens of "enacted prophecy", how Jesus brings His kingdom, all these hinge on how you read that battle.

This story of 'a day to remember in Nain' is not, therefore, just another resurrection story. It's a story of Jesus declaring war. Something we sometimes miss in such a slender text. But Sergio, he wouldn't have let us miss that. If you read the bible, a good discipline with tricky passages is to do that thing your dad sometimes inexplicably did when he was reversing the car. You have to put your left arm (modify as appropriate for all my many international readers) across the back of the passenger seat – as this somehow makes reversing seem cool; probably because you get an excuse to steer with one hand.

So, left arm up, and reverse, just how did we get to Nain of all places?

Well, we can comfortably start with the "cornfield Messiah", remember that story? The first one we told in this book. Jesus claiming to be Lord of the Sabbath and all the controversy that courts.

We move through Him appointing his twelve apostles, twelve being a non-accidental number, a kingdom metaphor for His restoration, reformation in fact, of the twelve tribes of Israel.

In some readings that kind of makes Jesus the new Abraham. He was hip to that, of course, because that was how Abraham *would* bless the whole world.

Jesus has been healing, exorcising and everyone knows He has power because the healings and exorcisms are real.

Jesus has been teaching controversial sermons (Bonhoeffer will later dedicate the bulk of "The Cost of Discipleship" to one sermon on a hill. Luke's version of it is stripped to the bone and focuses on love for enemies).

Jesus teaches on judgment and says *"why do you call me, 'Lord, Lord' and do not do what I say?"*

Jesus heals the servant of a centurion from Capernaum and, upon observing the manner in which this Roman centurion can cope with His authority to do so, comments that "even in Israel" He has never seen the kind of faith this centurion shows. This might make the Jews a little huffy, perhaps they wanted Him to heal without zeal.

When you drive in reverse like this you can't help but notice that in 'the story on the way to Nain' Jesus has been an enactment (an embodiment in fact) of the prophecies surrounding Abraham and God's wordwide (and worldwide) covenant with him. Luke's Jesus even makes this easy for us to conclude, what with Him quoting Isaiah's reclamation of the world as His starting point (some of them already want to kill Jesus because of this audacity). Jesus then systematically lays claim to the Sabbath, the Nation, the (true) Law, Love for one another, a World redemption (even for Israel's sworn military enemies) and all this He brings to bear in an enacted ministry which excites everyone who sees it (for differing reasons). Luke, somehow, manages to ram all this in *before* we get to Nain. He wants to set up a mini-mandate *already* that Jesus is the great reversal because that is the perfect Jesus to approach the outskirts of Nain at this point.

Try seeing Jesus' presence here in Paul's military terms, those of the battle against *"the spiritual forces of evil in the heavenly realms"*. Jesus is starting to look like a serious threat to the border and He is moving with unlikely success.

Now, if you were *the powers of this dark world*, essentially the ruling oppressor behind this scene, then you'd most likely think to yourself: what I need here is a smack down. That's what's behind the veil of the "Nain incident".

I mean THE enemy, who can see what Jesus is up to, already knows after forty days of fruitless negotiation that diplomacy and compromise will not avail him. So, when he sees Jesus and his newly 'branded and banded' Israel making its way across the plains. When he sees Jesus capturing town after town winning the hearts of the people with a force that will go on to capture the twin treasures of Jeff and Jairus. He knows he needs to send out his elite strike force for a showdown. Jesus is not the only one who is skilled in the use of enacted prophecy; the enemy knows a thing or two about this as well.

So, cue music and take it away Sergio:

Panning shot: Nain has a city wall, a city gate and there is an open plain beyond.

Long range rising view 'crowd shot': We see Jesus' mission group, coming through the heat haze, headed by Jesus, coming to town, kicking up the dust in their multitude, feel the buzz of the animated crowd.

Close up: the city doors opening, 'a welcome', seems to hang, and falter. The only thing to leave the gate initially is a small black scorpion. It scurries quick enough because behind it here is another large crowd. In comparison to Jesus' companions, they look dead. Defeated, inanimate, they make their way out to the plain. They part on cue and make way to be headed up by a coffin. The scorpion runs under it. The way in to the city becomes increasingly blocked by streams of mourners spilling listlessly into the plain.

Long depth of field shot: Jesus is just visible and out of focus beyond the edge of the coffin. Walking purposefully, coming out of the desert, coming past the graveyard to meet them. The shot opens up to reveal the mourners' take on this, in their body language it's clear that some of them are none too happy about His approach.

Spin shot: That tension reaches Jesus' people, one of them sees the coffin, her face says she knows that dead people, and the articles around them, make you unclean. So will Jesus stand aside so as not to be contaminated if He wants to speak in the Synagogue this Sabbath? Will His kingdom procession give way just out of respect for the dead? Will He put off his entrance until tomorrow? If there is a large crowd off to bury and have a wake, who will there be left in the city to hear the message in any case?

Intense close up: Jesus' eyes. The disciples' heads come into shot framing him. He stops. The disciples catch the mood and look up and down the field and then at Jesus. They see Him looking, watch Him wait.

Three sixty motion: All the way around both crowds, both scenes faster and faster and faster. The scorpion makes his way to the center ground and both crowds pivot around him and respectively close in on him from the front and the rear. He freezes, pincers lifted and the crowds spin faster and faster getting closer and closer as he stands eerily still, almost, beckoning them close.

Freeze with intercut crowd slo-mo: The back of Jesus' head, the coffin bobbing just in shot over his shoulder getting larger and larger, the faces of the mourners looking less and less glad. The frisson of gesticulation among the entourage to move aside and let them come uninterrupted straight through.

Profile shot: Jesus' eyes alone, in open plain, a coffin enters. It stops impossibly close to his head. The mother of the dead completes the frame with grace. She obscures the coffin, before Jesus. She looks at him and cries new tears. He reaches out a hand to her cheek. "Don't cry", some of the mourners, in silence and slow motion, are appalled; Jesus' disciples are rabbits in the headlights.

Jesus steps towards the scorpion.

Ah Sergio, we need you more than ever.

Soon afterward, Jesus went to a town called Nain, and his disciples and a large crowd went along with him. As he approached the town gate, a dead person was being carried out – the only son of his mother, and she was a widow. A large crowd from the town was with her. When the Lord saw her, his heart went out to her and he said, "Don't cry".

Then he went up and touched the coffin, and those carrying it stood still. He said, "Young man, I say to you, get up!" The dead man sat up and began to talk, and Jesus gave him back to his mother.

They were all filled with awe and praised God. "A great prophet has appeared among us," they said. "God has come to help his people." This news about Jesus spread throughout Judea and the surrounding country.

This story centers on "sons", and how Jesus' enacted prophecy (which forcefully brings in the kingdom) faces off death itself. And that's not just in the case of a corpse of one son of Israel, not at all.

This crowd, in witnessing the force of the kingdom come are, of course, just the crowd, they are a bit hapless really. Their excitement around what Jesus is capable of in miracles and teaching has grown, and with it His entourage and the general buzz. In this instance, Jesus actually gives them en masse a role in His prophecy, they are, for one night only, the kingdom people.

This mother was a widow we are told. So the death of her only son is no small matter. At this point in His ministry when Jesus meets the literal children of Israel (His proto Eve – Jairus' daughter, His proto Adam – this son of mother Israel) it is telling that they are all dead.

For the mother to be a widow with no male relatives and no one else to marry her, is to have lost her rights to her property and her standing; it will pass to another. Israel, of course, is a widow too in this story. She has lost her husband (God), she has no redeemer (the prophets are gone) like the physical woman in this symbolic re-enactment, she has no son to protect her (yet?) and so she, too, in consequence lost her property, her standing and self-determination. Cue Roman occupation.

The contrast between the two crowds has a role here. They stand toe to toe; one for the people of death and loss; one for the people of the "not yet kingdom". They too, meet on the plain. An implicit challenge. Stopped together, a resolution imminent, death, clearly the stronger force. The kingdom can come another time, after all what's Jesus going to achieve when a whole town is in mourning? Take your circus somewhere else Messiah-boy, no room at the inn here.

"Don't cry", an appalling, stupid thing to say. Her son is dead, her hope is gone, we haven't even got him in the tomb yet and you and your holy junket have the brass neck to say that this is not a time for crying. What's going to stop such crying? God may well wipe every tear from every eye when the kingdom comes, but you can't wipe these tears just because it's ruining your mission meeting. You can take your copycat kingdom carpet bag to another town, go sell crazy someplace else, we are all stocked up.

Jesus touches the coffin; He deliberately makes Himself unclean, a Rabbi becoming unclean for no good reason. Well here's a showboat. He touches the coffin not as He slips by it, surrendering his status as clean by way of consolation; He touches it by standing in front of it and making it stop. Death's muscles bristle with power, the pall bearers' feet stumble. Death is running its course, Jesus makes it stop.

What does He want us to do? Take the coffin out of the way; take death back to the house until He has passed by? Well there's a cheek. There are some things that are more important than what you want to do in this time, Jesus and the death of this son is certainly one of them. How dare you prevent us from processing death to its final place!

The wind blows where it pleases.

Then Jesus, more forcefully than in Jairus' daughter's case, makes the same request. In Susie's case Jesus just said 'little child arise'.

In this case He is forceful. He says *"I say to you get up"*. Why the personalized distinction, why not just get up? Because another 'I' had said to him "lie down" (in the dust). Jesus wanted them all, and that someone else in particular, to know He was reversing that command, He was overturning it. He was smacking it down.

This boy splutters into life and sees the son through the bandages of death with the smell of myrrh in his nostrils. Jesus gave him back to his mother, which makes me feel he was only young. In any case, Jesus restored her inheritance, gave her a hope, proving along the way that death itself could not stop (would not stop) what He was starting.

Figuratively, as this enacted prophecy comes into view, the mother stands for Israel without hope, husband or inheritance. Jesus restores her inheritance, by resurrecting a son. This (first) resurrection shows her that, against all hope and against her own power to reverse things, God, her lover, has come in rescue. He has brought her life out of death and He has done it through the resurrection of a son.

We have to look too at the crowd Jesus leads in His train – the kingdom people erupting in joy. The other crowd, the death people, are transformed. We have to look at a whole world symbolized by these two crowds where they become one, a joyous, rapturous merging into a "one kingdom" people.

They were all filled with awe (understatement) and said a great prophet has appeared. That's because they knew that both Elisha and Elijah healed the dead sons of widows, it was their badge of authority in Israel and outside. They were taking this as "a sign". As well they should. This is not just a hailing of a prophet though (the prophet?). Immediately sparks fly in a discussion on the rationale for His arrival. The speedy conclusion, fueled no doubt by some of Jesus' own "followers" at this point, is that "God has come to help his people". Hmm, interesting, what do God's people need help with the most at the moment, why it's Rome! Oh, this is good stuff…

The text says "this news" and I would argue it's this news about a forthcoming opposition to Rome perceived in Jesus – through the cultural expectation of what 'one like Him' would do (indeed others have in the past) that spreads. In another place we find that Jesus withdrew from a crowd and an area because He knew they intended to come and make him king by force, so don't think I am making this stuff up. Oh and incidentally he raised that dead kid to life, how cool is that! Who knew!

Jesus knew, from the moment Death broke cover to challenge Him outside that town, that the stakes were getting higher. From the moment Death wanted to say to Him 'thus far you can go and no further', the enemy was mobilizing. Death's easy recruits, God's own people, had been harassed into being complicit with the enemy's Public Relations machine. Easily convinced to accept Death as the great leveler, the amoral conclusion. Death the all in all. Then the transformative power of Jesus meets Death on that plane and kicks his scorpion arse. God is the great leveler, even of you. God is all in all, take your sorry little sting back where it came from. This son shall live.

What is going to happen is heralded by the resurrection of the son of Israel. In a few moments Jesus is going off to meet Jeff, Mary and Susie, adopted son, transformed daughter, resurrected child. There will be no stopping Him now. The Son brings life, and Death hath no dominion. For now though, the crowds in Nain must be thinking 'what happens next?'

P.A.R.T. Why? – Because we have to! That's what happened next. Jesus converted all these mourners with the power of resurrection. Jesus redoubles the kingdom crowd, absorbs the mourners, and Jesus, ever the one for a bit of dinner suggests that it's time to get the barbeque lit. That's what happens, the defeat of death is not anodyne or religious or half-baked. It's an excuse for at least a whole night of partying. Songs of mourning will be replaced by songs of joy, and we daresay a few new wineskins might be hastily opened.

The boy sits and talks with Jesus, why wouldn't he? The boy's mother keeps rushing up with another lamb kebab whenever Jesus' plate is empty and kissing his laughing face on the cheeks again and again and dancing off. The disciples are in the mix telling tales of Jesus before this point. There's rejoicing and dancing and music and praising God for what He has done.

In corners, serious chaps are doing some seriously sullen thinking, some because they don't like all this, and some because they are thinking militarily. And Jesus fixes the gaze of the enemy across that (temporarily) happy campfire and in the portent shadow of the sullen.

'So you like sons who live...', thinks the enemy.

'No', thinks Jesus, 'I like Sons who die for sons and daughters who live'.

'Rome favors a smack down approach too you know', thinks the enemy.

'I know', thinks Jesus.

And fade...

So, here's a Gadfly moment for the last two chapters on the hermeneutic of Jesus then.

- Am I saying that we follow a Jesus who actually supports a necessary internal, personal critique of the purpose of scriptural authority?
- Am I saying the advancing kingdom of Jesus needs to be read through actual lives of real people that God – in His sovereignty – willfully harnesses into "living scriptures" so as to create the "thin places" in this world today?
- Am I saying that it is not coherent for the church to read the bible to be 'about Jesus' but that we actually have to read the bible through Jesus, so that the church, mirroring His praxis, becomes the enacted satisfaction of His story?

Yes, that's exactly what I am saying.

Prologue to the Final Two Chapters

For the last eight chapters I have been trying, with limited success in places of course, and hopefully with a little dash of narrative brilliance now and then, to say something significant to the modern church, looking all this time for "a new reading" of that. I've been trying to do this without reverting to just criticizing the church for its failings, which any fool can do. More fool me if this is all that I have expended so much effort for.

I've been genuinely wrestling not to write a "sermonologue", because I set out to write something helpful; something deep. The monologue inherent in writing is inescapable of course and this can make it a dangerously impersonal task. There is always a risk of beating people up with ideas and offering them no redress. There's always a risk of pounding on the door of prototypes and stereotypes that say nothing to, or of, anyone's real experience. Too many Christian books fall into this class for my liking. I'm sure I've come close here, at times, to doing just that.

To minimize that risk, I have tried to reach out from the pages as if you and I were at least locked in conversation about these things and, who knows, maybe one day we will be. I've been trusting that we do have a shared life, you and I. That's why I have spoken to you about the bible in the way I have, assuming that you know it well, so as not to be patronizing, even if I do come off a little preachy and up myself.

There is good reason, of course, for the "preachy" part. This is simply because I am a preacher. In my journeying for an authentic expression of "church" these last few years, I have successfully evicted myself from all but a few of my opportunities to speak. I have chosen to burn instead in another way. The fruits of this are in your hand. I have wrestled for what I think God's church, in its very bones, maybe ought to be like. I've tried to offer this to us both through a complex "reading" of church.

That's because, to me, these bones are knitted together in the womb of the bible.

So, what I have really been attempting to do is "illuminate" that pre-existing script, straining to rise to the calling of every preacher, to shine some innovative light on the church through the bible to reveal more of something that it affirms is beautiful; something holy.

Now that we are coming to the end of that, you have every right to ask me: "So what exactly is it then that you were trying to say Mr. Arthur?"

That's a great question.

That is where the real danger in a piece of writing like this lies; that I run out of steam; that I simply bring things to no conclusion. Worse than this, I could round things off in an unsatisfactorily "samey" way by paraphrasing everything that I have said already and then saying it again. How annoyingly sermon-like would that be?

Before setting off on the last bit of the journey let me just pause then and say something simple for once:

I owe you my gratitude for reading all this stuff. You honor me in the reading of it.

As we bring our conversation to a close then, I want to run a final risk. I want to leave all that has been said, trusting that you have heard me. So, hopefully, together at this point, we could just step off the edge of it into something new.

Right?

Here then, is my final Gadfly moment.

- Am I trying to say that I think the modern church is missing a sacrament?

Yes, that is exactly what I am saying.

An assertion like that forces us all full circle. We (and I) have to say precisely what we mean by "church" and, if we are honest, there is a problem for us here. The problem is that the 'pluriform' of expressions that we collect under that term may actually be more different than alike. Onlookers could even be forgiven for saying no two expressions of it really *are* the same thing at all. The millennia of waves of theology, ecclesiology and 'missiology', that just keep rolling out from the church and attempting to crash on the timeless shores of the human condition maybe do little to ease our definitional anxiety. Church was, is, and steadfastly remains a wrestling matter.

We can conclude that even before rationalism and empiricism, recently re-enforced by post-modernism and buttressed further by new-wave atheism, have sought to delimit us, or neutralize our claim to influence. Before we, ourselves play that constant game of leapfrog with technology, culture, sociology and even soteriology in our perennial struggle to define an alternative church movement.

Defining Church, for a lot of us a lot of the time, is to be straining for something 'contemporary but continuous' which, when you examine the ritual baggage it brings with it, is always just out of evidential reach. In our evidential, behavioral definition of church it is obvious we are wrestling to protect that which, though we recognize it to be anachronistic, is yet of great import to some. As to whether this genuinely protects our continuity or hampers our relevance to Jesus' 'word and world', well, the jury is out.

There is *one* thing, however, that defines *all* church. That is sacrament.

Which means that if I want to define a new one, I have to say precisely what I mean by sacrament. This immediately raises another kind of wrestle, of course. Each (or is that every?) church tradition varies as to how it locates sacrament: is this best effected in a far away heaven; at a distance in an inner sanctum; close by but on the other side of an altar; just a wafer on the tongue away; penetrating all the way inside the spirit of a private individual through an altered state of perception?

Wherever it is believed to be enacted to one side, the fact *that* sacramental experience is sought remains the unquestionable core of what any church is up to. The church, in all its diverse forms, therefore, stands or falls on access to the divine. This common bond of church as a place of sacrament is where there is hope 'in and for' a 'contemporary continuity'. It is also what makes it possible to say something new to "the church", for all its ancient diversity, and somehow still be addressing everyone in it.

To (mad as it seems) offer the church a new sacrament at this late stage we have to say something new. This new thing has not been a call to new wave mysticism, monasticism, transcendentalism or charismatic experientialism. It is a call to the sacramental intimacy...

...of risk.

In my last Gadfly moment then, I'll attempt to conclusively set out the form of this missing sacrament along with some of the smaller discrete risks inherent in it. It comes in four final forms. These do rest, a bit like an uncertain child on the shoulders of an over-confident parent, wobblingly on top of the rest of what I hope I have already said to you. So, in these closing two chapters it should not be at all surprising *how* we will attempt to take a deeper look at a hermeneutic of church through a hermeneutic of Jesus. This will lead us inexorably to "reading church through reading Jesus."

Reading church has to be predicated upon:
Intimacy with this world
Intimacy with each other

Reading Jesus is defined by:
Intimacy with the bible itself
Intimacy with Jesus Himself

To do this we will be using the same tools we have been using all along, and then our journey will be at an end...

A Reading of Jesus 3:
The King of the Half-told Kingdom

In this our final "reading of Jesus" we will lay out a concluding argument that the kingdom of heaven that Jesus gave was "incomplete". So, having already defended this point by referencing the kingdom parables and Jesus' proclamations/instructions to His disciples (and indeed church), we now turn to the crucifixion. We will see that even the crucifixion itself functions as a controlling story for Jesus which remains deliberately half-told. I want to suggest that the crucifixion of Jesus thus stands as the quintessence of God's imperative for a hermeneutic of church read through a hermeneutic of Jesus.

In responding to this hermeneutic the church can be seen as required by Jesus to become a sacrificial servant community, experiencing intimate communion with God and each other. Once this is achieved, that community will be unstoppable in holding this same kingdom out to the dark world in and through their radical discipleship to the resurrected person of Jesus – even if that costs us our lives. Easy…

So, we need to ask if, when the whole New Testament screams from the rafters all the way from Eden to the Jordan, that all the thin places till now proved transient, then how is this one – God's church – going to become permanent? To understand the answer to that question we have to go back to the church's origins and deal with how they came to the conclusion that it would be. We have to come back to the crucifixion; for you cannot really talk of Jesus lest He be crucified for you…

Jesus said: "I am the way"
If the disciples who were trying to decipher Jesus' kingdom parables and proclamations just needed time to unpack and understand fully what Jesus might have meant when He said He

was "conferring the kingdom" onto and into them, they weren't going to get it. Within a few short moments of Him telling them all this, all hell breaks loose. Jesus faces Gethsemane, the disciples are pants at everything, Jesus is arrested, abused, "numbered among the transgressors" and brutally killed. The disciples emerge from that wreckage, as a group and individually, threatened, blinking and bleeding. Importantly, nobody said 'so this is the kingdom then?'

But it was.

So, we in turn have to deal with this. We have to examine that wrecking and we have to ask, as they did, how on earth could that be "Jesus coming in His kingdom?" Having faced, with Jesus, the apocalypse of the death of the Son of God, the disciples needed to face a final challenge alone. In fact everyone who would believe in Jesus, every disciple, would have to face this challenge as well. Jesus had predicted the manner and the meaning of His death in His life. They just hadn't understood it; they didn't take Him literally enough. Their vision was still too blurred with ideas of the Messiah. So He had prayed for us whilst He had breath that clarity would come and He said it was all finished when He died.

All who were to subsequently follow Him would have to see past this death if they wanted to believe what He had said. The first time around this must have been nigh on impossible. I mean, come on Jesus, precisely *how* will something as formidable as Death and Hell be defeated through the kingdom of this church given what has just happened? How would the Eleven even be capable of believing that the gates of Hades would not prevail against them now? They so clearly have prevailed! Where, in the name of all things sacred, would the church Jesus said He was founding get the power to get back up from a smack down as final as this?

Well, they needed to realize something else about Jesus' kingdom stories and sayings. These had actually been setting the stage for *and* pointing to a thing He called 'the day of the Son of Man'. They had to go on from there and actually grasp the fullness of what Jesus' proclamations about that had referred to. Grasp the fact that the Son of Man would *actually* need to endure "his day" to fulfill these and other prophecies in order to satisfy the wrath of God on all flesh come down.

They would have to understand that Jesus, the Rabbi, wasn't always speaking metaphorically about the implications of the Kingdom come. After all, it was only then that Jesus could prove He was not just another trader in the marketplace of the heavily contested kingdom narrative. He was the outright owner of the market.

Many of Jesus' stories and pronouncements had pointed towards a perfect destruction. Jesus had taught them that they needed to recognize the kingdom in this – precisely because it was not what they were expecting. They would have to know it when they saw it. Jesus was predicting for them how it was He who would personally bring this kingdom with a single-minded and shocking finality. The *reason* His parables pointed inexorably to a perfect destruction was because they pointed to the crucifixion.

There needed to be 'a way' that Jesus' kingdom could come with a finality to end the hung imperative of destruction in all of those parables, an end to the landowner's justified wrath. That way lay in what Jesus had really meant in His conversation with Nicodemus that night:

"just as Moses lifted up the snake in the desert, so the Son of Man must be lifted up".

He was referring to an Old Testament event when the Israelites were still in the desert with Moses but had started the military campaign to found the original kingdom. To take the land God had promised. God had, however, instructed them to travel around Edom and they:

"grew impatient on the way; they spoke against God and against Moses".

God sent venomous snakes to attack them for this and many of them died. Realizing judgment was upon them they turned to Moses to intercede with God for them (again!). God gave Moses the way for the people to be put right with Him. It was a way which, at this point in the history of God's relating to the nation, took an uncharacteristically personal form. He required a personal faith-choice from every Israelite. God told Moses to make a bronze snake, to fashion a symbol of all that was going wrong. He was then to *"lift it up"* on a pole with an offer. Anyone who was bitten by a real snake need only *"look upon"* the symbolized punishment and they would live.

The snake Moses lifted up on that pole, at God's behest, represented deserved punishment for sin. It also represented a testimony that there was still *a way*, an imperative, urgent way that such sin could be dealt with – a way of salvation. The way was to show faith in the transformative patience and justice leveling grace which promised to lay aside the coming destruction. Jesus predicted to Nicodemus that for the Son of Man to come in His kingdom He himself must be lifted up just like this.

It's a simple fact, of course, that out of the many that occurred, you and I know about the crucifixion of Jesus. He wasn't crucified in such an outrageously public manner because He had to be. He had made it plain that He was laying down His life, that no one was taking it from Him. He practically has to shout this at Peter in Gethsemane to stop his pathetic, misguided call to arms. Whatever is going to happen, says Jesus, I'm allowing to happen. He wanted to be lifted up; He wanted us to be able to "look upon" the one we had pierced. Jesus meant to bring a solution more final than the temporary atonement power of anything that Moses and the law could ever have achieved. When He had finished teaching and showing them this way, He executed it.

It's tough this. Jesus, in acquiescing to the crucifixion in Gethsemane not Golgotha, demonstrates to us that He did not passively or accidentally take the wrath of God onto Himself. He was not, as some have said, a casualty of history or a martyr to philosophy. He wasn't dealing with His own personalized response to the wrath of God in an ascetic kind of way because He had somehow misinterpreted how "peace on earth" might reign. His was to be a visceral and final reckoning with the enemy of men. That's not the devil, not men themselves, the enemy in question is God Himself.

Now if that seems a little sharp-edged, how else do you explain, except by ignoring them, quite how plain nasty some of the wrong sides of Jesus' kingdom parables and sayings really are? Even that great celebratory wedding feast has a door through which the unfit are to be thrown out. These parables contain profound exclusions. They are like that because, on top of all its other functions (easily another whole book's worth), the crucifixion of the man Jesus in the first century and our continued telling (nay celebration) of it, has to take this whole world to this same edge. The power of experiencing the Jesus of the half-told kingdom is this then: in the perfection of sacrificial love He will demonstrate its supremacy over all other things. He will take the creation and us within it to the most shocking edge imaginable. So, here are three, necessarily incomplete, functions of Jesus' crucifixion:

- It is a demonstration of the reality and finality of God's wrath
- It is a prophetic act
- It is a recruitment poster for the church

The finality of God's wrath

Jesus was, in and through this death which He acquiesced to, actively modeling and experiencing the full effects of God's wrath. The weeds are burned; the fruitless trees are violently uprooted. Jesus deflects these onto Himself to demonstrate the justified wrath of the landowner. Join the army or build a tower, we must first sit down and count the cost. We must look upon the one who has been crushed. Tarry in the crushing. It has to define our motion. In the appalling hiatus of the crucifixion, Jesus isn't just being a martyr prophet to Israel's necessary plurality. He is actually enduring, and, therefore, modeling for us, the real wrath of God coming onto any real person.

This is no longer a weed in a field or a tree in a story, it's a real person like us, like me. A person like Him? Right in front of my eyes Jesus is showing this is a reality, not a metaphor, not a philosophy. What we are asked to wrestle with, therefore, anachronistic as it might seem for me to mention it in this way, is quite how appalling that is. That death. Jesus left nothing to chance, no stone unturned, no protest accepted. He fully tells it like it is. Proves it.

Read the words of Psalm 22, apply them to Jesus, rightly so as He applies them to himself with His closing, prophetic breaths. Ringing in the ears of the hearers of this song, Jesus calls His followers to a half-told story written, before you and for you. There is no other way that we might be saved. The original hearers of the time, brutal and misguided of course, say Jesus the miracle maker is rallying a final miracle to show off His power and His cause, so let's see what happens next. Of course nothing (apparently) does. His breath leaves Him; He sings the psalms no more. God crushes, utterly and utterly forsakes. His Gethsemane moment is passed into. That God rejects is a part of His story, is a part of His song. God will do this and His justice is unbearable.

Who is it that God rejects here? If He is nobody then this particular rejection is not of any significance.

It's a prophetic act

The crucifixion had the people of Israel as its first audience, this is not accidental, because salvation comes from the Jews, always has. Jesus was a prophet and, get this, He did not give up the office even in death. So His death, coupled to all the other functions it performs, is a prophecy. The witnesses are being shown the antithesis of the 'now kingdom', shown it in stark relief. In the manner of His death they (fore)see what awaited them if they persisted in holy xenophobia and revolutionary war (a same old storyline that God is no longer blessing). Crucifixion was applied by the Romans as a brutality of the time to punish sedition against the Holy Roman Empire and the Lord of that Empire, Caesar.

In the Denarii controversy, Jesus asks to be handed the coin for paying the tax. It bears a portrait of the most powerful man in the world (a graven image) and it bears the inscription 'Caesar is God'. Carrying his currency was complicity with that claim, enforced or otherwise. That's why the temple had money changers after all, who in their right mind would offer such a coin to God? The controversy over this coin is not about tax, it has a darker side and Jesus knows it. As N.T. Wright constantly points out, the man or men crucified next to Jesus were not thieves, they were bandits, revolutionary bandits, what we like to call terrorists; what terrorists like to call freedom fighters.

The worried Jewish leaders were protesting to each other that Jesus' activities cannot be allowed to continue lest:

"the Romans will come and take away both our place and our nation".

This *shows* that they understood the Roman machine and how it smacks down revolutionary freedom fighters, even confusingly unorthodox ones like Jesus, and how they all might be caught in the crossfire and the fallout. To avoid this, when the Jewish council have had quite enough of Jesus, they bundle Him through the judicial process. They wash their hands of His kingdom and speedily effect His crucifixion by the Roman war machine. This is doubly ironic in that they were probably doing that to take advantage of the popularity of Jesus' ministry to make Him into a cautionary spectacle for future upstart Messiahs as well.

The Jews thinking and acting this way shows that, despite the absence of a military agenda on Jesus' part, they could very much see a "worldwide implication" for the kingdom He was trying to announce through His miracles and preaching. They feared for the temple, they feared for their lives. So, Jesus is actually aided by them in this to be a prophet of God to His nation. He is aided *in the act of being crucified* (let that sink in). He dares to go beyond anything Ezekiel achieved in enacted prophecy. He prophesies right in front of their eyes, not the brutal expediency of Rome but the horror of God's wrath falling.

With that crucifixion (speaking loud and clear and long into the heritage of the prophets before him, even Caiaphas) Jesus shows that the wrath of God *is* coming on the nation of Israel and her plans. A wrath that has been promised from the beginning if they broke faith – cut this fig tree down!

Jesus had fed them some very useful evidence for His trial when He had dared to prophesy against the temple. He prophesied its destruction no less, which was not popular with those who were all the time looking for its (temporal) fulfillment. He said its destruction connoted the cancellation of the code it stood for. His God desired mercy, not sacrifice. So how the hell does the crucifixion show mercy? Well, tough as it is to take it, Jesus shows them in the crucifixion, as Caiphas had obliquely prophesied, that the total destruction of Israel (and the temple since, in some senses, they were synonymous at this time) was not necessary. It was not necessary if they accepted the perfect destruction of the one man. For that act to have any power to claim this, other than some kind of Socratean level of commitment to a philosophy, it has to leave open a hung prophetic imperative of its own, a half-told story waiting for an ending: Does it matter who it is that dies here?

If He is nobody then this is a horrific expedience but unimportant.

This is a part of why Jesus wept over Jerusalem, because she could not see from the scriptures how this was going to work. She was blind. Most of the Jews of the time threw His prophecy and His crucifixion back in His face. So, in around 60 A.D., His prophecy was fulfilled. The Romans did come and every man in Jerusalem, who hadn't left his coat inside and ran for the hills, was crucified. Their place, the temple, was burned to the ground.

Game over.

The recruitment of the Church

Or it would have been game over, were it not for the second audience Jesus is modeling to in the crucifixion. They are, unexpectedly and ingeniously, handed that game. This is even though they are seriously ill-equipped to even see this at the time. Those who mourned would be comforted, those extraordinarily ordinary men and women He had chosen to have faith in the power and the agenda of what He was doing would look upon this crucifixion very differently soon. As would, in the course of time, the church that they would create. As would you and I.

From Abram forward, Israel's fate was always bound up with that of the world. Ever since His promise to Abram about all nations being blessed, God had kept the church in the wings of His garment, to be His chief story-carrier. Jesus hands the baton through His sacrifice and death, even if they don't see it straight away. It is we who are given the second-half of the (Jewish) story to carry. A story that *starts* with death and loss and despair, and has the audacity to suggest these are a victory. That death, loss and despair are stripped of their power only because of the identity of that one man in His death. Who is it that does this?

If He is nobody then nothing can really happen, can it?

Who is this man? His miracles, His parables, His praxis were, He claimed, a prospectus for a new hope and realism in God. One born of the Spirit and blowing where it pleased. The fate of the world in His narratives seemed to pivot not on its own deeds but on an exterior source of grace. Someone who could level the game. Someone who is "other". Jesus' mission appeared to be this intoxicating anomaly where He was, against dangerous competition, willing to offer "other" or as He called it, *the way*. This He did with healing fingers, this He did with arms that embraced babies, this He did with hands that washed feet. For a season it was all so very tangible, He was all so very tangible.

But it had ended.

The opposition from within and without, the culture of the world and the powers He set His kingdom up against came back with a smack-down so final that no person, no movement, no soul, not even a tangible heaven-bringer like Jesus, could ever get back up from it. He is erased from His chosen venue of the kingdom with a brutal finality. His enemies are vindicated.

Though He never said He was bringing one, there is no overturning of Rome. Though He said He fulfilled it, the stricture of the Law of Moses and its (mis)representatives tightened its yoke back around the necks of the people. Though He never said they would do anything else, His followers turned on Him or fled in His time of tribulation. Though He claimed to have tied him up and robbed his house of its treasure, it was Jesus, not Satan, who was tied up and robbed by His executioners. Though He called out to a God He said was His ultimate trust, in His final moments, He was left mourning His own abandonment.

It was obvious, not just to the mourning disciples but to the world at large, that whoever Jesus had been and whatever He had expected God to bring as a new expression of kingdom, this had catastrophically failed.

God did not hear Him.

God stayed in heaven.

His name was hallowed, but distant.

His kingdom didn't come, it was stillborn.

His will was not done on earth; it was viewed from afar as before.

His daily bread was not received; it was discarded at the city dump.

The forgiveness for trespass, only led to a deeper trespass.

The forgiving one was not received; He forgave for no earthly consequence.

Temptation remained, it sifted, and all were found wanting.

No one was delivered from the evil one.

Not even the one who has said He would lead the deliverance.

All of Jesus' storyline of the new kingdom, the new Adam, the new wine, the new garden, the new trees, the fecund fields, the great harvest, the miraculous catch of fish, the good shepherd, the streams of living water, the resurrecting one, the transfigured one, the mysterious bridegroom, are laid bare before us in the crucifixion, all taken away, all is gone, emptied. The smoldering wick, extinguished. This is what the world does.

Whoever Jesus was, it was folly to take on the world even for a brilliant moment. Should such a light have come into this world, it was utterly put out. Jesus gave all the wealth of His house for love, and, in a bitter irony, it was utterly scorned.

Look at what they make you give...

In His death on the cross we have the final intimacies relived, Moses hasn't brought the Promised Land at all, Elijah cannot finish the story, Samson has been crushed, these and a thousand other prospectuses of the so-called loving God in heaven, are gone. Jesus, in this, has pushed himself to the very edge of intimacy not with God, but with us. He pushes Himself to demonstrate His alignment to what He called *"greater love"*. He has so much faith in this idea that He models and endures it. He lays down His life for His friends. He was a man of His word.

And for this our hands strike Him, for this our fingers pull out His beard, our rods beat His back, it is for this that our spear pierces His side. He dies our death, completely relinquishing His right to the ultimate intimacy with God He came bearing all along. He foolishly traded it all for a final intimacy with the futility we were all so obviously born to.

And the *'watcher of men'*, just watches after all. Everything is really meaningless after all. He who said *"the wind blows where it pleases"*, is like us, born to be one who experiences the folly of 'a chasing after' that wind. How will this same storyline ever overcome death and Hades? Jesus you fool.

The crucifixion of Jesus, therefore, is the ultimate expression not that God meets us at the edge, but that God meets Himself at the edge. It is the terrible expression of the total insurmountability of the price of intimacy. Jesus' dying is the ultimate realization of the fullness (or folly) of His own kingdom agenda to attempt to pay the price between humanity and holiness. The bitter consequence of such a mission is that He alone tastes fully what can separate us from God not knowing if, in so doing, He will reverse it or be crushed by it. God the innovator, God the impossible, God the satisfaction, either accepts Jonah's offering to save those in peril on the sea, or He doesn't.

He swallowed the first Jonah up for three days and then transformed that whole prospectus from a defeat to a petition borne to the foot of the mountains of death, a petition for God's holy temple to be all in all, for death to have no lasting dominion. What happens in the crucifixion is that God is called upon again, for three days, by Adam-Jonah-Jesus, to finally and irreversibly level the mountains of this (our) death, to be our great leveler, to close the path to misery, to finish the way into intimacy and this time dare to leave it open...

If you are a disciple, bleeding and blinking in the sunlight after the crucifixion; if you are the church; if you are a person hearing its story in reading or in person after all this time, what you think happened next defines your place in this world.

Wake up Jonah.

God hears.

Jesus is resurrected.

The second-half of His kingdom story is allowed to begin.

And then something even more unexpected happens...

Jesus hands the second-half of His great half-told narrative to us. The kingdom can now be unlocked, and He hands the keys to us. The key to the extraordinary power of Jesus' claims for His church is found in the fact that He was capable of surviving death. Jesus showed Himself as what He indeed claimed to be – the resurrection and the life.

The crucifixion was recruitment.

He made Himself the completion of the human prospectus writ large on our very own story. That makes Him *the way* – home.

He conferred a kingdom that outstretched every expectation and interpretation of it to become the satisfaction of humanity. To take this kingdom to its completion He then sets the church in the UK and beyond into motion as the ultimate expression of it. This He does with a warning to *never* let it become lukewarm.

It is in the Son of Man suffering many things and being rejected; it is in His prophetic praxis as the end of the line of the great prophets; it is in the audacity of the recruitment of His crucifixion and His death; it is especially in the impossibility of His resurrection that Jesus has inaugurated and transformed His church into the evensong of this world.

What kind of trust is this?

Chapter 9

An Intimate Reading of Church

So when Joan Osborne so hauntingly sings "What if God was one of us?", we can now respond "thing is Joan, He was, and because of that we will now show you how *absolutely everything* has to change..."

Jesus is not like Moses, some religious man who pops up and makes a noise about the rules. Jesus did not, as 1John has to vociferously rebut, come to offer a spiritualized, comforting allusion for religious people to have superstitions about. Jesus was visceral. From first to last He was an intimacy project with the human race, one that could receive kisses and tears and one that could disrobe and wash feet.

To be this, He was wholly incarnate; we can accept no substitutes for, or challenges to this. He actually risked birth and the perils of life to be bone of my bones. He really had all our bodily functions, and the desires that come with those, to be flesh of my flesh. He grew weary, wept, felt longing and knew joy to be Spirit of my spirit. Also, He died. Death of my death. This He did exactly as one of us would. That's how He died for us, as intimacy with us. For the incarnation to happen at all and then terminate in the crucifixion is the ultimate act of intimacy without compromise.

Ours is a God of intimacy without compromise and in this chapter I want to say: like God, like church, it's painfully simple.

So how do we stack up? Well, historically we can already compare some of the approaches of the mainstream church in its relating to the world. Although it is a massive over-generalization to even go here, let's just look at some of those through Jesus' intimacy without compromise lens. These will be embarrassingly poorly sketched. Just let that wash over you, see it as splash of stereotypical contextual color.

1. Separatism We don't need to name any names. For the separatist movement, "the world" is a deeply internalized pejorative. These churches will not only draw a line between themselves and the world, but they will build a stout wall on that line just to be absolutely sure the signal is clear. "Salvation is found behind these walls and in our cultural expression of the doctrines of that term", is writ large on every brick. Sometimes it's in the King James version.

2. "Stoicism" Further up the compassion scale are the 'stoics', a mixed bag of churches both charismatic and traditional. They have thrown a lifeline of sorts over their wall but still think testifying that "The Wages of Sin is Death!" is a cool thing to do. Deconstructing their internal public rhetoric does reveal a note of compassion for the world. However, the rest of the melody blurts out that the world is sick. The world is pornographic. The world is addicted. The world is an infection to be cut out of the church, it is evil. Clear, crisp and clumsy as hell, literally.

3. Traditionalism Where the separatists perhaps want to reject the world (condemn it even) and the stoics would indict the world (convict it perhaps) the traditional churches, on the whole, want to save it (convince it). They tend, therefore, to major on the upside of Jesus. Their rhetoric surrounds the offer of life and freedom. Anachronistic hellfire posters are kept to a minimum and cafes and crèches are advertised instead. This church wants to buy the world a cup of tea and have an apologetic chat.

4. Activism The activist church loves the world whether it likes it or not. They are heavily connected in global mission, fairly hard-hitting in a home-grown social action portfolio, big on justice, straight down the middle doctrinally and spiritually. They are also creative in engaging with and meeting the needs of their communities and often crafty in evangelism through this.

They remain warm to this world and its people. It is an important identity point for them.

These models and their many variations are still out there today, and often calling themselves *the church*, so who has got that right? Which of these would seem to be Jesus' authentic, attractive, alternative world order loving the world in intimacy without compromise? You know what I am going to say.

We need to journey for the answer. We are offering this world the whole incarnation of a God who was 'one of us'. That leaves the church a burden of proof in its relating to this world in His name. This is going to have to involve proof that we are: following Jesus' lead; seeking to copy Him; giving Him what He asked for. A three-pointer, I know, sue me.

When we have journeyed through these three points, we will see that the church must be intimate with this world not separate from it. We will also see a need to expand our reading of Jesus' half-told kingdom into the church's self understanding. That will include two facts. One that we might affect "the kingdom of heaven" ourselves by asserting some of our own needs onto its realities (fundamentalists and Calvinists alike will need to remember that the nearest exit may be behind them). Two, when we understand the magnificence of Jesus' intimacy agenda, we will hear a call of Jesus. Empowerment to bring such a kingdom starts when we also prove *within the church* we have learned to be intimate with one another as a sacrament of risk.

Following Jesus' lead?

The venue for wrestling with Jesus on the subject of intimacy with the world has to be the gospel of John. When it comes to "the world", the mentions in the synoptic gospels are all in single digit country. John, our star player, has fifty-seven references to "the world" and nearly every one of them is from or about Jesus.

John's Jesus is saying something about the world and He is saying it to the church.

Wrestling with John's Jesus quickly reveals that He is not really interested if the only thing churches can prove is that we *believe* that His love will *"overcome the world"*. The risk we must accept to be the church that He inaugurated is that Jesus is expecting us to *express* that His love overcomes the world; to be its demonstrably living proof text. The kingdom church will be the one that "follows Him in" loving the world rather than "believes in His love for" the world. I know. Shocker.

To read like this we will need a hermeneutic. I'd like to suggest that, on this occasion, perhaps simple is best, we could try "just reading" the text. This will bring two dangers.

First, 'just reading' the bible (in English!) on this subject might show how obvious its meaning becomes. This is something that has led theologians to disenfranchise us from such affordable serendipity by corralling together and telling us that not all of these words (in John or anywhere else) are reliably Jesus' words at all. They suggest some statements were put in His mouth by later editors, when Christian theology was more complete and presumably more controlling. They do not, I note, agree on which statements. Like they would know in any case, were they there?

Second, when we simply want to *read Jesus* like this. It does not allow the thoughts of Paul and the experiences of the early church to inform our position. This disallows the evidence needed by the churches which seek relative inoculation from the world in complex philosophical arguments – like pre-destination for example. Without trying to sound smug, my hermeneutic is coming from examining Jesus and not Paul, Peter and James. Jesus said the more important things.

So, let's deconstruct a selection of John's texts of 'Jesus and the world'. In those we will see a manifesto which is, first to last, of risk and sacrament. We should see it in *Jesus' reversal of evil*. We should see that as the call to intimacy. I'm going to suggest that these form a healthy reading of the church through a reading of Jesus; one that is a challenge to put down faint interest, high disdain or citadel concern for this world and replace these with an intimate "Jesuit" risk.

Faith in Jesus' Reversal of Evil. Jesus considered the darkness of this world to be reversible, however big or small it gets, and He was living under occupation remember. If the evil of this world had not been, in some way, reversible why would Jesus have come at all? God could have just sent a postcard along the lines of 'will the last one out switch off the lights'. More crucially, if evil were not reversible there would be little, if any, point in the intimacy of Jesus' incarnation. Its pinnacle, the crucifixion, would just be a horrific nihilistic mess. It's not a mess (not like that anyway) and, in my view, Jesus calls His church, more than she knows, particularly through that very act to be consequentially and intimately associated with this world. We must look upon the crucifixion as evidence which demonstrates the extent of *Jesus'* faith in the reversibility of evil, not ours. So John says:

John 3:19 – *This is the verdict: Light has come into the world, but men loved darkness instead of light because their deeds were evil.*

Pointing out that evil will not please everybody. As Jesus says:

John 7:7 – *The world cannot hate you, but it hates me because I testify that what it does is evil.*

And then, by way of remedy to all that, He says:

John 12:31 – *Now is the time for judgment on this world; now the prince of this world will be driven out.*

If the church is intent on copying Jesus then Separatism won't fly here. Jesus only allows us to be testifying that the world is evil *if* we are trying to do something about driving that evil out. This will be at some cost to us says Jesus:

John 15:19 – *If you belonged to the world, it would love you as its own. As it is, you do not belong to the world, but I have chosen you out of the world. That is why the world hates you.*

If we choose to accept His intimate mission, to love the world as He does, then the world might hate us for it – just as it hated Him. That's why Jesus doesn't expect the world to be loving you *"as one of its own"* any more than it did Him. In the person and mission of Jesus, perfect love has no expectation of reciprocation. In fact, Jesus goes further and takes no license at all to return any hatred either. So He says:

John 12:47 – *As for the person who hears my words but does not keep them, I do not judge him. For I did not come to judge the world, but to save it.*

And John says:

John 3:17 – *For God did not send his Son into the world to condemn the world, but to save the world through him.*

So, if He is instructing the church to take something like this same attitude, Stoicism won't really cut it. We don't call down fire on them (even in posters), we don't reel off evidence of their corruption in our closeted meetings and pretend that we "love them" when this is conditional on them coming to their senses, one of our meetings or both. We just come close with the offer of Him.

Jesus tells us in advance that if this makes for tough going we are not to retreat into our buildings and rehearse our justification orthodoxies, we are simply to be reminded that this world hated Him first. The stoics would do well to rehearse more often that when it did, His choice was intimacy right to the end. Intimacy even with those at the foot of His own cross. Is that sort of intimacy the church's benchmark in relating to our world today, really?

So what are the implications of simply reading John's 'Jesus and world' so far? Well, as we honor Jesus' faith in the reversibility of evil (that we nonetheless testify against through seeking to reverse), as we care not when the world hates us for this (apparently judgmental) stance, as we refuse to embrace negativity towards them in response (or defense), something happens to us. We reflect Jesus' selfless love and we take our part in His *remaking* of our world. Why have we sought to make our calling more complex than that? Everything else should serve that agenda as we now attempt to be the people through whom heaven touches earth.

If His agenda is our agenda, then Traditionalism and even Activism certainly come in for some review of attitude, if not praxis. Even they should not be able to think some of the things that they have been thinking about this world up to now, including if these have been thought privately. The church will have to internalize the fact that the only thing Jesus will permit us to hate in this world is our own life in it. As He says:

John 12:25 – *The man who loves his life will lose it, while the man who hates his life in this world will keep it for eternal life.*

Jesus' manifesto for the world and the church is the reversal of evil through a non-judgmental and unconditional love. It is important that any church philosophy or practice which undercuts this through retreating into tradition and pretending that worshiping God is the real focus (hence why it uses up most of the resource and time), misses Jesus' call to a reckless love. Similarly, any church philosophy that creates evidentially little more than a philanthropic mission club persevering on biblical evidence, apologetic reason and core values of "necessary separation" from the world also misses it. Missing that call is to miss Jesus' tripartite sacrament of risk:

Risk one is Faith. Not just "oh yeah *faith*", it has to be faith in the right thing. Faith in some Gnostic myth of the irredeemable corruption of this world can and does legitimize separation, stoicism, quiet traditionalism and even activism. However, that is not what we are being called to have faith in. The risk that Jesus (and Paul) clearly wanted us to accept was that we are called to respond to the world's evident present corruption with blind intimacy and care. We are to respond like this right up to when it crushes us if necessary (although let's not go looking for that action if we can avoid it). That's faith.

We accept that it is a good thing that Jesus is calling His church out of the evil of this world, but not out of the world itself. We need to be blindly accepting of this, however painful or confusing it gets for us. It is a sacrament of the risk of our faith. Faith says He knew what He was doing when He called His church. Faith says He is overcoming this world through us. Faith is a risky thing. For one thing it perpetuates the risk Jesus took in trusting us with His kingdom.

Risk two is Hope. To risk the intimacy with this world Jesus expects is really an eschatological thing. It proves for one thing that we Christians believe that a life which is continuous in death is actually valuable in life. We prove this not by focusing, as earlier Christians made the mistake of doing, on our heavenly terminus. We prove this all the more when we behave as those who are not called in Jesus to be immunized from, and passing through, this world singing songs and studying the bible to pass the time. There's no hope in that for them, not even at Christmas.

Our hope for them is shown when we do not effect even a passive rejection of, and escape from, the world – something we could vouchsafe by curbing some of the derogatory attitude and language we do use about this world and its people. We live out the hope for Jesus' renewal of this world. Before their very eyes, we demonstrate their value to us, their value to Him. Against the odds, we display our hope for this with our very souls when we take risks for them that they did not ask for or know they needed. He is renewing the world through us. Our behavior should infect others with this hope. Hope is not a quiet thing. It's a risky thing.

Risk three is Love. There is a practicality to "following Jesus in loving" that is not the same as "believing in Jesus' love for" the world. Following Him simply and inescapably equates to loving the world, sacrificially if necessary, as He did. Our Jesus went a whole lot farther than singing 'This Little Light of Mine' in testimony against the terminal darkness of this world. He allowed Himself to be crushed to show that His coming announced the love of the Father. He said that such a love would, and I quote, *"overcome"* this world.

In consequence of this the church needs to be famed for an actual, not theological, love for this world and its people. We behave as those who believe God loves the world today through the things that we do to love it. Our love is our identity in Jesus' love when it is marked out by the same levels of risk He took.

So how do we stack up?

Well, we can already see certain challenges. This is a world which will accept the church, albeit passively, if we just stand on a soapbox, or a street corner, shouting. It's a world which will accept and publicly wheel us out if we will be 'national treasures' or cultural bedfellows (probably bunk beds) and indulge them with cosseted traditions. It's a world which will perhaps accept and even appreciate us when we rescue its detritus. None of that will really cut it for Jesus. Jesus wanted the church to explode on the world's stage, so we will need to raise our whole game.

Jesus did not commission us to set up a memorial to His beliefs or His behaviors on our way out of the door He had opened for just us. He opened the door for all. This He did through intimacy without compromise. Then, intriguingly, He gave those He saved first a role. He set us at the threshold until the last moment. This is what the potent of my quotes from John's Jesus and the world should make clear. Jesus asks God:

John 17:18 –"*As you sent me into the world, I have sent them into the world.*"

Everything I've just been saying, everything sacramental or risky in the church should hinge on that word "As". We are to be "as" Jesus in this world. The church's relationship with this world has to be forged in the furnace of Jesus' identity with it in His birth and especially in His sacrifice for it in His death. He requires us to share His intimacy without compromise.

To do this our churches must embrace an identity *within the crucifixion and resurrection* of Jesus, not about them. We will give up our encrusted orthodoxies that reach for in-depth under-standing of Paul and Peter and James and asks them to save us from that challenge by miring ourselves in the more important matters of ecclesiology. These "mere men" will not avail us. They were an imperfect (eek!) reflection of the one who called us (and them). They did their best, but they do not define Him, He defines them. So it must be with us. He must define us. The option to bash out some alternative definition on a doctrinal anvil of our own making which conveniently sidesteps Jesus' call to sacramental risk is not the church He called. Sorry. Rather, His call (and the blessing promised with it) makes the church the intimate, evident focal point of God's *refusal* to reject this world.

This is not even a refusal which we are personally unfamiliar with. We are the beneficiaries of it ourselves. That's why we cannot give a signal that we have given up on everyone in the world and gently close this door on our way out. To be the church, we have to hover. Even if that means we have to be, as He was, lifted up in order to do it.

Jesus said as long as He was in the world He would be its light. He then said to us, I need you to hover in the world *as I have been*. Do we get that? He didn't die to save the church, He died to save the world. The power of that death is released through His church. Its people draw upon their own experience of the reality of being saved by and cleansed by Jesus and seek to sacrificially love the world by trying to become famous for *our own refusal to write it off*. Harmonizing with our founder, though dusk arrives, the church is found faithfully expressing this sacrament of intimate risk by returning to the world marketplace looking for some to hire. This only underscores the meaning of the dusk, it does not avoid it. The church is being called by Jesus (in my reading) to be constantly identifying herself in Jesus' own *urgent* intimacy with the world. That is a critical part of the gospel.

It's such a shame that we have so damaged our reputation already by transmuting this into a smug fear of hell or a complacent search for heaven. It should have been a forceful combination of the faith, hope and love Jesus showed this world, as we re-express them in the sacramental mission of the church. It's such a shame that even in the places where we do seem to accept this mission we do so in a broody way, as if tasked by our master to do this and not because we have been asked by our friend.

Jesus is the invitation to the mother of all parties where the guests live exemplary lives of reckless love. It is love, not righteousness, that is the existential sledgehammer of the modern church movement on the world. Love is the surprising offer of a glass of champagne.

Now, for the sake of my wife at least, I need to stop and address all this bold spiritualized rhetoric with some hefty practicality. Let me (just the once) quote Paul:

Love must be sincere.

And that, for Christians (like me or otherwise), is inconvenient. Here's a snippet of my story:

As I write these very words, I am waiting for a friend I've known for ten years to come and have lunch with me. I'm hoping he doesn't come. You will need some details to make sense of that.

The severe diagnosis that my friend has had around his neck since childhood doesn't matter. The ease with which I can dip into his life in times of crisis and drop off shopping or sofas (that I don't want anyway) to a flat that I couldn't spend more than minutes in is irrelevant. The way we used to routinely sit in my (nice) house and "hear confession" surrounding substance abuse and grievous misjudgments – to which I gave feeble absolution over a sandwich – is of no consequence. The long absences, wondering if he is alive or not. The irony of his request that I pray for him that night right in front of three policemen who were still holding him down on the casualty ward floor. The goodbye hug in a mental hospital at four in the morning that followed. His frequent re-acquaintance with those services over the years. Not even my whispered prayers that God might grant his fervent wish to die – in some kind of "release of contract" manner. None of this matters.

After my many and obvious kindnesses, I've woken up to what matters. What has become clear to me, years on, is that for all this my love is not sincere, it is mechanical. Or at least it was, before I started writing this stupid book. I've realized that care and inconvenience cannot be surrogates for the love that is required of me. I see that if I am to seek to be Jesus to this friend,

331

and all the while remaining *authentically me* in the midst of that process, that I need to take a risk. A sacramental one.

That's why I've invited him to go out for lunch, because lunch doesn't give me any power. Lunch doesn't help him or solve a problem. Lunch offers time which has been given, not taken. Lunch offers affection not pity. Lunch disarms my mechanical love. He is half an hour late. Truth is he stands me up more than he sees me in any case and, even after confessing all that to you, I'd honestly feel more relaxed today if he doesn't come. After all, I've got this really important writing project that I want to finish.

Here he comes now.

How apposite.

Imagine, if you will, a worldwide church movement which amplified this crushing little mandate of "sincerity". A church that did not approach the needy only through charity. That did not care for the community with a genteel superiority predicated on a mild judgment of those who are "worldly". That did not organize its festivals and feasts or perform its weddings and funerals with a pregnancy about sharing our beliefs. That did not stand slightly apart, but aimed to stand in the midst with the kind of unrelenting commitment Jesus evidently had.

Now, I know you are feeling got at, but if I get at you, I only get at myself. The thing is, what if the church, as individuals and corporately, were to sincerely love the world around them? No conditions, no strings, no agenda, no polemic, no theology, nothing. To take the kind of intense love we can all have for daughter, father, lover and recklessly seek to (also) direct it at the other, the stranger, the one whom we do not know. Not because we want them to join our club, or accept our beliefs or even hear our gospel of Jesus, but because we want, in as unalloyed a manner as is conceivable, God's passion for people (which we have personally experienced) to flow to them through our very souls.

What if it really wasn't all right to set the bar any lower than that? If every energy that was dispensed in a church passed this benchmark internally and externally. Don't blame me for this. I'm not asking you for it, far from it. I'm being swept up in the (frankly devastating) realization that Jesus is asking me for that in my relating to the church and the world, those within and without. If the church is to be the true broker of Jesus' conspiracy of grace, therefore, and not just a bunch of people who believe in the doctrine of it, then I suppose we are to be defined by that kind of love.

"By this" says Jesus, the world will know. How will the whole church, and not just individuals and societies within it, be as irreducibly and intimately compassionate towards other people and this world as He was? A pretty argument in an apologetic tract or DVD presentation is not really going to cut it. That is not going to prove to anyone that Jesus still is the lover of this world. It's we who are going to do that part. This 'proof-living' was His ultimate trust when He gave us the kingdom.

Taken as a unity, Jesus' manifesto for the world and the church is the reversal of evil through a non-judgmental and unconditional love, an intimacy without compromise. What have we made of it? This is not to be a hallmark on the church, only visible to those who come close to look, it should be read like spiritual Braille by everyone who so much as brushes past.

Seeking to copy Him?

Just loving the world intimately is not as soft an agenda as I am making it sound, however (I know, I'm not even making it sound that soft). That love cannot be unfocused, it has to be, as Jesus says, "wily". The truth is, that it has to be steered with one and the same purpose that Jesus gave it. It can't just represent Him, it is still required to copy Him. So, the purpose of this love is only found in those other harder things that Jesus said about bringing His kingdom.

If we want to be found creating an authentic church – one

wherein these sacraments we have been discussing can be revealed – we will have to be a people wrestling with Jesus' view of the kingdom. After all Jesus *did say* He hadn't come to bring peace on the earth but to set it on fire by His baptism and clearly bids His church be baptized with Him in that. Is it important to church identity that Jesus *did say* He did not come to bring peace to individuals and families but division of their closest ties and then bids us to be the true church and grab a sword? If Jesus says the kingdom of heaven, now that it has been revealed in and by Him, requires forceful men and women to take hold of it, then what is the agenda for the next church meeting?

It remains pretty critical really that Jesus *did say* the church founded on His discipleship would become renowned for doing greater things than He did and lead an onslaught against which the gates of hell and death would not stand a chance. Well, that brings us up a bit short doesn't it? Is that sort of discipleship the same as the one we teach in our churches? If Jesus' call to authentic kingdom cannot be solely an intellectual concept, as we wow one another with the latest trinket of Hebrew epistemology, what are churches to think about? If it cannot be solely a spiritualized concept, from one of our worship-high refrains or deepest lamentations, what should the core substance of church cultic behavior be? If we know our liturgies should reflect the sense of urgency and, dare I say it, extremism that He gave the kingdom, then it will not avail us to try and *just* build them from prayers, talks and songs will it?

So, what will we offer?

Our offering will certainly include visibly accepting that the world is worth saving with the tools Jesus gave us. The first of these is to realize that we are not essential to the task. Jesus' call to authentic kingdom maintained in His practice, His teaching and most of all His death, that the kingdom has always been advancing without us. He teaches one of His most profound kingdom parables aimed directly at that conclusion. We need to stop trying to bear the burden of responsibility for God's kingdom. It's God's kingdom, not ours, we are not responsible; we are just invited to be culpable.

It would be very empowering for the church to conclude that Jesus could have wrought His victory over sin and death all on His own, but instead He came risking intimacy with friends in the middle of it. In that, He paved the way for a kingdom of love that the world had never seen or expected. It was radicalism. It was a risk. The purpose of it, as Jesus said, was to show us a new "way" and give us a new command, oriented around "a greater love" than the one the world already knew. One which, let's face it, even in its religious manifestations, was getting us nowhere. OK that's easy to say, but what would reverse this? What would get us *somewhere*? Well, we need to be reading the church through reading Jesus. He asked us to copy Him. He asked us to go into all the world and make disciples. He dared us to be more insistent with God.

So, there are a couple of the reciprocal risks that I think the church should now be taking in this way of love. I haven't made these up to court controversy; it was courted long before I was alive to bang on about it. Don't think I'm suggesting for a minute that these describe my average week either, they don't. I'm completely falling back on Jesus for my steer here. When it comes to how churches become kingdom churches, I think we'd do worse than to copy Him, to give Him what He asked for and (maybe this will come as a surprise to you, but I hope not) to become more insistent with God.

Copying Him will not be easy. Jesus brought the kingdom, after all, without a committee meeting in sight (I don't count the trinity as a committee, though I am sure some people might want to). Jesus barges into the synagogue, having not earned His way there; He is an oddball, the curious case of the carpenter who knows too much without having studied. He takes the stage as a peculiarity, a distraction even, He is given an intellectual hearing, but He almost always turns it into a living demonstration.

Jesus finds a woman at the back of the church who is crippled, who is maybe considered, given the cultural sensitivities of the time, cursed. He suggests that He can see they might, in this case, be right. Maybe she is hiding at the back, maybe this is the only seat the community will give her. When it comes to this woman, whom Jesus suggests was oppressed by Satan (yup, it's not just white-suited Zealots who use that language), He then, without her permission or request, brings the kingdom forcefully to bear on her. He heals her and takes she, who was written off as cursed forever, and restores her to the shocking shalom of a Daughter of Abraham. This is done as a complex testimony to them, to her and to us. Then He moves swiftly on.

As my friend Dave Gooderidge points out, what we have here is not a Jesus who walks into a room and says "here I am", but one who walks in and says "there you are". Will the church copy Him in this? Are we ready to take the initiative of bringing the kingdom that nobody has asked for and without their permission to do so? Is the church walking into rooms across this land and saying, "there you are" and delivering the kingdom with authority and power, free of charge and much to everyone's amazement?

Copying Him will not be easy. Jesus brought the kingdom in the face of opposition from the popular press. When the editorial policy of the local red-tops is to start suggesting that Jesus is actually batting for the opposition, He is quick and fierce with them. In one interview He says if, on the evidence you have seen, you think I'm working with Satan to drive out demons and steal the hearts of the people, who is it that your side uses? But, I tell you this, it's not whether I am working for you know who that ought to worry you, it's how you will escape judgment if it turns out that I am working for I know who, and I am the finger of God among you.

Jesus didn't win any popularity contests with the established church, with the powerful industrialists, the military establishment, the bankers or the politicians of His day. He just kept on bringing the controversial call to an authentic kingdom and ignoring the potentially lethal level of opposition He was generating as if it were a minor irritation.

Copying Him will not be easy. Jesus brought the kingdom, after all, without a doctrinal apology in sight. When the disciples and the Pharisees trot out their half-acquired orthodoxy of original sin, familial culpability and temporal punishment:

"Who sinned, this man or his parents that he was born blind?"

Jesus is short and shirty with them. You want original sin do you, how then, if you are so hasty to judge others, will you escape it yourself? You want the sour grapes your fathers eat to set the children's teeth on edge? Then look to the tombs of the prophets that you have had to build and look at the tombs of your own hearts as you plan, in my case, to further capitulate to the calling of an ugly people riddled with corruption.

Jesus crashes through their pathetic philosophy of merciless theology and says that He has come to break its worthless cycle once and for all. He says, don't ask me to endorse your principles of the kingdom of God, I am the kingdom you fools. Ezekiel and Jeremiah knew all about my day, the day that would come when those sour grapes would turn sweet. I'm making new wine from such as these and putting it into my young wineskins. Ezekiel and Jeremiah said a time was coming when a new covenant world would appear, they said the law would alight on men and women in an integral and holistic way. On that day it would become possible for them all to know God of their own accord. On that day they would be rescued from their infirmity and sin. Well, I am that day.

In the church today then, our discipleship is supposed to

follow a Jesus who said, so that you know I have the power to forgive sin, take up your mats and walk. A Jesus who said, now that you have seen God among you as healer, stop sinning before something worse happens to you. We follow a Jesus who said, neither do I accuse you, now go and leave your lives of sin. This is heavy stuff. We find in Jesus a call to an authentic kingdom that flatly replaces impoverished doctrinal proof texting of a capricious riddle maker God with a God who is simply both sovereign *and* risky. Jesus does not seek legitimacy in quoting the scriptures; He seeks it in fulfilling them.

"Neither this man nor his parents sinned"

says Jesus with possibly a hint of despair at how they want to box Him in to their ideology, and leech legitimacy from His obvious authority. God has simply exercised His sovereignty over this man's life. God has had Him born blind (yes, God made him blind!), God has left him blind for forty years not for sin, but for this moment. God planned that I was going to encounter this man so that he would demonstrate my authentic kingdom.

Watch out if you copy what I do, says Jesus, mine is a kingdom which will call into extreme question who it is that can see and who is blind. The religious elite more than once have to ask, are you trying to insinuate that we are blind? Jesus more than once replied, it's obvious you are. In an award winning piece of heavenly irony, God finds the case for Jesus. He sends a man who has been blind his whole life right into the Jesus mix to leave an unswerving conviction of proof that the reason he can see now (and oh how he can see) can only be that the prophets of God's reversal walk among us again. Will the church copy Him, can she take this mantle? Will she wear camel hair? Or is she too busy being dressed in fine clothes and living in palaces?

Jesus says to the scripture monkeys, you've been reading this stuff your whole life and you haven't read a damn thing.

So, if the church were to actually copy Jesus, rather than just say we want to, even just in these simple ways, we will see the same highly confrontational principles emerge. For one thing, our authority would come about because our bodies cash the checks that our mouths are writing. We, like our Jesus, will be comfortable owning the preternatural as a badge of identity and a mechanism to call this world to account. We, like our Jesus, will not judge people through a pretentious thought cloud made up of scripture. We, like our Jesus, will seek to see the living scriptures written in the people we confront and heal. We, like our Jesus, won't wait for permission or, worse still, popularity to enact the kingdom; we will view this world as under the sovereignty of our God. Because that is copying Jesus.

Giving Him what He asked for?

When we have squared all this away, our tripartite sacrament of faith, hope and, above all, love and authority; when we have harnessed these to copy Jesus' own kingdom agenda, there is yet another risk we must take. For the church to place itself in the 'authentic kingdom bringing' seat we will just have to go ahead and obey Jesus more quickly and more generally. Take the simplest of instructions from Him:

"Go into all the world and make disciples".

To what degree do we lean into that and just try to get this personally and corporately? I recently visited, in my job, one of the world's largest cigarette manufacturers. I have to tell you that my skin was crawling. I think cigarettes are evil... please cut and paste your relevant arguments here... As I walked around the offices and ate in the canteen and watched the people going about their stuff, I wanted to scream what my mind was racing with. I would never work here, it is against my faith. Then I realized Jesus might not have been so hasty.

You see, the idea that there were even five hundred people in an office in the UK who would be bereft of any chance to meet and hear from a Christian in their workplace bothered me; the workplace where we spend such a great deal of our time and where the ethical challenges will be the greatest. It dawned on me that having no Christians there would not be acceptable to God. I became convinced that He would have men and women right there in the midst. For them not to be there would mean, in our easiest of societies, that the church had not gone into all the world. It is too easy to read Jesus' call to go into all the world as if He had been giving a geography lesson. He wasn't.

In giving Jesus what He asks for, we Christians maybe need to be a little less up ourselves about this world and about ourselves, otherwise we will anaesthetize the church from her calling. We may need to examine whether we let our cultural defaults pre-define what "all the world" can mean. I hate to make this sound mundane but when I finally cut my (glorious) long hair, people who had never spoken to me in church felt empowered to pat me on the arm and tell me to my face how it now looked "so much better". If I had a fiver for every Christian eyebrow raised at me for working in a bar or being a Psychologist, or working for a big corporate, or riding a high-powered motorbike when I have a small child, I'd have quite a few.

I'm keeping the examples trivial; you'll know of more important cases yourself. Have we made a cultural norm of pre-defining the arena for the action of the "acceptable face of" the kingdom of God? Of pre-defining "the world" that Jesus spoke of Christians going into with His authority? Does this pre-definition run the risk of excluding most of the places where our serious life expressions are found and our most serious decisions are made? Are we failing to bring the kingdom home *to ourselves* and lodge it in our beings – insert your favorite quote from Chariots of Fire.

So, heaven forbid that my gifted son or daughter doesn't go to University, but God can have the gap year – sorry, that feels like a bit of snipe. If it is, then that's because I want to ask: do we too readily accept cultural norms about School, University, Job and Church propriety itself? The danger in that might be that we prayerfully dedicate all sorts of decisions to God once they are, as near as damn it, already made. We pre-decide how "all the world" is defined for us. Then we seek blessing in that, often-times mourning it to be a meager one.

Is this the right way round? Do you tell God in advance what you are willing to give? Jesus seems fairly heavy on rejecting everyone who ever tried that. Do we give Him what He asks for both out of the pages of the scriptures and, more scarily, during conversations of surrender. Or have we decided to lead Him to culturally endorsed, pre-prepared altars of offering and decision that doesn't so much respond to the call to authentic kingdom as politely redefine it?

One thing seems certain. If Jesus had been a conservative evangelical; if He had no interest at all in risk as one of the defining characteristics of the life of God; if He had preached faith proposition which didn't rip out and replace your identity; if the disciples had been a committee: then Jesus would have got about a lot less, spoke to fewer needy people and got in a whole lot less trouble, that's for sure. And if we set up structures that desire that, we are not giving Him what He asked for.

Reading a Church as Half-told Kingdom

I need to say this again. Jesus left the kingdom half-told. He may want us to respond to His world through the same intimacy He had. He may want us to have manifest faith in His ability to reverse its evil through non-judgmental and unconditional love. He may want that love to be sincere and our response to His call to the kingdom to be authentic. He may want us to accept His manifesto and actually copy Him in what He did, not just allegorize and neutralize it. This may free us to want to give Him what He actually asked for in the substance of our life choices, in our coming and our going. This is all the stuff you are so familiar with in every stirring sermon, rousing song, festival high note or (decidedly preachy at this point) book.

For me though, the sacrament of risk at the center of Jesus' call to authentic kingdom is actually *best* defined, mindful of all of the imperatives of all these superlatives, by what we cannot say. Reading church through reading Jesus leads us to one further inescapably risky conclusion:

- We cannot say the *definition* of the authentic kingdom of God here on earth has been *fixed* by Jesus already.
- It cannot all be one-way traffic from Him to us; because that's not love…
- If the church does not respond to the authentic kingdom of Jesus, it's certainly not because we are failing to give ourselves enough challenges! It may be because we put ourselves in a position where we refuse to issue God with any.

You haven't misread that.

Jesus' ultimate gift to us when He gave us the kingdom in all its edgy half-told beauty was that He gave us the keys. He gave us the right to complete it in a way that recognizes the incontrovertibility of the involvement of our being in it. He could have brought the kingdom without us. We are not essential to the task. This is His love; the kingdom is also *for us*.

You see the temptation out of the self-critique we have been indulging here is to think that "the answer" to giving Jesus the kingdom He asks for lies in defining a church made up from a radicalized counter-orthodoxy to the ones we have. That doesn't work, it's just a reaction and creates an "anti-church" – one that makes too much of its identity from trying not to be an orthodox church. This misses the blessing in urgently seeking the church Jesus style, the ingenious and paradoxical kingdom church; one where He expected us to have the audacity not to allow all the kingdom traffic to be one way. This coming from the Jesus who, remember, said ask for anything you want in my name and God will grant it. I think we should be doing way more with that text than just opening prayer evenings with it.

I don't think we do ourselves any favors preaching the whole time that this Christian gig is about God saying "jump" and us saying, "sorry, bad leg". I think we, as church and as individual beings, in committing our lives to Christ, have earned the right to pressurize God. It is we who should be asking Him to make His kingdom more authentic (relevant, applicable), for us. This is how we find we can offer God a new intimacy, one we perhaps least expect: trust through pestering. This trust is not an innovation on my part to make my book interesting; I think that trust through pestering is the key to the missing sacrament of risk that Jesus is asking His church for.

Jesus, to my reading, isn't giving us this key to unlock His shiny pre-ordained kingdom church; rather He seeks our participation in the *definition of the whole kingdom*. If we but moved the cultural baggage out of the way, I think we'd see that more clearly and it would revolutionize some of what we focus on in our churches. For a start we'd stop pretending, sotto voce, that it is "exciting" to know God and be part of His work when it is evidently not.

Bringing in the kingdom actually would get pretty exciting if we accept Jesus' mandate for audacity. An audacity which says to God, wouldn't this be a more authentic kingdom if we, the ones who are called to bring it, were to have a share in saying what we think it should look like? After all, why must we wear out our spirits in constant, and often anachronistic, humility chasing after what we believe it looks like to you? Now before you go getting all conservative evangelical on me and start quoting scriptures about not talking back to God, just hear me out. This is not my idea, it is Jesus'. I think when He conferred the kingdom on us He took this huge risk in giving us a role in shaping it. A role we sometimes tragically overlook.

Don't believe me?

Ask yourself, why else would Jesus tell us a parable of a cheating employee who ends up being praised by the employer for his audacity in playing the system to his advantage? Why else would Jesus say the kingdom of heaven is like a friend of yours who calls really late at night with a really inconvenient request that you have no intention of fulfilling – who ends up getting it for his sheer audacity? I mean, imagine a church meeting with such manners in play! Jesus, what are you doing? You are applauding the contrivances and the bugging where people bring the agenda they have set themselves.

So, why would Jesus liken petition before God, in a bizarre counter-morality tale, to a petition before an unjust judge who is being pestered to death? Why does Jesus (with a wink and a smile) let that story end ambivalently when the judge realizes that giving the justice he thought best to withhold is actually the natural solution to this pestering presence? We might ask, while we are at it, why these incendiary parables are never engraved on our church banners. They stick to the Gadfly brain though. Jesus why are you talking like this? It's almost like you want your authentic kingdom to be full of people who bug you.

Is Jesus actually daring His church to care more for something than He does? Is he daring us to be bugging the life out of God? What a church we might unleash if we did. Taking Jesus' lead, and treating God in the way these parables reveal, does not say much about Him theologically, but it unveils a world of invitation into edgy intimacy with Him. Risks are afoot which speak of how close to the edge we might just be dared to go. Risks are afoot because we will accept ownership of an expanding kingdom that we take a part in shaping rather than just seeking to be the caretaker of the ageing one we have inherited keys to from ecclesiastical history.

Now, if you think I've gone a bit punch drunk with all this writing, if you think Jesus couldn't possibly have endorsed such an irreverent move then just read with me for a moment. Let's look at how one of the best living examples of this in Jesus' life shows Him at this His most glorious edginess. I'm guessing you have never heard a full-blooded sermon on 'Jesus the racist', even though, for a brief moment, that seems to be who He chooses to be.

Jesus said: *Do not give dogs what is sacred.*

Matthew and Mark both contain an encounter between Jesus and a woman, one says she is a Canaanite, the other says Syrophoenician. Whatever that means she is by nationality, she is at a double disadvantage if she wants anything from Jesus. First she is a "she", next she is neither a Jew nor even a derivative. Let me slightly merge the two accounts of the tale.

The context is key, the context is actually a big religious debate that Jesus has just had a few days previously with the Pharisees over ceremonial hand-washing before eating. This is something Mark is at pains to, very helpfully, point out is <u>not</u> a Law of Moses but a *"holding to the tradition of the elders"*. So a jazz law then. An envoy of the teachers and Pharisees came up to Jesus and said:

> *"Why don't your disciples live in the tradition of the elders instead of eating their food with 'unclean' hands?"*
> *He replied, "Isaiah was right when he prophesied about you hypocrites; as it is written:*
> *"these people honor me with their lips,*
> *but their hearts are far from me.*
> *they worship me in vain;*
> *their teachings are but rules taught by men".*

As they begin to take more than a little umbrage at this hugely disrespectful and insulting left, right, left combination from

Jesus, He goes for the haymaker. Possibly quite angry now, He starts telling them they have *"nullified"* the word of God. Just to really raise the temperature, He then holds a hasty and brief public seminar. In this address He pronounces that He not only thinks that the optional "traditions of the elders" on clean hands are a nonsense but, for good measure, He says nothing you eat can make you unclean. In that statement He overturns all of Jewish food law. All of it.

You have to stop and see what a whirlwind of revolution Jesus has just sent running through the whole of Judaism. He, a mere man, has just deconstructed some of the sacrosanct codes that God Himself had put into place. He has just cancelled parts of what is written. Who does He think He is? If we can't live by what is written, how can we live? Moses gave us these words to be our very lives. If we don't have these, to whom shall we go for the words of eternal life? "Good question" says Jesus, maybe just with His eyes.

The teachers and the Pharisees will go home that night just a tad on the dark side it has to be said. So it's no surprise that the disciples have failing Public Relations top of mind. They try to tactfully point out to Jesus that the Pharisees (a quite powerful machinating bunch of elitists) might be upset if Jesus was, as He clearly only appeared to be, repealing Moses. They then ask Him how to read His *"parable"*: sub-text so that you are not actually repealing Moses. He snaps at them too, perhaps still a little angry, *"are you still so dull?"* So it wasn't a parable, He really does think He can change God's law. Wow.

It is onto this *stage of reversal*, unaware of all this tectonic theological horn-locking behavior, and the extreme fallout Jesus has caused Himself by it, that our woman now walks. Who will she be, will she be a "normal" person, or will she be a kingdom enactment? Keep your eyes on Jesus to see. Watch Him closely and think, what is really going on? Just what kind of kingdom does the man want us to see? Here is the story:

Jesus withdrew to the region of Tyre and Sidon. A Canaanite woman from that vicinity came to him, crying out, "Lord, son of David, have mercy on me! My daughter is suffering terribly from demon-possession".

Jesus did not answer a word. So his disciples came up to him and urged him, "Send her away, for she keeps crying out after us."

He answered, "I was sent only to the lost sheep of Israel".

The woman came and knelt before him. "Lord, help me!" she said.

He replied, "It is not right to take the children's bread and toss it to their dogs."

"Yes, Lord," she said, "but even the dogs eat the crumbs that fall from their masters' table."

Then Jesus answered, "Woman, you have great faith! Your request is granted." And her daughter was healed from that very hour.

Now, let's read that more slowly. What's going on, where are we exactly? Well we are in Gentile country, an odd locale for a Jewish Messiah mission. Matthew doesn't say, but Mark puts us in a house. Well, that's already interesting because it makes this intense exchange even more intense, especially if it wasn't a Jewish house.

What's going on, the woman is what precisely? Well she is audacious, she, a woman, crashes the party of an important Rabbi and "shouts" for His help, maybe repeatedly. She is not showing a wild load of respect for what's in today's busy schedule. Whatever else is going on in that house, she is intent on interrupting it. Her interruption points to a world outside of this (religious) house where children are suffering from things she knows the people in here have the power to do something about. So, she comes in and presses an insistent demand for intervention.

(In an important point of back story that we never see, there must be a question about how it comes to pass that this little girl has been exposed to the demonic.)

So, she comes like the persistent widow incarnate. So, Jesus, for His part, slips into the role of the unjust judge. Her demand is a Jewish demand; she calls Jesus the "son of David". Is she playing to the gallery? Is she challenging Israel to a competition? Is she authenticating the source of God's Christ? Is she just playing politics with Him and saying the right things to get His attention? We don't know, but it is an interesting thing to say if you are from Canaan.

What's going on, the disciples have what sort of grip on the situation precisely? There seems to be a fair bit of moving about language in this story, was it a really big house, was it a courtyard? Who knows? The disciples come up anyway and what they do to Jesus is *"urge"*. How do you read their urging? It goes one of two ways. It could be an urge for a compromise. Look Jesus, this woman is making a scene, what do you say, a little bit of free healing for the heathen today, just so she can be on her way?

Alternatively, and equally believable, they could be looking for exclusion, that this woman should not be crowding a Jewish savior and Jesus should put a stop to this. It would certainly discourage any potential repeat performances so far away from home: what with this being Tyre and Sidon after all and, well, heathen-ridden.

What's going on, how do we read Jesus here? Well, 'racist' is one way of putting it. Jesus initially says, maybe to just His disciples in private, maybe as a pronouncement in the room or across the courtyard:

"I was sent only to the lost sheep of Israel."

Xenophobia, if not all-out racism perhaps? This feels to me like a gauntlet from Jesus to all in earshot who are complicit or otherwise with its sentiment. Cleverly, one way or another, everyone there will be brought up sharp by this.

If the "urging" of the disciples was in favor of or against the woman's case, it has failed. So, the woman herself comes and kneels. She brings the case to the judge. Short of physical restraint, the disciples are thus dialed out of the encounter. The woman brings it head to head. She has the sense to be humble but she may not be any less insistent that Jesus should help her. She confronts Him with her suffering again, implores Him personally, this time with eye contact. Jesus accepts this intensity and plays His cards with eye contact, and it is not a pretty thing He says:

"It is not right to take the children's bread and toss it to their dogs".

She ought to get up and leave at that point; her petition has been smacked down with a racist chaser. She is a dog and she needn't think she is getting anything from a Jewish miracle worker, her face doesn't fit, wrong shoes, wrong bag, wrong dress. Does Jesus look away at this point expecting her to leave? Are we letting the full force of this land?

But wait; is something more interesting and intense happening? Has Jesus seen into her soul? Is He merely reflecting what He knows she thinks He thinks of her? Is the racism heading as much in the other direction and Jesus is only underscoring it? Is He, like He does with the woman at the well, revealing that He sees into her life? We don't know, but it is fascinating, this charged encounter. She lets the slap land full force, and considers her priorities. Then she says, and we don't have the tone for this, so it might be with anger at Him:

"even the dogs eat the crumbs that fall from their masters' table."

There's a world of interest and pain to me even in the placing of the apostrophe in that sentence. How does it feel to be a

Canaanite these days? Who are these masters who, perhaps true to today's form, speak of them as, and treat them like, dogs? Is this Jesus turning out to be one more in a long line of them? Has she perhaps felt the sting, not of racism, but of disappointment. Had she expected Jesus to be so different?

But Jesus lights up inside and that world goes out the window:

"Woman, you have great faith! Your request is granted."

I'm caused to wonder, for those who were having late-night campfire discussions, where this further exchange puts Jesus and His mission praxis on their Jewish score-cards. Should they chalk this one up to a blip? I'm also caused to wonder if the healed daughter and this audacious woman are actually present shortly after at the feeding of the four thousand, which we believe will have been a gentile crowd. The feeding when Jesus makes the new children of Israel toss their own bread to a pack of four thousand dogs. Does He just, as He looks up to heaven to give thanks for the bread He will multiply in the sacrament of their inclusion, wink at her?

What we are seeing here about our Jesus is a call for a more insistent kingdom; a call to great faith that hinges on pestering trust. When it is coupled to those readings from John's gospel that we have already considered at length, does this demonstrate the authentic kingdom? There is a model for church in the insistent woman who crashes the party. Of course there's another in the Pharisees' view of propriety. Can these teach us anything new about our approach to Jesus' kingdom?

Well, yes.

Start by comparing the groups in these stories; see them as representative of archetypes. Look at their behaviors and attitudes and start comparing those with the authentic kingdom Jesus might have brought into painful juxtaposition.

We can see the dowdy religious who have taken God's law and "modified it" by adding a bit of dignity and polish in the solidification of traditions for the way things should be done and should stay. We can see Jesus' excited converts and seekers, who maybe hear Him turn the money changer tables over, see Him repeal Mosaic Law, as He seems to run riot through the whole rationale for God. We appreciate the disciples, worried face, who don't know how to read this edginess that puts them between past and future without a watch. Also, we see this particular woman who helps Jesus to land a completely incarnate kingdom into the middle of all of this. In so doing, she offers Jesus a platform (much like the man born blind) upon which to dance His controversial steps.

Jesus is taunting us in this story:

- Is great faith actually found not in endurance but in a risky journey of bugging the life out of God and not taking 'no' for an answer?
- Does God actually want a transactional kingdom which He does not (completely) define beforehand?
- Will He risk being tricked or pestered by us?
- Has He mandated His kingdom church to be a bunch of audacious callers at midnight?
- Does God require this so He can see He has caused Jesus' likeness to be in us?

If the church doesn't know how to rise to the (to me at least) evident calling of that kingdom mandate, then at least let's be dogs looking for crumbs, that would be a start.

This is why the story of the Syrophoenician woman alone remains one of the all-time most fascinating kingdom definition duels in the whole bible. Jesus and this woman locked in a risky sacramental intimacy around faith, spirituality, identity and healing in a context that transcends all the pre-conceived social and religious values. Values that say God is predictable; values that say just because we are human we should come from a humiliated perspective. And when it comes to the bible she doesn't come on her own, she is in good company.

Do all of these stories not reach to the raw authenticity of what wanting to be a part of His kingdom to come could actually mean to us? Does God want to see what that is worth to you not solely in ritual, theological or intellectual ways but in the very viscera of you? I mean, part of His authenticity is that He can be visceral too. How else would He have come up with the crucifixion?

Is the authentic kingdom church today really founded on such haunting persistence and counter-cultural intimacy and risk? If the church was to become this woman, kneeling before Jesus again today, what impact would that have on our sense of identity? Well, for one thing we would drown out all the dissenting voices of tradition, take away all the proprietary cultural filters and just make forceful eye contact with Jesus ourselves. Then we would risk making our demands.

How will He react to the intimacy of a church where we have learned the sacrament of bugging the life out of Him for what is important to us and for what we think our world needs? A church which seeks to express an intimacy with this world which is not only the same as His, but is as effective. For one thing, I think He would light up inside and the world would go out the window as He marveled at the great faith in Him that we have thus discovered. Something He had been hoping and planning for all along.

In the light of such a gaze, I think the church would forsake the safety of its conventions of endurance, pack a bag and begin to truly journey...

I also happen to think, that to help us with that journey, He would say to us, do you see how intimate you have become with me for the kingdom to come? Now, why don't you remember this when you deal with each other in the (journeying) church...

Intimacy with each other?

So far, so good. We reject the models we have been given, because these are more about safety than sacrament and we take the risk of being a journeying church. We copy Jesus more audaciously; we don't set the rules in advance for what we will give to Him if He asks. We learn to kneel before the father with as many demands as requests and we understand that an intimacy project with the world will lead to intimacy with Jesus who loves the world and wants to save and salve it through our unrelenting faith, hope and love. These are to be spurred on by our experience and remembrance of His life, death and resurrection. And the world is to go out the window.

This mandate is still dangerously unbalanced, however, if we leave it there. Such an identity points us towards two further and greater intimacies. First, we need intimacy with each other in the church, where our love for one another must dwarf everything else we do. Second, the reason we need that is because it will complete the evidence for our fundamental intimacy with God. Admittedly I could have just read Jesus saying you need to love your neighbor as yourself in order to love the Lord your God with all your heart, mind and strength...

Jesus modeled a very counter-cultural set of behaviors for receiving love (whether this be perfume or tears), and for giving love (whether this be blessing babies or washing confused feet). His church, of all people, should be elevating and offering Jesus' model of love, not our own interpretation. We should never stack this high and sell it cheap – to make the church romantically attractive. We should make it plain that love comes at an absolute premium. This will just make it all the more shocking when we give it away for free. To show that we have fully grasped this, one of the most full-blooded aspects of a church experience – evident to participants and obvious to onlookers – should therefore be our intimacy with each other. To be His church we must love *within* and that love, also, must be sincere.

So, inside the church, it is not permissible to just tolerate those we are stuck with, we have to love them. This love cannot be done from a ritual, aesthetic or poetic distance, it needs to be obvious with a full and transparent accountability. Jesus hasn't called His church to polite tolerance; He calls us to call each other to stand up to the full height of genuine stubborn, planned love. This should never be solely reactionary; it's not just a form of crisis response. It should never be, perish the thought, only done as a professional discipline. For me, the risks we'd take unfettering such a kingdom *inside the church* would be evident in:

- The lessening of the sanctity of familial love
- The need for ministers to forego clinical distance in their professionalism
- A love for enemies
- A realized importance for the appropriate recognition of sexuality
- The elevation of the supremacy of friendship in the church

Let's briefly look at each to make the case.

Family love: To love well, we have to take risks. One of these is counter-intuitive from the off. We have to sit loose to genetic family. To take no credit in our own culturally endorsed conventions of that kind of love. Are you a good wife, a wonderful dad, do you dote on your grandchildren? This is all to the good, but beware, Jesus warns that if you love those who love you back, this is of no credit to you. Concocting a patchwork community and calling it the church – where we all individually love those who love us back – might make it feel the result is a rich blanket of (familial) love around us, but He says that if this is all we achieve we will be poor, wretched and blind.

I'm not saying that these familial loves are inadmissible, on the contrary, they are an essential heart to a church. We just need to treat them appropriately. In the economy of God's kingdom they become proving grounds and learning spaces. You cut your teeth of love on these before you throw back your head and roar. They are the generational training grounds of grace. They should stock you up with an abundance of love designed as a contagion. So it's not wrong at all to seek the most intense possible love in a family setting. What's wrong is if we don't, thus loved, deliberately seek to spread the infection.

When Jesus was challenged that *His family* was outside (come to take control of Him before He ended up dead) He retorts that He has no family and flatly rejects the authority of their love over Him. We can't make an idol of a 'higher love' restricted to families. If we confine our appetite for love there, or if we all ration our use of it by channeling the lion's share through conventional norms of marriage and blood, then this is not Jesus' church.

Jesus' call to His disciples was to redefine the church into a country of 'love and family'. We cannot pretend that aggregating across the islands makes just as good a country. This is not the intimate church He spoke of or what He meant by greater love.

Against professional love: There is a special sub-class of Christians that need to get the principles of Jesus' love the most recklessly and that is the ones who would lead the church. Our leaders and our Ministers cannot afford to be those who love with a professional duress. Leaders must qualify their calling in that they are giants of genuine love, the bible calls for nothing less. To be His priests, in the particular expression of church leadership, cannot be a call to be some aesthetic realization of the divine expressed in a compulsory love. You, of all people, have to be His very joy and community embrace. You of all people have to be outrageously loving, as Jesus was from babies to prostitutes.

When the people of the church accept what a tough calling their Ministers have, therefore, undertaken, a reciprocal love response is called for. In that response we hold leaders particularly accountable for honesty about the weaknesses and struggles of their calling to love. Specifically, we cannot tolerate that they should slink off and set up an "out-group", with other leaders, where they might unburden themselves safe from our gaze. Rather, it is with direct eye contact in place that they hold us accountable to become giants of love to them. It is we who are called to outrageously love them and hold them in place, not some professional club.

If we (all) embrace the role of the grace community then when leaders do fall, love will be able to restore them without schism. This can only happen of course if our churches are founded on a model of intimate co-accountable relationship with (servant, friend) leaders in the first place. This is not something many traditions (or leaders) encourage in the first place, or at all.

Love those who hate us: As a defining characteristic of His church, we must love those who hate us. Jesus said, as the second half of His economy of love, that we must love our enemies. As a soft-handed, middle-aged, middle-class churchgoer in one of the safest lands on earth, I can't know what this really means. What I can grasp in Jesus' instruction here though is the following. If we love our enemies and are found loving them at great cost and with intensity, especially if they loathe us, it is we who will experience at first hand the full weight of God's grace *to us*. This is not of the earth. When we are seen to love our enemies, the power in it might be, precisely, that we are seen for who He is.

The importance of sexual love: As a defining characteristic of His church, we must be a community that rejoices in the full released potential of sexuality. We must embrace a bold dialogue with this, the strongest of human intimacies, to give our people a map and a compass in this area and have the compassion and strength to help them to use these. This is how our young people especially need to navigate the unknown country. In our increasingly sexualized world, we have to talk about it openly, truthfully and meaningfully in public and in private – commensurate with relationships which have both the strength and the safety to bear such conversations. Modeling ourselves on the friends in Song of Songs might not be a bad start. They were concerned that 'love to the beloved' be fully realized and that illegitimate barriers to this (God honoring) experience be removed.

Re-visiting supremacy of friendship: Although it sounds like a diminution to put it this way, we need to see friendship as the cardinal love of the church. I know this will feel like I am restating Chapter three of this book but I do feel, now that we have come so far, it is appropriate that we return to this subject. If we are honest we have managed to conceptually separate "love" and genuine friendship. Jesus would find this a nonsense. We cannot *just* love. We have to be friends within that as Jesus has instructed us. Friendship is more than love because friendship is the spiritual *and* tangible expression of love. It is one of the strongest hermeneutics found in our bible for that reason, after all, Jesus loved Judas. The most shocking thing Jesus said to (all of) His disciples was the thing they proved least ready to hear:

> *"I no longer call you servants, because a servant does not know his master's business. Instead I have called you friends..."*

If this is the outright expression of His kingdom come in this world, what have we done with it in the church? One of the things we have perhaps done to it is to fail to see it as sacramental. To reclaim that we might need to dwell a little more fully on the evidence before us that Jesus' behavior shows it is precisely so. Perfect love may cast out fear, but those who fear, need friends.

When we differentiate the way friendship is done in the

church in the ways I have been describing (Jesus' ways). When we, therefore, lessen the sanctity of familial love, when ministers forego clinical distance, when we love enemies, when we give appropriate recognition to sexuality, wash each other's feet, then we find friendship becomes our "cardinal sacrament". We realize God gave us friendship to make us 'whole beings'. We realize friendship, in the church, is an altar where our sacrificial capacity for love can be freely given at any time, in reciprocal recognition of His.

That stunning fact has at least four implications for my hermeneutic: In it we are independent of God; it is the power in our worship; it validates our assertion that we see others as valuable; and it makes the church into a necessary plurality.

Friendship is an independent trust: God has made us individually capable of friendship, this is core to our identity and, in this one critical sense it is something about us which remains "independent" of God. The capacity for friendship is as integral to my human free will as it was to Cain's. It is a trust. God gives us this capacity so that we might choose to be friends with Him. This He does trusting us with something which is wholly ours so that He, who needs nothing, can accept something from us.

Friendship is the power in our worship: Worship rituals, even those surreptitiously found in the freer churches which say they have none, have been millennia in the making. Ritual will always suit us better than relating because it is easier and lazier. This why it has to go. Also it tends to be dull (sorry) it alienates those who haven't capitulated to it, the very ones to whom it is supposed to be a beacon. Ask yourself why it is necessary in leading worship or prayer for the leader to talk in an (sorry, dull) artificial voice. Imagine her talking to her children or friends in such an odd way.

Our friendship with God becomes holy when our conjoined expression of it wells up and spills over. That's why there are huge risks from ritualized stagnation masquerading as the authentic vulnerability required to make our worship experiences intimate. Let me say it again, it is not the beauty, lyricism or ritual of our worship that will make our church holy, it is the profound friendship between the worshippers. Friendship expressed in and as worship is the quintessence of the 'necessary plurality' of the church. Such worship shows how we can thus participate in our friendship with the divine together or, as Jesus puts it, "as one".

Friendship calls us to see validation from others as valuable: So friendship is the fabric of that which is holy about all of us. This is not the reserve of an ecstatic few, it's the job of the whole community. It is not difficult to draw near to when we see it as a "natural sacrament". Think about what we all feel quite intensely at marriages and at funerals (the bookends of Jesus' prospectus for His church movement) – and maybe slightly less so at the things involving babies. Don't we discover something about ourselves in these events? Don't we feel our longing for others (in love, in pain, in hope)? That is why we elevate these experiences as sacred. Consider if that might be why Jesus turns up so forcefully at weddings and funerals and why He likes babies. By copying Him and by genuinely offering and receiving these kinds of friendship – as we were designed to – we practice, and participate in, a deeper communion with God. And even this is His initiative. Why should this surprise us?

We still, in today's western set up at least, have to avoid post-modernism though. So these experiences cannot be understood as self-referential, it cannot be a selling point for "what church does for me". Friendship is validated in and by others, it's a plural experience. This validation is what gives us the evidence that Jesus Himself is pouring out of us. This is how our friendship is sacramental.

So, let me just summarize my main claims here, and, for brevity, let's do that Rabbi style:

- To not value friendship in the church, or see it as the reserve of a sensitive few who can find the time, creates a community made up of absence, a rehearsal of Eden, a focus on loss.
- To reclaim Eden the Church is a venue where ritualized relating is replaced by Eden's original signature piece, on the part of mankind and of God, the transparency and risk of allowing yourself to be known.
- To set artificial limits on the intimacy God calls us to, even if these feel like a necessary defense from the overly needy amongst us, from the potential for sin, or even from fear, is to fail to be human.
- To help us reclaim our humanity the church has to promote the vulnerability we all know is the full cost of friendship. The church has to accept the risk of becoming famous for our wild extravagance in this.
- To confine friendship to the gilded cage of family and marriage is to overlay an anachronistic definition of 'family' on the bible that neither it nor Jesus validates. If we do this, even as reaction to abuse by dysfunctional others, we dishonor His most intimate instruction.
- To promote the idea of family the church has to accept the risk of demanding that it include strangers. We thus redefine its substance and augment the fundamental power of its diversity.
- We cannot be hierarchical friends. It is a crashing irony to say we commune when everyone defers to elitist authority structures and accepts a rigid and self-imposed praxis of over-spiritualized 'one to one' from formalized ministers.
- The church might just flipping well accept that its founder and savior expressly told us in no uncertain terms that we are not to do this and that should be more precious to us than it is.
- We cannot commune aright if we only seek God vertically

at a distance because this is to ignore that which is horizontally sacramental right next to us.

- The church must accept and rejoice that it is at times through these people, and not some super elevated sense of individualized spirituality, that He wishes to come to us with visceral intensity. It is through me that He wants to call out a sacrament to the one standing next to me.

- We should not pretend that Jesus modeled His friendship as anything other than a shocking sacrament of intimacy and risk. No one will believe our claims to be on His side of sacrificial love if we are no better at it than they are.

- Friendship with each other is an authenticating force for our claim to be friends with God. It is central to Jesus' shaping of His church into a necessary plurality – because it takes a village to love a person.

The trick of our enemy is not to destroy friendship in the church; it is to render it optional, or worse still, to make it ordinary.

Towards an intimate reading of church?

So what am I saying? Can I summarize all of that stuff in three short paragraphs? Well, not very easily but here goes...

We need a more intimate reading of Church. This needs to be commensurate with both the person and the mission of our founder. We need to have observably accepted that the person of Jesus in birth, life, death, resurrection and relationship is an intimacy without compromise with both the Christians and the whole world. The Church needs to be likewise. The models which we have created from our historically literal and latterly systematic readings of the scriptures, particularly the broader New Testament, have delivered a Church at various fundamental levels, removed from the world. It was often more interested in a heavenly home than dwelling "in the midst". This doesn't mean there hasn't been compassion and even profound love at work, but it has not been, and arguably still is not, the defining norm.

We need to reverse the church's tendency to judge the world on God's behalf as guilty of irreversible evil. Jesus called us to accept His *manifest faith* in the reversibility of evil and the separation of its substance from its perpetrator – something all Christians have, in any case, personally experienced. The church is to testify to this common experience by promulgating hope and love in the face of evil. In so doing we reflect the intimacy of Christ's refusal to reject the world even as it killed Him. If we copy Him with that pure motive it will redefine the Church and, in that, the world will be unable to write off the Church as ineffectual.

We need to better use the tools He gave us for this sacramental risk-laden task. He called them "the way". His fusion of servant friendship and sacrificial love was to forcefully advance a manifestly super-natural kingdom. This kingdom cannot be "an object" or "an artifact". It has to be etched, sometimes (of course) in blood, in the visceral and present lives of those it affects, not written in liturgies for those who sing about its past.

As today's agents of God's reversal we, therefore, dedicate all of life to copying Him in the most fundamental aspects of our decisions and our being. Central to this is the acceptance that Jesus' kingdom is conferred on us, and in us, to finish. Recognizing Jesus' provocative stories, proclamations and relations with real people, we will bug the life out of God to finish that Kingdom. The most critical venue for this, as set by Jesus, is our unswervingly intimate love for one another expressed in intense, genuine, friendship in the church. The world at large may still choose to write this off, but it will not be able to ignore it.

Chapter 10

Reading Church Through Reading Jesus

The subtitle of this book is "reading church through reading Jesus" and, with only 30 or so pages to go, it is time for me to now put my cards on the table as clearly as I can and say what I think this means. This will, of course, be somewhat difficult to do. I have been banging on for nine whole chapters now about a "hermeneutic approach" and clearly you have got my number by now. I'm referring to a spiritual hermeneutic not a rational one. I'm trying to be a bit, you know, deep.

Even the Old Testament encourages a conversation with God which it describes as something where *"deep calls to deep"*. The New Testament writers inform us that the spirit that Jesus left now gives us access to *"even the deep things of God"*. In one and the same conversation our own spirits are now enabled, and expected, to share their depth. When that does happen there is trouble ahead because, particularly in our century, the rational part of our brains can feel a little bit left out of that conversation and get, well, jealous. So, in this chapter, I want to attempt a three-way conversation from the off. That won't be easy because what I have to say *is* a little bit "mystical", but in a good way, I hope. Even so, the rational part of us will struggle to keep up. But here goes...

Our journey towards this final set of readings of Church through reading Jesus started a long time ago now. We spoke of that tendency over the history of our movement to "refine" the Jesus we speak of and to only read Him in certain ways. Using some stories about Him, I tried to say that I felt we need a bigger Jesus. One who is more immanent, more intimate and more threatening.

I've suggested that relating to God is more of a "wrestle" than we perhaps allow. Using stories which point to Jesus, such as Gideon, I've suggested that we can unwittingly create a distance between ourselves and God when we acquiesce to culture and expectation. In this we concoct an image of God as someone who requires our best to be pre-prepared and offered on the basis of the storyline our history has already given us. This might be quite the opposite of what He does require and accounts for the tendency for church to be, well, a bit boring. In reality God might not want a static cultural best from us. He may want us to ache to give Him our undefined "first". It is in wrestling for that we learn to participate in His best.

We read some stories that point to Jesus' intimacy and brought into stark relief some of the most impassioned things Jesus actually said (and modeled), therefore, about His mission and His church. These spoke of forgoing ritual and distance between ourselves and God. We, who are through no explicit fault of our own tossed on the dual seas of individualism and post-modernism, may need, therefore, to copy His search for the art of authentic, accountable friendship. We need to do this especially with each other, but also through that with God.

We also approached a more difficult reading of Jesus. In his treatment of certain kinds of people and certain kinds of offer we saw that friendship with Him is tempered, in His words and His deeds, by a note of exclusion at times. We concluded that this was a beneficial thing. However, the fact that Jesus seemed to be saying that "terms apply" to the free grace of God is something else the church must wrestle to get right.

We approached some of the grand meta-narratives of Jesus' ministry, particularly in examining the "feeding aspect" to His character. Jesus did show that the church He established was to be modeled as a place of sustenance. This has rich practical and spiritual meanings. Feeding was used by Jesus as a sacrament of inclusion in His community (church). We concluded that this call cannot be replaced by a pastoral sensibility where we just try and feed one another "in His name" through an intellectualized commitment to sound teaching or emotional commitment to thoughtful counsel. His unequivocal desire is for us to actually feed on Him to be included in Him. It is clearly the spiritual dimension of this that His most controversial sayings show.

We explored a wilder country in some of the great precursory stories that point to Jesus, such as Moses and Samson etc. Their challenge was to an intimacy with God through crisis and loss. We reflected on Jesus' own existential crisis of Gethsemane and the cross. In reading these stories we concluded that the suffering and sacrifice which are so prevalent in our most powerful and useful bible narratives, and which so especially define the span of Easter, are evidence for the real cost of intimacy with God. God may desire our experience of Him to be neither 'centering', emotionally self-referential nor ritually comforting. Rather, "the edge" is where God appears less as we have defined Him from a distance and more threateningly, as someone who will allow Himself to be seen up close. This may be an encounter where suffering and death pass out of reality, as a sheer intimacy which transcends them is offered.

Just in these recent chapters, we have been facing up to the challenge to rediscover the joy of the hermeneutic of Jesus' commands. Interpreting Jesus in a more full-blooded way means that our church, to be Jesus' existential and phenomenological kingdom church, is being called to intimacy. So far we have looked at this as both intimacy with the world and particularly intimacy with each other but there is much more still to say on that subject.

Standing on the shoulders of all of this then, comes my central and final two points. The first of these is that church has to be something that we read into existence through its treasured core text – this cannot be done through understanding alone. We now need a profound and spiritual intimacy with the bible. Crucially this gives way to the final intimacy. Bible reading, given all we can now know and believe about Jesus, should never now be done in a way that is experientially, rationally or spiritually divorced from seeking a profound intimacy with Him. That is the destination of the church's "reading of Him". So we need to read church through reading Jesus.

Intimacy with the bible

The church needs to become more intimate with our core text, or at least less bemused by or alienated from it. When Moses received the Law arguably he knew, as happened very quickly thereafter, that it would be written down. The kingdom was, initially, to be a matter of words. People put their trust in "a written thing", and the term "it is written" arrived with gravitas. So, at the heart of God's prospectus for His people, Moses wrote:

> *Take to heart all the words I have solemnly declared to you this day, so that you may command your children to obey carefully all the words of this law. They are not just idle words for you – they are your life.*

Maybe we'd do well to re-open this dialogue in church today. To ask what do we *really mean* now when we still say "it is written". Is our very life revealed? What do we and others actually see on a close inspection of the churches' relationships with the writings at the center of our faith system? One might be forgiven in 2013 (in the mainstream church movement) for seeing something which is overly intellectual. Yet we are still compelled to ask: where is the reader experience? Is it, like so much of the bible's own content, rooted in the risky and the sacramental?

In reading the bible, and I hope you apprehend that I mean something which transcends just picking up the words with your brain through your eyes, I think we need to take more risks. These concern authority, rule making, the calling of young people, and our overall paradigmatic orientation to 'solo scriptura'.

Authority: We should not primarily be using the bible as our ultimate authority in some of the ways we have traditionally been doing. Take the default position of the doctrinal proof texts we shout at the heart of the world. Is that really the best we can come up with? Was the church really to be called into being by so thoroughly neutralizing the existential passion of its central premise? We should not primarily be seeking to use the bible to identify with authority propositions which are a cultural or even a spiritual form of community control. Take the way we use isolated bits of text to legitimize church rules and power structures, were we really to domesticate the bible for this orthodoxy's sake?

What would happen if we challenged aspects of the ancient, oligarchic dichotomy separating those who wield the authority of the bible from pulpits and church covenants and their patient listeners? What if we questioned the required complicity of those expected to acquiesce? Challenged the unquestioned rule that only those "trained" to do so could direct the central, often corrective, authority of reading? Well, for one thing, we'd be getting closer to Jesus' use of the scriptures and the way He communicated them to all.

Jesus' model was undoubtedly to question the authority with which others were using the scriptures based on comparing the scriptures with their loves. This He did by demonstrating that the scriptures conferred authority on Him not because He had studied theology with a sociology chaser, but because He fulfilled them:

"This day this scripture is fulfilled in your hearing"

says Jesus and they are outraged. Because He messed with the certainty of its esoteric plasticity and said this is no mere work of fluid illustration, this is pointing to a real thing that is now arriving.

Can we imagine a setting where, even just within our churches and with our church leaderships, we insisted on a fulfillment model for our use of scripture as a standard? If they asked us only to accept their authority, not on a cultural demand characteristic of membership in a community, but on the degree to which they could personally and evidentially emulate the one who makes the scriptures a dynamic expectation of what is going to happen? That would be an exciting form of "biblical authority" wouldn't it?

Rule making: We should not primarily be telling people in our churches that they can use the bible to seek a certain kind of rationale, code, rule base, or any sort of fixed communication from God on high about His expectation of them. Apart from this being a hideously one-dimensional agenda of rational control, we automatically implicate exegetical skill and theological training in such a reading. This is disenfranchising all but a few from the authority to read well. What would happen to the church if people personally approached, without fear or apology, a God who doesn't really want to ask them something as limiting and boring as 'what do you believe?' What if, through a risky process of trial and error, we are asked to experience the bible through a 'being in it' not a 'knowing from it'?

The calling of young people: We should not primarily be using bible study notes to con our young people into thinking God has a conservative evangelical doctrinal expectation of their behavior. Jesus was not a suppressive of young people; He demanded life-changing agenda of risk from them most of all, His young wineskins. Are we offering young people a motto in Christ that sincerely says "sell all you have and come follow me"? What would happen if church leaderships tell young people, as I believe Jesus would, to run like the bright young things they are after the kingdom? The one Jesus says might cost you your life.

What if we set out from the off to fill their heads to bursting with the scripture as it tapped into the edgy genius of their un-world-weary potential; if we set them off to release the now and not yet kingdom of Jesus' words. If we were found saying, read this, and when you find any bit which is speaking directly to you, get out there and make it a reality for yourself and those around you. Leave the conservative part (of finding you some transferable skills in the middle of this for example) to the adults, you just get out there. We will be right behind you with money, time, love and bandages.

A truer paradigm: What if we, the church, are not called in reading the bible for a paradigm of just being 'Christ believing', or to have a soul prospectus so dull and a calling so limited as to want to fix things down as 'bible based'? What if we didn't want to pursue something so profoundly dry as 'sound teaching' the whole blessed time? What happened to the edgy genius of the young Jesus let loose in our midst, ravaging the value systems of the world, challenging its authority and searing the hearts of followers and detractors alike? What if we open the bible intent on following Him as the one who says *"the wind blows where it pleases"* only to reveal it's a hurricane?

These are only some of the risks. In them I am asking, are we facing up to a bigger Jesus? Are we wrestling to bring God our first not our best? Are we seeking the bible for guidance on the spirituality of authentic friendship? Are we engaged in a dialogue at all with the God who meets us at the edge? Are we joyful in a full-blooded kingdom Jesus, as we read and through whom we read? Are we at all willing to at least test some of our cherished assertions in the fires of unpredictable experience? Do we journey or endure?

Does wanting this make me appear nothing more than a liberal heretic? After all, if I'd said at the beginning that I don't believe in the authority, inerrancy, and inscrutability of the bible as the rule of life for the church, you wouldn't have bothered to read this book in the first place. I do believe in these things. Remember this is a hermeneutic piece. The key to reading *me* in these last few paragraphs is the word "primarily". I do believe that all these things are crucially important and deserving of our energy, argument and attention, but I also believe they are secondary.

To me the primary function of the scripture, as Jesus says, stands not in its authority per se to give us rules, but in its testament to His authority – so that we might come to Him and have (spirit-filled) life. They were to be a mechanism of approach; we've run the risk of turning them into a wellspring of control and reproach. The primary task in the church's use of the writings in the bible, therefore, is not to achieve an intellectual (or even spiritual) form of clinical distance from them so we can apply them to ourselves like medicine. It is to reach for an existential intimacy in the reading of them. A living sacrament attuned in and through these scriptures, in everyone's hands, to a living Jesus.

I like a man called Keith Judson. At the time of writing he is a regional minister for what he calls "The Association of Baptist Churches in the West Midlands". Preaching at my church in helping it to journey towards finding a new minister, he made that old "benefits of Baptist Association" pitch. Then, most unexpectedly, smack in the middle of that he said so profound a thing as I will never forget. "To be a Baptist church is to recognize that the bible is not our final authority, Jesus is our final authority". He restored, in that moment, a hope in me for the traditional church, and he survived without being lynched at the door. We became friends over this sentence.

When I speak like this of intimacy with the bible, I haven't just made this stuff up just to sound funky or be confrontational. It is not just a part of my hope for God's church. It's a hope I think people all over the church ache with. I'm just the one writing it down today. I think maybe there are many others, of course, whom we must convince to leave their places of safety and understand how *unthreatening and liberating* it might be to ease the door of the bible wider. To remove the ancient security guard who cannot remember why he is there. To let more people pass through and run around in a temple where they are not told off. To let people read it not as a challenge of comprehension but as a sacrament of relationship and risk. And, of course, to accept the threatening part, to let risk in the bible beget risk in the church.

So, if we are to accept intimacy with the bible like this, in the hope that it leads us to something sacramental, we will need to acknowledge that the sacrament part functions in at least four ways:

1. Accept a deeper function for the text and its interpretation
2. Own the possibility for a legitimate spiritualized reading
3. Read the text for an interchange of being
4. Expect it to facilitate experience of spiritual community

Challenging the functionality of a sacred text: How sacrament works for you will depend on your definition of sacred, won't it? As a boy of ten, and a brief member of a Sunday school in Paisley, I was easily given the impression that the bible was sacred. Why else was it accompanied by music as a massive copy was carried aloft down the aisle? Why did people stand in reverence until it was placed on the back of a large lectern guarded by a golden eagle? Why were its weighty, gilt-edged pages turned with such solemnity?

When the heavily embroidered bookmarks would swish out of place, with a textile gravitas fit for the textual gravitas on offer, words from something called "a testament" would be read in a "respectful", unnatural sing-song tone of voice that rendered them alien. Then at the conclusion of this "reading" to them – that seemed to me, even at ten, a wholly passive exercise in control – the people were to murmur "praise be to God for His word to us".

As a man in his mid forties, a member of the modern church movement, and now a believer in Jesus Christ, I am still easily given the impression that this bible is sacred in the modern church too. So many people are constantly quoting it. Many thorny life debates are, to the minds of some, already settled with great clarity in a few phrases from its ancient pages. At times you'd be forgiven for thinking that the whole prospectus of the church, when faced with the uninitiated believer, seems to be to cram them with this hasty orthodoxy. This reveals staggering arrogance to insinuate that, as much as it matters, what these ancient, complex, intoxicating manuscripts really mean for their life has already been uncovered.

We thus, even if this is an unwitting by-product of our zeal for the bible, hazard strangulating these writings with our sectarian cultural norms. It seems we fear to take the new believer and set them on the bible's unpredictable steed because it might bolt with them to an undiscovered country of giddy, paradigm-loosening, value-challenging joy; the authority-challenging joy like that of our highly controversial savior? We daren't give them the bible's full untamed Jesus. We daren't let Him loose among the pigeons of their heart. Sometimes, it seems, we daren't bid them read at all, we are so busy asking them to listen to what we think it says.

Onlookers and participants in the church alike could be forgiven for thinking the primary relationship with this bible for the average church person involves reciting atomized, and inherently malleable, portions of it to each other over and over with a necessary gravitas. This recitation may, surreptitiously, be saying more about our agenda for God than His for us.

As a churchgoer, I can see the bible must be important. Easily a full fifty percent of the time spent in church is given over to a – hopefully spirit filled – individual standing up and sometimes explaining, sometimes exhorting, sometimes interpreting the bible. Although, to be frank, their usable text seems a slender affair also, because the same parts (not always interestingly) come up over and over and over, whilst some parts never come up at all. None of this seems to deter people from behaving as if the whole sacred thing, which sadly many have never tasked to read in its entirety, is the final authority in matters of life and faith. The laziest of all our orthodoxies.

It shouldn't come as a shock that neither the recent, nor the modern proposition, nor our common practices for using our "sacred text" are what I am referring to when I want to wrestle for a sacramental use of the bible. The problem with them ought to be so obvious. They are not the least bit intimate. We do not need a tired combination of mere allegorical application and a 'designed praxis' based on systematic doctrine. We need a lexicon for the life of the church. This can only be brought about if our approach to the text expects a living intimacy that can be experienced between the spirit of the text and the spirit of the reader. Such a spiritualized reading, in private and in community, could be sacramental.

Opening the way to spiritualized reading: To risk this sort of relationship with the bible, we need to try something new. We need to dare to believe at times that Jesus' fulfilling of it, and not merely our rationality, can arbitrate our experience of spirituality through reading and inspire consequential belief and behavior. These can be stimulated around an idea of reading for communion, of deliberately reading the text "before God". One of our uses of the bible, by no means the only one of course, has to be spiritualized reading.

Let me give you a very small, very personal example. As with all my real examples it is not the sort of whitewater story that is usually favored in books like this. I've chosen something very simple because, however it feels, I am serious when I say that I do not want to beat people up. My wrestling is for the church. Of course gentle waters are always caused somewhere along the way by deeper, more dangerous currents.

Your challenge is to tell me, even in this uncontroversial example, whether you think this is a legitimate modus operandi for God's holy word. I'm going to suggest it is. This is where, doctrinally, theologically and in all sorts of other ways, you'll find I have a pulse. Here's a snippet of my story.

I used to be a part of a church leadership and now I am not. The details of my failure here are immaterial and I won't be telling you them, because the time for rehearsing my pain is long gone. Let me ask you instead, for a moment, to picture a scene in your own church if you will. This is one that objectively happened in mine.

Picture having to have your church meeting in another venue because so many people wanted to come. Picture a united leadership who, with one voice, wanted to make a mission recommendation that was the largest financial, emotional and spiritual commitment ever seen in the church's seventy-year history. Picture a church meeting that ends with cheering. I thought I'd relate that meeting in a book one day. That book, maybe some ten years later, would be about how, with God's help, we had pulled it off and created a new paradigm for church in the UK. No joke, a completely new paradigm.

We (and I) suffered a smack down from the enemy soon afterwards that ended all this with a swift and profound finality. Should have seen it coming.

Fast forward to two years later, which is the point I want to take you to. I was, although still attending and thinking and contributing, heavily disenfranchised from church. I was next to completely out of community with it. All that you have read of me so far ought to tell you that church matters to me a great deal, but what could I do? My faith, not in God, but in His church was all but gone.

The "spiritual image" that would come to dominate my

internal visualization of the end to our new paradigm for church, of the end to my part in that, and of how I consequently felt about my own faith expression in a church building, was a shipwreck. My prospectus for any church, and my view of myself as a Christian activist in one, were thoroughly (maybe deservedly) shipwrecked.

So, I was sitting in my friend's (centuries old) house in a field in Brittany. I was awake early and troubled in spirit, nothing new there. I turned to my bible and I read. Remember, you have to be the judge, is this a legitimate use of the text or not? Without aforethought, the discipline of my own reading just at that moment had brought me among others to this passage:

> *Before I was born the Lord called me; from my birth he has made mention of my name. He made my mouth like a sharpened sword, in the shadow of his hand he hid me; he made me into a polished arrow and concealed me in his quiver. He said to me "you are my servant, Israel, in whom I will display my splendor."*
>
> *But I said, "I have labored to no purpose; I have spent my strength in vain and for nothing."*

Just then, to the one who thought of himself as completely shipwrecked, a life raft floated gently into view. Then I wept for some time.

Trust me, were I to give over the remainder of this chapter to an exegesis of this bit of messianic prophecy in Isaiah, I would not let you down. I know how to treat such a text, I can revel in what it is supposed to mean as well as the guy, or girl, in the next pulpit. That is the easy part. *I know how to read this text.*

What I need to ask you to understand though, is just how on earth it can be that this text knows how to read me?

I haven't got the words to tell you how profoundly close this reading brought (all of) me that morning to God. In the reading of it, at this particular juncture in my unique emotional and spiritual history, I was, in fact, dispensing and receiving a sacrament. A life raft of God's making slipped into my view because He was simply saying at the end of this sacramental exchange:

'To sense that you are one who is known, is a pre-requisite for believing you are one who is loved.'

You decide then, can this be a legitimate address from God using the vehicle of His scriptures bonded mystically to my identity or not? But when you do decide, be careful what you wish for. To let such a text loose in our lives, even as this un-sensational little example of it shows, breaks *all* the comforting, conservative rules of systematic theological exegesis and then some. But tell me this, just how intimate do you find the God of systematic exegesis? Of what inner use to you is a text that slavishly follows the unimaginative conservative rules that speak only of "believing" and say nothing to, or of, the mystery of being?

An interchange of beings: I believe, without a doubt, that one of the ways the scripture works, and indeed endures, is that God can be speaking directly and supernaturally through it to His friends. For the present purposes, if you believe this to be a credible way in which God can speak, then that has dramatic implications for the whole church's legitimate use of the bible, doesn't it? For one thing, at times like this, it makes it possible for the reading of it, in and of its simple self, to be a sacrament. We can afford to bring our own experience to bear on it with more intimacy, therefore, and risk experiencing God as more unfettered than we imagine. To experience that dialogue predicated on love not control.

If we can, in such reading, encounter God being to being, love to love therein, consider how profoundly a communal version of that sacrament would deepen our feeling of being what Jesus calls *"as one"*. When we are found to be expecting God to turn the text into an intimate touch-point, we will feel He is there in person. Such a principle of 'sacramental reading' is, I think, foundational to His authorship not of this text, but of us. It is an interchange of beings. The established church recognizes this, it really does. This is why we have a stubborn ritual of the public reading of these texts embedded in our DNA. The problem with that sentence, of course, is 'ritual'.

So, it is not whether we should read the bible this way or that which matters here, this has been inappropriately dividing the church for millennia. What matters is that we are found expecting God to take advantage of the pregnancy of our reading. He alone, predicated on what the very text tells us we can trust about Him, can turn our reading into a wholly intimate interchange between His being and the collective of a spiritual community.

Facilitated spiritual community: Seeing the bible, albeit falteringly, in these sorts of ways, it stops being correction and starts to make it connection. Can you see your church and its leaders wrestling with our unassailable inherited defaults when it comes to bible interpretation? Are they recognizing for you that our established cultural orthodoxies in the inherited disciplines of our approach to reading our bibles – like the dowdy communion furniture upon which they sometimes sit – risk saying nothing at all of God's laughing call to vibrancy? Can you see your church members refusing to consent to be third parties to someone else's ecstatic dialogical praxis and expecting instead that the bible will facilitate the spirituality of our connection with God and each other?

Jesus gave us the right to have an expectation of the scriptures which was predicated on His fulfillment of them. What have we done with that? Have we helped the church to read these texts not as a source of orthodoxy, a community form of control, a pocket salve for pain, or a panacea for the existential and moral complexity of the life of the world, but as an evidentially intimate way to meet and hear God as a community? You might say we are already doing that, but I beg to differ. What we often do is make the bible enduring when it should be, as it says of itself, a lamp to the path and a light to the feet. Each image speaks of facilitating a journey, of uncertainty and bravery and nothing of endurance or constancy.

If the church, counter-intellectually at times, was setting this text free in our community life in these experiential ways, I think it would help us understand not what we can know about God, but how we are known by Him. It would facilitate, indeed validate, that we are a spiritual community. We don't reject every other use of the bible of course. What we do is expand our reading to risk letting the bible be about believing *and* about being. When we do that it becomes a source of communion, an intimacy with its author.

Now we get to it, isn't this, after all, the very definition of sacrament? That He, the rule-breaker risk-taker God, is found to be present *among us* and, like He is in so many of the stories in the bible, not just watching, but journeying with us? I think that having intimacy with our bible like that would better prepare us for the central intimacy it actually points to.

Intimacy with Jesus?

I like the preaching of John Bell of the Iona Community, did I mention this? From time to time over the 23 years (eek!) that I have been listening to his talks and mulling over his view of Jesus, I have written to him to thank him for saying (and being) a profound thing to me. In a letter to him in the spring of 2011, I hit upon an idea to help summarize what I believed he had done for my faith and my life. He had ignited and sustained in me, over two decades, an image of an intimate Jesus. It was obvious that he himself had arrived at this in and through his evident love for an authentic engagement with the bible and Jesus therein.

This in turn had helped create in me that same profound passion, but I couldn't think of a name for this. So, in a fit of fancy thinking, I called it "a hermeneutic of Jesus". That idea grew in my mind and, with a hefty nudge from my friend Mark Greene, it has now grown into this book. The central premise of this book has always been that we need a hermeneutic for the church based on that hermeneutic of Jesus. Or, to put that more simply, I've been saying we need to have a reading of church through a reading of Jesus.

For the church our reading of Jesus will, by necessity, be forged on the anvil of intimacy with the bible as I have just suggested. However, the mettle of it, by greater necessity still, has to be heated in the fires of experience of this same Jesus. This is my view. To be authentic this experience has to be, as I have tried to suggest, not one of liturgy or doctrine (pleasing as these may be) but found in a risky sacramental journey; a journey through which Jesus both carries and calls us to intimacy with Himself.

I've used those sorts of words all over this book to describe that journey and tried to bend them to my appeal. Words like authentic, necessary and costly. I've added qualifications, or expressions, of them like 'community', 'risk' and, of course 'kingdom'. I've called these things at various junctures 'sacramental'. This might have struck you as a bit odd. To me a sacrament is something that testifies to "other" and the possibility of reaching out to that other in a way that fulfills something in your own being very deeply. That's why marriage is a sacrament. That's why, to my understanding, God's primary image of "the kingdom of heaven" is a wedding.

Now then, since the church knows without a shadow of a doubt that her identity, on the lips of Jesus, is a calling to be the bride of that wedding, we must approach the groom.

What will we do if we find him to be given to a profound and confusing "otherness"? What will we do if we find him to have a threatening and unsettling nature? How will we approach a groom who is not waiting in a perfumed chamber for us but has gone off on a risky journey and wants us to pursue and meet him on the road? Moreover, how will we understand this sort of marriage when the relationship is, despite our emotive liturgies around it, not actually freely given at all but massively, massively expensive? What will we do when the master of the banquet hands us the bill for all this champagne?

So, let us draw our conversation to a final close by simply looking at those questions and then it will be time to say goodbye for now.

The profound and confusing otherness of Jesus: The Jesus we are to know cannot really be textual, conceptual or comfortable. The images we are offered by the bible should leave us in no doubt at all about that. If your Jesus is a first-century baby in a manger and speaks of innocence, holiness, vulnerability, birth and potential, that is clearly very good. However, the same Jesus is hung up to die for you lamenting that the dogs surround Him, that He is able to count His bones and that He is utterly forsaken even as He is pierced to bleed and die a horrible death on your account. That death is willed by God Himself. That Jesus is on offer too. These are one and the same Jesus, and the bible is unashamed in offering these, and many, many more, images of Him all the time confirming what Paul knew too well, we are only ever capable of perceiving an incomplete image.

When that is clear we understand, of course, that it is only by His own initiative Jesus is *made knowable* to us at all this side of time. That's what makes His incarnation so staggering and not just a transportation mechanism. Through it Jesus offers Himself to be known by us. He does not offer Himself however as 'same' come to convince. He offers Himself as 'other' come to compel.

That is why at times we need to concentrate our reading of Jesus on the one among us whom we *do not know*. The other. The offer of friendship with God comes from one who is other to me, who wants to be other in me and who will repeatedly present Himself as other in the other. All are differing forms of one and the same intimacy. So, let's try, falteringly of course, to unpack some of the more metaphysical implications of that little spiel for the church here on earth.

Buckle up.

Jesus is other to me. John's gospel puts it like this:

> *Jesus knew that the time had come for him to leave this world and go to the Father. Having loved his own who were in the world, he now showed them the full extent of his love.*
>
> *The evening meal was being served, and the devil had already prompted Judas Iscariot, son of Simon, to betray Jesus. Jesus knew that the Father had put all things under his power, and that he had come from God and was returning to God; so he got up from the meal, took off his outer clothing...*

And you know the rest. Importantly it was against Peter's protest that Jesus insisted on washing his feet. He insisted in order that Peter might have what Jesus called a *"part with me"*. Peter was perplexed that Jesus was not experiencing the same emotions as he was, it discomforted him. We too must start the journey of intimacy with Jesus by recognizing that if we seek the control in this relationship Jesus will have to correct us too. His offer of *"part with me"* comes out of a profound "otherness". We are invited to commune with that otherness in a relationship with Jesus who says:

> *I am from above. You are of this world; I am not of this world.*

We cannot approach Jesus as if this were not true. We cannot demand relationship, as Peter repeatedly wanted to, on our terms. There is a profound surrender in accepting Jesus as the one who is other to us; an acceptance which is essential to even have a faith.

When that is done, our system has to prepare itself for another existential shock. Jesus is also other in me. John's gospel puts it like this:

If you love me, you will obey what I command. And I will ask the Father, and he will give you another Counselor to be with you forever – the spirit of truth. The world cannot accept him, because it neither sees nor knows him. But you know him, for he lives with you and will be in you. I will not leave you as orphans; I will come to you. Before long, the world will not see me anymore, but you will see me. Because I live, you also will live. On that day you will realize that I am in my Father, and you are in me, and I am in you.

How long have you got?

The church simply cannot celebrate from a distance, be this intellectual or ritual, that Jesus is other and expect that to be enough. More than a few churches seem happy to stop there – and that includes some that say they don't. He set out the opposite stall in His teaching. His appeals to His friends underscore His rightful status as "the other without". He says it is right that we call Him *"Lord and teacher"*. Then He washes our feet and tells us we can have no part in Him (we cannot become His kingdom) unless we accept Him as the one who is also the 'other within ourselves'. This is as a compass for the journey and a captain for the soul (remembering we do not accept Platonic soul-body dualism in Christianity). The presence of Jesus as other within you is, very clearly, a spiritual intimacy, one that leads somewhere.

It makes us aware of, and despairing of, our own sin. This is not a Jesus who, because He loves me with the fullest of loves, overlooks my faults. The Jesus resident in me is psychologically and spiritually complex. He becomes, as the psalmists were falling over one another to point out, the absolute reference point to the whole of what "wrong" can mean. He does this in a way which is other than our very selves. We are recognizably inhabited by the spirit of Jesus in a way that consciously amplifies the difference between us and Him in this matter. This is why He called Himself a "sword", something that we find at times divides the very sinews of our metaphysical beings.

It makes us sensitive to that which is holy. Jesus says 'the world' (without the Spirit) doesn't recognize the Spirit and we do. We contain within ourselves a pre-conditioning to hear and see the divine which His presence within us brings to life. This creates a resonance with God. This is fueling of our ability to pray in particular and our expression of praise in general. We become strangely confident that in these we are not saluting God with an unfamiliar voice from a long way off. Our call is not empty in that regard, neither is it permitted to be audacious. We are greeting Him using a familiar (and beloved) voice which we can nonetheless feel is other to us; a strange resident who inter- cedes in the greeting.

Jesus' residency is not just about community with the divine however. It invests us with a deep compassion for other created beings like ourselves and causes a holy hatred of injustice to them to well up. A hatred that becomes both a passion (that which motivates action) and a compassion (that which feels as others feel). These of course are the dual expression of the person and mission of Jesus. What we find, perhaps to our surprise, is that these are of course coming from within us now.

It is in such experiences we sense the divine, it's as simple as that. We are chosen and permitted to sense Jesus' presence in the world through recognizing it in our very selves; a presence which is constantly insisting that I allow Him to wash the feet of my soul. This is the way, perhaps most mystically of all, that I become conscious that I am, as Paul says, "in Christ".

This active, oftentimes painful, otherness of Jesus is a mystical thing. Accepting the existential implications of that is not, as Paul repeatedly says, something we can do rashly or flippantly. He says it is like a kind of death which we survive. In that allusion, of course Paul is folding us into his hope of relationship with the one who was the first to survive death.

It is when that relationship becomes vital that Jesus, a shepherd to the end, prompts our (mystical) spirit to help it shape what our (temporal) physicality wants to be and do. To acquiesce to the force of His prompting is to accept the full challenge of Jesus. The reason Jesus offers Himself to us as the other within is *not* that we respond to and love Him more in and of Himself, but that we love Him the way He called us to, through loving one another.

His greatest desire, the thing He said was the defining context of His own sacrifice, was the thing He gave the title "greater love". Then He set up His kingdom to take that greater love to the world. So, it is not a surprise that Jesus also approaches, agitates, and inspires us through appearing as 'other in the other'. As John's gospel says:

> *"...that all of them may be one, Father, just as you are in me and I am in you. May they also be in us so that the world may believe that you have sent me."*

Jesus *also* presents Himself to me, therefore, as the 'other in the other'. This He does through both Christians and "people of the world". In the one He creates community and in the other a longing for it. So the church does not own Jesus like Noah owned God – as He fled into His presence and, in so doing, condemned the wickedness of the world that was left behind. The church owns Jesus in order to move towards and love the world. We can expect Him to come to our aid in this the toughest of tasks, but it shouldn't surprise us that this aid is manifest through the Jesus who approaches us as the challenging stranger.

In His earthly life we read that our Jesus was insistent that all could eat and be satisfied. Jesus repeatedly gave audience to the illegitimate. Jesus was the one who says that it is the unlikely outsider who is the exemplar of great faith in God. There's no reason why we should expect Him to stop all that now and come and take a seat on the sofa. If we read Him right, we can expect Him still to be craftily creating interactions which are designed to agitate communion with Himself through communion with each other. This He does as an inconvenient reality not the rehearsal of an idea.

This Jesus who greets us through the other unique people around us, therefore, is a further, and almost limitless, expression of a Jesus that we *do not know*. That is disquieting. Jesus' desire is for us all to be "one" so we can experience residency in the Father collectively in the way that He does naturally. So seeking to know Christ *through other people* has to become as attractive to us as our own knowing of Christ. If we stand next to, but do not know the actual and potential adventure of Jesus within, the person beside us, we will never achieve that communion.

So, the church has a duty to help Christians to have the humility to want to experience Jesus "in the other" and, hardest of all, to understand that He is there in a way which is neither superior nor inferior to the way He is found in me. This has numerous implications:

The Jesus of the other disallows "my Jesus" from being definitive. He can never be limited like that, limited to my idea of Him. "My Jesus, my saviour" is a lovely praise song, but it is also a substantial arrogance.

The Jesus of the other will not clash with the Jesus in me. If they do, this might be an issue of pride. The Jesus in the other will recognize the Jesus in me and together, if allowed, they will agitate one another. He wants us to amplify one another.

The Jesus of the other will be recognized when the leadership of the church does not restrict or dominate the definition of Him. Good stewardship and sound teaching and their benevolent motivations to one side, we are called to a Jesus who washes our feet, not one who tells us to wipe our feet.

The presence of Jesus in so many others will mean that He fills the church, and the world, therefore, with a deeper idea of Himself than that which any single one of us will be able to describe, contain or experience.

The presence of Jesus filling His particular body, the church, like this (and all His churches in such ways) will mean that He can never be limited or dismissed by those outside of the church. He will be evidential, this will be our onslaught.

So, when the church is slightly dazed by the implications of all this and approaches this profoundly confusing Jesus, our whole prospectus stands or falls on whether we can, as individuals and as the plural church, accept Jesus as other. Jesus offers the church a tripartite intimacy with Himself as 'other to me', 'other in me' and 'other in the other'. Our belief, sacrament and praxis have to accept them all.

From my Gadfly point of view, the evidence that we have read the church through reading such a Jesus is testified in our acceptance of the whole offer of Him. The test of that will be found if we examine the dominant reading your church has of Jesus:

Is your reading actually focusing too much on Jesus as other? Are you holding an aesthetic conversation loaded with a gravitas intended to keep Him at a distance? One that continually emphasizes Jesus as a *completely* "holy" referent. A conversation which is brooding constantly on an iconic and comforting religious function for Him? One that even elevates the crucifixion itself out of the blood-saturated human-crushing horror that it was into some kind of grandiose spiritual appeal of the otherness of a distant, mysterious and confusing God.

Or, is your reading really focusing too little on Jesus as other? Are you emphasizing the converse position and seeking to hold a conversation with a Jesus who is not permitted to be holy enough? Are you re-anthropomorphizing a risen Jesus and hailing him through the limitations of our cultural reference points as if he were *merely* a friend? A malleable companion for life's highway who brings advice and comfort. How easy to dismiss as imaginary something so close to a psychologically graven image as that. Where would the challenge to our very existence, and that of the world order, come from with such an internally referenced and compliant savior?

Are you, by default or by design, reading for a culturally convenient Jesus? One where the focus of Jesus as 'other in other' is insufficiently universal. It is there, but qualified, so that Jesus signs an exclusivity contract opened only to include your church family or movement. Is your conversation a whispered denouncement of any other conversation with Him which might be held outside of the parameters of your comfortable orthodoxy and control? How many more centuries do we need of that self-defeating nonsense?

Are you attempting to read alone? Has the focus of reading Jesus as 'other in me' come to dominate your understanding of Jesus and emphasize the personal faith of Christianity? Is the Jesus of your conversation a private savior offering Himself as a wholly personal God in whom we can each establish a post-modern salvation for a single platonic soul? Is He the sort of Jesus who did indeed endure the cross because it had only been for you?

Even though I have used emphasis for effect, you can recognize, I hope, that the misaligned focus found in such readings is a possibility for the church. You can also recognize that each reading would be generating a complex but incomplete view of Jesus. Rather than being a forgivable oversight, this means that any church founded on limited readings will be limping from the off. So, if we are using something like them, or even if we have a perennial tour of all of them through our ecclesiastical calendar, we need to ask to what degree we are just, in fact, using a pre-recorded polemic and passing that off as the church.

I realize that I am laying out a tough challenge for any church. I'm suggesting in fact that we may be pushing a proposal onto the world which is really only part of Jesus. The part with which we are the most comfortable. That we may be building our church communities around something that is really only an idea of Jesus; one which will appeal to like minded or compliant people who accept that idea. I know I am saying that if we do fail to approach the whole of Jesus' complex proposition from the bible, it is probably because we are, individually and corporately, fearful of, or embarrassed by, the full spiritual, emotional and community intimacy He really called us to. I understand that I am accusing the church, if it thinks and behaves in these ways, of taking Peter's vow. Of a modern spiritual equivalent of saying "no Lord, you will never wash my feet". So when the finishing line is in sight and after all my protests that I don't want to, it appears that I have written this book because I do want to beat up the church, right?

As I said way back at the beginning of this book, we have to judge the church to be a part of it. That is an inescapable fact I have come to, and why I am writing. So, when it comes to intimacy with Jesus, my judgment is simply that we have risked being content with courtship. I think the church (myself included) may rehearse a near intimacy that means we don't want to get married. If we are honest, we find the offer of communion with an intimate Jesus may just be too threatening and unsettling.

Jesus is threatening and unsettling: The thing is, the conversation Jesus is offering His kingdom church is of the end to courtship and so it speaks of consummation, of ownership and of surrender. Confused or otherwise by His profound otherness, it is imperative that the church be holding that kind of conversation with Jesus now. Jesus says His kingdom is an invitation to the mother of all parties, and that party is a wedding.

We have rehearsed many times throughout this book why Jesus is threatening and unsettling. If you want a Jesus of the Immaculate Conception it comes to you through the poverty of an unmarried first-century teenager bearing all the shame and threat that goes with that. She unleashes a stream of prophetic praise to God reflecting through the mechanism of this child-gift, a God who wants to scatter the proud, bring down rulers and send the rich empty away.

If you want an innocent baby being born in humble circumstances and laid in a starlit manger you need to bring to mind that this manger is in the occupied territories and in a moment He will become a refugee fleeing for His life as the machinating local royalty, complicit with the oppressor and only interested in power, will unleash an atrocity on his own citizens killing their babies.

If you want the advent of God's promised savior to stir the long still waters of biblical prophecy you have to remember that the prophecies which come are as ambivalent as the man himself would become. They speak of the rising of many but they speak of the falling of many too. They speak of a cost and a sword that will pierce the very souls of those closest to Him.

If you want a teenage exemplar who "all throughout his wondrous childhood" obeys his parents so that "Christian children all should be mild, obedient as he" you are confronted with the only story we have of that childhood. One where a teenage Jesus ignores the fact that His parents would have been anxiously searching for Him when He has been missing for three days and then sulkily points out that, if they knew Him better, they would have realized where He was and where His real priorities lay.

If you need the man Jesus to be a blessed savior who surely does say 'come to me all who are weary and heavy laden and I will give you rest', an easy yoke and a light burden, you have to reconcile His definitional intent. The light burden He offers is the cross, the easy way He offers may lead to imprisonment, torture and death and the rest He is giving is that, if you haven't come to consider these things momentary, then you were not worthy to come to Him at all.

If we want to seek personal completeness and wholeness through knowing, loving and serving Him, we discover that He thinks this is impossible with us. He only offers to give us His wholeness. If we seek Him for the way to heaven He, more than any commentator in the scripture, says watch out you don't end up in Hell.

If we want to have Jesus as our leader we will exasperate Him when we are slow and dull, we will disappoint Him when He looks to us to find faith and a spine to go with it. We will struggle to keep awake for an hour. We are as likely to flee the hail of bullets He walks into. The loving gaze He fixes on us knows these things about us in advance. And yet the fellowship cup He stubbornly offers to be shared with us is still mixed with Myrrh.

If you want what He actually offers, "a part of Him" and dare to say you want to be like Him or with Him in any way, He says you must drink His cup and undergo His baptism. We know from the facts that these offers hang in the air still, and these are not states of blissful companionship on a pilgrim road through life. If we read Him, we have to read Him right, because we have a Jesus who says:

> *"you diligently study the scriptures supposing that by them you possess eternal life, these scriptures testify to me and yet you won't come to me to have life".*

I do think we want that life. In part we do already show that we *want to* hold that conversation in our worship. Of course we do. In most churches we are drawn to sing emotionally heavyweight things because we know in our spirits we are not messing about here. But it is easy to hide in worship, it is too conveniently vertical.

In part we already want to hold that conversation by the meticulous care that goes into much liturgy as a designed evocation of truth. But it is easy to hide in the routine of what we consent to in liturgy because it is cyclical in rehearsing how we are the same. It's even easy to hide in the cut and paste of our use of the scriptures with one another – because it is just too orthodox and safe.

Jesus approaches us in and through these very scriptures even as we seek to create our hermeneutic of Him. Great care is needed, therefore, if we are to create the right one. He may very well accept the tears of the contrite, lift up those who cannot lift up themselves, and forgive the unforgivable. However, in the final analysis, when it comes to *His completed mission* Jesus of the scriptures is not offering a baby in a manger, a dutiful son of His parents, a teacher-reformer of wilderness and welcome, a friend at the communion table or even a man dying on a cross for our sins. The bridegroom who approaches the church is threatening and unsettling because He does so in a victory which transcends these images and presents Himself to us as:

I saw heaven standing open and there before me was a white horse, whose rider is called Faithful and True. With justice he judges and makes war. His eyes are like blazing fire, and on his head are many crowns. He has a name written on him that no one knows but himself. He is dressed in a robe dipped in blood, and his name is the word of God. The armies of heaven were following him, riding on white horses and dressed with fine linen, white and clean. Out of his mouth comes a sharp sword with which to strike down the nations. "He will rule them with an iron sceptre". He treads the winepress of the fury of the wrath of God Almighty. On his robe and on his thigh he has this name written: KING OF KINGS AND LORD OF LORDS.

Now that is a threatening and unsettling sight to see pull up in the church drive at your wedding.

When I look at Him, even through the painfully limited hermeneutical lenses in this book, when I read Him like this, I see that relationship with Him *is* marked out by risk. Intimacy with Jesus is not to be with some timid partner come to validate my world and augment my sense of comfort at its confines as I have defined them. The merest glance at Jesus' claims about Himself certainly make Him intimidating, but the merest glance at His actions towards those whom He loves should make Him intoxicating.

He has not come to fulfill you, not as an equal partner who fills up the other half of your glass. He is the unexpected deluge. He lays waste to the room and everything in it and leaves you paradoxically laughing and alive in consequence. Soaked to the skin with this Jesus, that's what the church needs to be after. It's part of what our sacrament of baptism is pointing to after all. It is what our church's (missing?) ongoing sacrament of risk and intimacy ought to be fully striving for.

So, when it comes to our wedding, who does the church want to meet us there? Is it an anodyne Jesus who only inhabits an unthreatening quarter of our peace-made hearts and offering us a love of our own making which might be diluted by our culture and rendered insipid by our own commitment to it? Or is it a bridegroom who wants us edgy enough in ourselves and in our actions in the world that we allow the proper threat of a Jesus Christ – who is the incarnation of a love that is as strong as death – to unsettle us into His activism?

Our reciprocal intimacy should be never to have such a poverty of ambition that we seek to approach another groom. One we can cope with, or one where we cherry pick those parts of Him that suit our orthodox needs for ritual, comfort and song. Our groom needs nothing from us, we can't fashion some externally facing token of agreed cultural practice and think this will be a suitable sacrifice that values Him; we know He has no pleasure in static traditions. The bride is not expected to bring any wedding gifts other than her very self. He has not come for the dowry; He has come for the bride. We need to be willing to lay everything else down and approach a Jesus who expects us to accompany Him and then tells us what we need.

Jesus is on a risky and costly journey: To accept Him, we must be prepared to meet him on a risky journey which appreciates the massive cost of knowing Him. So, and obviously I am using the language of metaphor here which encompasses the personal and the corporate experience of Jesus, after the wedding, the groom expects us to come with Him. It simply won't do for the church to sit for a wedding photo and then leave it on the mantelpiece of this world growing ever more sepia-tinted, anachronistic and romantic – a static best referencing something that is gone. It simply won't do for the church to merely fortify a marital home fit for the groom when He returns. If this has been our desire then we soon will have to face up to the fact that inertia is formed in a comfortable camp.

When the church reads aloud about her husband today, which Jesus does she introduce? Are we saying more about our values as His followers or the one whom we follow and love? Have we fallen into the trap where we are saying more about convening repetitive meetings for their own sake rather than as a way to take time out to commune intimately with each other because we are all on this perilous journey? When we reference the bible and share what we feel it portrays of Him are we selectively rehearsing and defending our static cares about how things appear or are done, are we really using it honestly enough for it to reveal the mystery of Jesus through the mechanism of the journeying church?

When we leave our bizarre behaviors and attitudes unexplained or offer a single method, prayer, philosophy or experience as definitive; when we absentmindedly consent to some kind of Gnostic saving personal faith with a distant ephemeral Jesus waiting in a far away heaven to reward us after death. When we fail to rise to the risk and the commission to bring the thin places that reveal heaven is currently coming here, coming with passion and with a forceful Jesus at the head of it. When we just make Him really boring; what are we doing?

If the church falls into these traps, we are failing to journey with Him, we have decided not to turn up for the wedding. He feared this would happen; it was in His wedding song – the one His kingdom stories warned us about. If we don't accept His journey of risk we realize the fears of a disconsolate Jesus in the Revelation who has found His church lukewarm. A Jesus who understands His church has allowed herself to become unsure of Him because she is paralyzed with worry about the cost of the wedding.

All right, perhaps I am laying it on a bit thick but this is heavy stuff. The bible doesn't give us these powerful and disturbing images of Jesus for a laugh, they are to be considered warnings. Jesus doesn't teach parables where useless servants are condemned for their failures because He never saw it as a possibility that His church might fail Him. If we want intimacy with Jesus it has to be based on an authentic Jesus like the one we can quite easily read about in the scriptures. A truer reading of church is read through a whole Jesus.

Have we messed this up and over-complicated Him? Have we messed this up and under-complicated Him? What ends would we be serving in so doing? What has the church been called, betrothed and beloved for? Surely none of us thinks that all that was done just so we would believe in His kingdom. Not when our wedding band is engraved with a covenant that says we are to become it.

So, the Bride's fidelity to Him is not just to identify and rehearse where our most outrageous hopes for the church and its mission could lie, we have to choose to go there. In so doing, as we have at various points in our long history, we set our faces and choose to pay the massive, massive cost of knowing Jesus. That alone shows we have accepted His trust and His pride as He presents us to His world as God's *particular presence.*

God's thin place.

So, let me say to the church (of which I am a part), if we want to be that people, we need to ignore how much it costs us and choose the missing sacrament of intimate risk. It was modeled for us in the crucifixion. Accepting that covenant the church cannot endure, we have to journey.

In so doing we become the new wine He wanted us to be. We accept the expense and become transformed into a sip of the divine.

You are to be champagne.

That's all I wanted to say really.

A Gadfly Farewell?

The subject of this book has been 'the church' and, without defining that term whatsoever (you know who you are), I wanted to say to you:

- More than ever, you need a bigger Jesus
- Wrestle with a God who does not want your best
- Regain the art of authentic, accountable friendship
- Sing a song of exclusion, just don't let it be the wrong one
- Be a place of sustenance and of counsel
- Try to risk a God of the edge not the center
- Rediscover the joy of the reading of Jesus

Maybe your church didn't need a Gadfly to remind you of all that, but I just thought I'd check.

You know the church we are all part of was forged watching an execution. We were invited to attend the funeral; shocked to see when we got there that it had been transformed into a wedding. This became the mother of all parties wherein we are approached by our God in an intimate recognition who then says to us:

'I'm really glad you could make it, did you remember the champagne...?'

Acknowledgement

There is no doubt in my mind at all that what we Christians call the Holy Spirit introduced me personally to Jesus Christ that summer day in Aberdeen and that this reformed my life and my future. However when it came to the subsequent job of deepening that relationship God had a different plan. To this task He set a man whom, at the end of this work which owes so much to his influence, I would like to acknowledge.

His name is John Bell, he is a minister and he works for the Iona Community, you have probably heard of him. I've never met John (except briefly and somewhat clumsily once over a bookstall at Greenbelt) but I have been listening "at his feet" for over two decades at the very same festival. This is almost my whole Christian life. John's tireless service of strangers like me and his unceasing appetite to explore intimacy with the whole of Jesus through (and beyond) the bible has been my primary inspiration. The spirit may have introduced me to Jesus, but John Bell has been responsible for shaping my affection for Him. I know he would be abashed that I give him so much credit, but I wouldn't say it if it wasn't true John. I just wanted to thank you in a way that you couldn't argue back...

John Arthur is a sinner saved by grace. He lives in Birmingham with his wife and daughter and two motorbikes.

His e-mail is J.Arthur@mac.com

Cover photography by John Arthur (lucky shot).

Circle Books

Circle is a symbol of infinity and unity. It's part of a growing list of imprints, including o-books.net and zero-books.net.

Circle Books aims to publish books in Christian spirituality that are fresh, accessible, and stimulating.

Our books are available in all good English language bookstores worldwide. If you can't find the book on the shelves, then ask your bookstore to order it for you, quoting the ISBN and title. Or, you can order online—all major online retail sites carry our titles.

To see our list of titles, please view www.Circle-Books.com, growing by 80 titles per year.

Authors can learn more about our proposal process by going to our website and clicking on Your Company > Submissions.

We define Christian spirituality as the relationship between the self and its sense of the transcendent or sacred, which issues in literary and artistic expression, community, social activism, and practices. A wide range of disciplines within the field of religious studies can be called upon, including history, narrative studies, philosophy, theology, sociology, and psychology. Interfaith in approach, Circle Books fosters creative dialogue with non-Christian traditions.

And tune into MySpiritRadio.com for our book review radio show, hosted by June-Elleni Laine, where you can listen to authors discussing their books.

MySpiritRadio